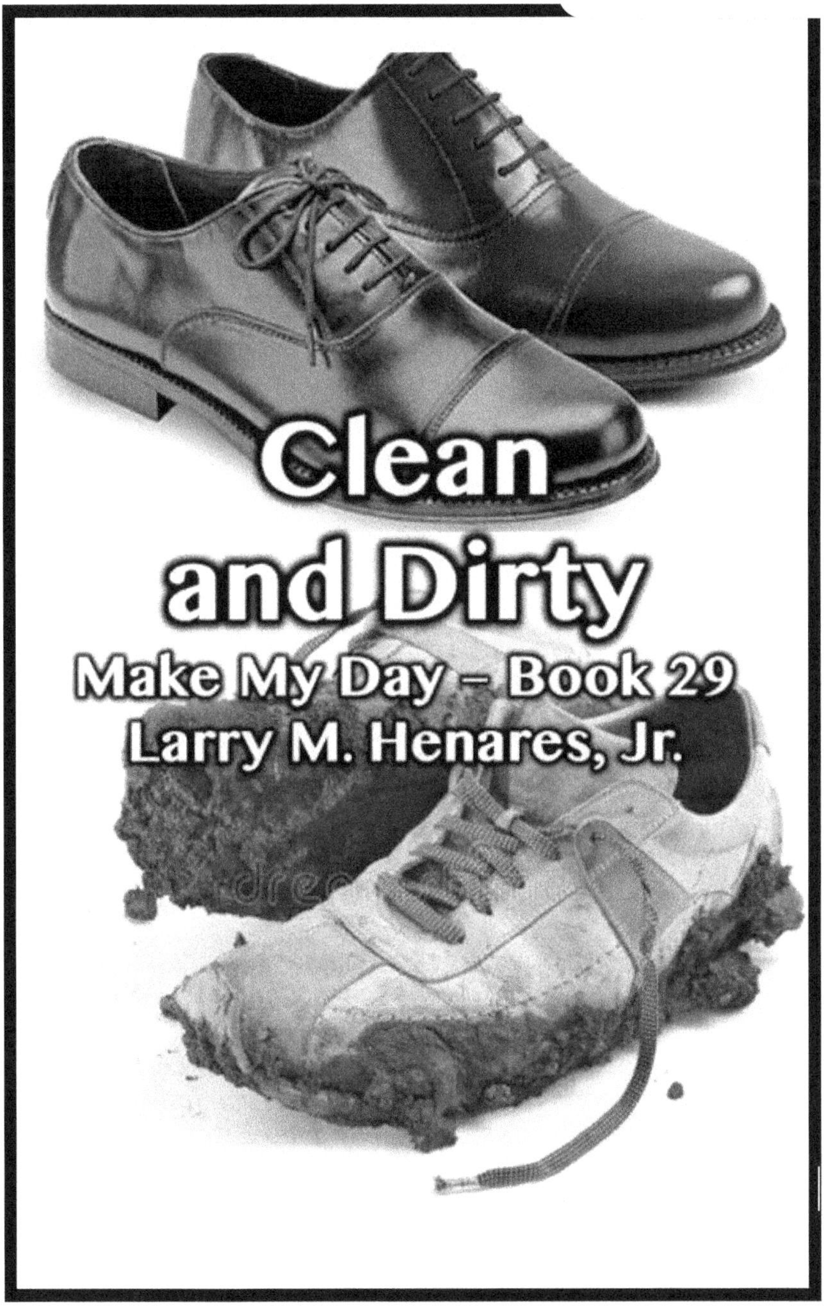

Clean and Dirty

Make My Day – Book 29

Larry M. Henares, Jr.

Published, February 2018

Dr. Hilarion M. Henares Jr., *known as* **Larry Henares,** *is a graduate of Ateneo de Manila, University of the Philippines, and the Massachusetts Institute of Technology, an engineer, economist, educator, big businessman, writer, civic leader, public servant, and hobbyist (guns, books, amateur radio and electronics).*

He is a writer known for his essays on economics, history, art and culture, a front page columnist in the pre-martial law Manila Times and the most widely read column in the Philippines, according to all surveys, the daily "Make my Day" in the Philippine Daily Inquirer, after the EDSA revolt.

ooooo

Tatay Jobo Elizes, Self-Publisher

This book is published under permission of

DR. HILARION M. HENARES, JR.

ISBN – 13: 978 - 1985825208
and ISBN – 10: 1985825201

ooooo

About the Book,
"CLEAN AND DIRTY"

Here Henares starts with the all-important Earth Summit Life in Rio de Janiero where in June 1992, 120 heads of state and representatives from all nations attended the Rio Summit, the greatest global meet in history. They signed the Rio Declaration, the Agenda 21, the treaty on global warming (watered down by the USA under George W. Bush), the world's greatest polluter) and the treaty on Biodiversity (with the US as the sole objector). It's been said that the Rio Summit is a qualified failure, since it produced nothing but ambiguous statements of intentions, rather than a firm and committed schedule of performance. But like Human Rights in the Helsinki Declaration of 1975, it has provided the people of this world a rallying point for for revolutionary action.

In perspective, on 12 December 2015, 196 Parties, including the two greatest polluters of the planet, China and the USA (under President Obama), to the UN Framework Convention on Climate Change, adopted the Paris Agreement, a new legally-binding framework for an internationally coordinated effort to tackle climate change, under intense international pressure to avoid a repeat failure of the Copenhagen conference in 2009. The Agreement establishes a global warming goal of well below 2°C on pre-industrial averages. It requires countries to formulate progressively more ambitious climate targets which are consistent with this goal. To achieve this goal, all Parties to the Paris Agreement will need to make profound changes to their economies. However, newly elected US President Trump announced on June 1, 2017 that the United States would withdraw from the Paris climate accord, ending any pretentions to world leadership.

Henares continues by recounting his observations and experiences on what its is to be a Communist in Romania (whose embassy rented his house in Dasmariñas Village) and in the Soviet Union, where in 1971, President Marcos sent him to negotiate a Treaty of Commerce and Friendship. In 1967, he was invited by Mao Zedong to observe the Cultural Revolution in China. He observed that these three nations were able to industrialize rapidly and give their people security from the cradle to the grave, which they couldn't do if they adopted the Capitalist system. In the case of the Soviet Union (and China), these two nations were able to to develop the nuclear bomb and assert their right to sit among world leaders in the United Nations Security Council. Later he asserted that the Capitalist System survived because it adopted the Socialist practices of Medicare, Welfare State, and laws prohibiting the exploitation of women and children... just as Communism in China survived and prospered because it adopted Capitalistic practices of free market and private initiative. Communism in the Soviet Union failed because its rigid bureaucracy could not adjust to the demands of the times. Swedish Socialist system succeeded because it adopted Volunteerism as a motivating force as Catholic religious organizations did during the 2,000 years of the Christian era.

Henares also wrote of what he feels the Supreme Court should be.

But the biggest part of this book narrates the early years of the President Cory Aquino Administration, full of high hopes and great expectations in the aftermath of the EDSA Revolution of 1986. Alas it was not a Revolution, but a Restoration of the prewar oligarchic feudal society, and the Continuation of the American domination of our economy and political system. He details how that Opus Dei headed by Bernie Villegas and Jesus Estanislao, and the so-called Council of Trent headed by Father Joaquin Bernas SJ and Jaime Ongpin the Constitutional Commission appointed by Cory to draft the new 1987 Constitution, and the entire economy, and political life of the nation, despite nationalistic forces under Joker that manned Malacañang Palace and leftist forces under Bobbit Sanchez in the Labor Department. Read on.

ooooo

BOOK 29: CLEAN AND DIRTY
TABLE OF CONTENTS

ooooo

EARTH SUMMIT

Part 1. Man's highest aspiration: Enough, not More!

The Earth Summit in Rio de Janiero is the most important summit meeting in this century. We met not as nations resolving conflicts, but as fellow passengers on spaceship Earth, with the common purpose of saving our planet. This United Nations Conference on Environment and Development or UNCED was also the first real bid for a New World Order by all nations and all peoples. On the agenda:

o A Treaty on "global warming" to curb the emissions of carbon dioxide and other "greenhouse gases." The USA objected to specific targets and timetables, since its industries and cars emit most of these gases into the atmosphere. Because Bush threatened to boycott the Summit, the treaty draft was amended to leave action on this matter in the hands of individual nations.

o Agenda 21, by which rich nations are pledged to help the poor nations develop their economies without harming the environment, at a cost of some $125 billion, only one percent of the GNP of the Group of Seven, and a fraction of their military spending.

o The Treaty on Biodiversity to put a brake on the loss of endangered species, by saving the forests they need to survive, proposing a plan for royalties to be given to countries for drugs and other products developed from their plants and animals, like vaccines derived from our monkeys and antibiotics from our fungi. This treaty Bush refused to sign, saying, ``I must as president, and will as a human being, keep in mind the needs of American families to have jobs."

It is not surprising that the only sour note in the Earth Summit was sounded by the USA, self-appointed leader and policeman of the world. In the founding meet of the United Nations Conference on Trade and Development (UNCTAD) about 30 years ago, the USA was the sole objector to many of the principles espoused.

On General Principle One (economic relations based on sovereign equality of states, self-determination of peoples, and non-interference in the internal affairs of other countries), the USA was outvoted 113 to 1; General Principle Two (no discrimination on the basis of difference in socio-economic systems), USA voting against, approved with Philippine vote by 96 nations;

Principle Four (to accelerate economic growth throughout the world and narrow the gap between rich and poor nations), the USA was sole objector, approved by 98 countries, including ours; Principle Six (diversification of trade between all countries, and increased markets for poor nations), USA objecting, approved 114 to 1;

Principle Seven (Reduction of barriers to trade with poor countries, and mutually acceptable relationship between prices of finished goods and raw material), USA objecting, approved with the Philippine vote by 87 countries; Principle Eight (most favored nation treatment and preferential concessions to poor countries), USA objecting, approved 78 to 1.

Principle Eleven (Net flow of development assistance from rich to poor countries without political or military conditions), the USA objecting, approved with the Philippine vote 92 to 5; Principle Twelve (portion of the resources saved through disarmament to be allocated to the economic development of poor nations), USA being sole objector, approved with the Philippine vote 83 to 1.

In the recent Uruguay Round of the General Agreement on Tariffs and Trade, the USA led the rich nations in frustrating the development efforts of poor countries by forcing them to accept as part of the imposed conditions on trade in goods, impositions on the so called trade-related activities such as in investment measures (TRIM), and intellectual properties (TRIP).

With such a record, the USA has shown that it is insensitive to the plight of the poor nations and determined to achieve an even higher standard of living at the expense of the poor of this earth. It is no wonder then that the USA is the SOLE OBJECTOR to most of the proposals in the Earth Summit.

The rich nations led by the USA, with only 25 percent of the population, consume 70 percent of the world's energy, 75 percent of its metals, 85 percent of its wood. The USA has 7 percent of the world's population but it uses up 32 percent of the world's resources.

We are beguiled by the American Dream of "unlimited growth and prosperity." Americans want More, while the rest of us do not have even have Enough. If the rest of the world rises to the level of the USA, even assuming that the USA stops growing, we will be using the world's scarce resources 4.5 times faster than we do now.

We must realize that there is enough for everyone to live a decent life, if the rich nations share what they have with the poor nations. Enough rather than More should be mankind's highest aspiration, and the true measure of man's advance on this earth.

Part 2. The Future is Now, in the Rio Earth Summit

Disaster stalks the planet Earth. The population will increase 2.4 times from 5.4 to 13 billion by year AD 2100. To sustain it, the world must produce 20 times what it does today. People continue to cut down forests for firewood, to exhaust the fertility of the soil, permanently impairing the earth's ability to feed itself. Only the Malthusian nightmare -- plagues, wars, natural disasters -- can offer hope in such a world.

The industries and vehicles of the rich countries are spewing out carbon dioxide in such quantities that it may trap the sun's heat (the greenhouse effect) and warm up the earth, causing the arctic caps, glaciers and icebergs to melt, raise the level of the ocean waters and flood major seaside cities.

Sulfur dioxide released into the atmosphere causes acid rain that poisons our environment, corrodes structures and works of art. Chloro-fluoro-carbons (CFC) used in refrigerators and handsprays punch holes in the ozone layer, exposing us to ultra-violet rays that cause skin cancer. Hazardous wastes from industrial and human pollution threaten to poison our seas, rivers and underground water.

A chart prepared by Newsweek shows the following:

o   15 million acres of productive land disappear every year: 40 percent of North America's, 71 percent of Central Asia's, 23 percent of Australia's range and cropland, and 160 million acres south of the Sahara have turned to desert.

o 60 percent of the Pacific Northwest coastal forest has been cut down; every year 5,335 square miles of forests are destroyed in Brazil, and more than 95 percent of its Atlantic forest has disappeared; India, Sri Lanka and the Philippines have almost no rain forest left; deforestation in the Himalayas causes floods in Bangladesh.

o By year 2000 AD, half the forests of Honduras and Nicaragua will disappear along with a third of Guinea's forest, 30 percent of Madagascar's and all of peninsular Malaysia's; nearly 4 million acres of forest disappear every year and with every acre die 50 to 100 species every day; these are the endangered species -- our monkey-eating eagle, Asiatic lion, giant panda, nail-tailed wallaby, spotted owl, black-footed ferret, ridley turtle, manatee, golden toad, humpback whale.

o 90 percent of coral reef (home to a third of fish species), in the Philipines and Indonesia are gone; the fish catch of northwest Atlantic fell by 32 percent since the 1970's.

To save the earth before it is too late, is the purpose of the Rio Earth Summit, backstopped here by Cecile Alvarez of Earth Savers and Jun Kalaw's Haribon Foundation:

* To stabilize population. It is not Cardinal Sin or the Opus Dei that cause overpopulation, it is despair over high infant mortality and harsh economic conditions that drives women to bear more children. We have two models: China's draconian one-child policy enforced with high fines and firing from jobs; or Costa Rica's approach, with its literacy rate of 93 percent, 90 percent Catholic population and readily available condoms, slashing fertility rate from 7 to 3.5 children per woman in 25 years.

* To use renewable sources of power, to conserve energy and to use fuels efficiently (saving 3 times more than the effort expended). The US now spends 28 percent less energy per dollar output than 20 years ago; Japan now uses half the energy that the USA uses to produce one unit of GNP; solar, geothermal, biomass and hydro power already supply 28 percent of the US needs; clean and safe nuclear power is already in place in all advanced nations.

* To use better substitutes. Like using guanaco (cousin of the llama) for better wool, instead of sheep which uproot the grass and turn the land into desert. Like using fiberglass instead of copper wire in communications, a single ultra-thin glass fiber replacing 625 copper wires; like using magnetic tape instead of photographic film coated with silver bromide -- thus saving our dwindling resources of copper and silver. Like using solar and

hydrogen cars. Just as silicon chips replaced the power-hungry vacuum tubes with electrodes coated with rare metals.

* To limit useless consumption: no more aspiring for more gadgets, dog biscuits, and toys of affluence. The Christian trait of self-denial instead of hedonistic self-gratification. The wisdom of Gandhi who said that if he had only one advice to give to his fellow Asians, it would be: "Reduce your wants and supply your needs. Your needs make you vulnerable enough without the added weight of unneeded wants."

* Above all, to address the concerns of the poor and the wretched among us. For there is no greater waste than war, crushing poverty, and oppressive governments.

The Future is Now.

Part 3. Green rights deter the rape of Mother Earth

The high moments of history are sometimes preceded by innocuous phrases that don't even merit public attention when first broached. "Consent of the governed" as part of Rousseau's doctrine of popular sovereignty, did not bring democracy to France, only the Terror of the guillotine, then Napoleon, final defeat, and then the Congress of Vienna confirming the divine right of kings.

Yet in the long run, "the consent of the governed" did dissolve like acid the pretensions of kings. In a little more than century, after the upheaval of World War I, most absolute monarchies in Europe ceased to exist.

Also the phrase "right of self-determination" introduced by Roosevelt into the rhetoric of World War II to incite Europeans to rise up against Hitler, was later used against the Allies by their own colonies declaring their own independence. In less than 20 years, all colonial empires of Britain, France, Netherlands and Belgium collapsed. Only the Philippines, "granted" its independence by the USA remained a true colony in mind and spirit.

The Newsweek reminds us that the term "human rights" was inserted inconspicuously into the Helsinki Declaration of 1975. And the words, "people power" was used in the EDSA revolt in 1986. In a few years, the rallying cry of Human Rights and People Power proved more powerful than Communist tanks and terror.

The premise of Human Rights is that universal freedoms have a standing above any system of governance, and the premise of People Power is that the people can have a successful revolution without taking up arms. Both made the logic of reform impossible to stop.

The same may be said of "green rights," "environmental protection" and "sustainable development" whose premise is that every nation must consider "the global environmental consequences of its internal economic decisions."

Prior to the Earth Summit, the poor nations felt that they did not create these environmental problems, that the rich nations have burned so much coal and oil to fuel their industries, as a result of which the atmosphere can no longer absorb the emitted carbon dioxide without falling into a greenhouse effect. The rich nations have chopped down all their trees in their period of development, and even now consume 85 percent of the wood being cut in the poor nations.

The proposal to limit carbon dioxide emissions to 1990 levels actually limit the growth potential of poor countries in their drive for industrialization, while allowing industrial nations to maintain the level of their development. The poor nations, led by India, are demanding that the rich nations pay for increased cost of development under the proposed new accords. This may cost $70 billion a year more than the current $54 billion a year spent on foreign aid. Compare this with the $900 billion a year in military expenditure. And the $50 billion net flow from the poor to the rich nation because of external debt.

Bush refused to commit any amount, saying that the era of the Open Checkbook is gone. But the European Community and Japan may ante up modest amounts, to be administered by the World Bank sympathetic to rich nations.

The poor nations threaten blackmail, to develop even though they may spew out gases that destroy the ozone layer over the rich countries, to burn their coal and possibly alter climate patterns that may keep wheat from growing in rich countries. "Why should poor countries preserve their forests to clean the air being polluted by the rich nations?" they ask.

The rain forests of poor nations in addition have a diversity of plant, insect and animal life important to development of new drugs and miracle cures. The poor nations demand that they be given royalties for the development of drugs from their forests, as a price for preserving those rain forests. George Bush objected, saying that this unfairly burdens US companies.

Nevertheless 120 heads of state and representatives from all nations attended the Rio Summit, the greatest global meet in history. They signed the Rio Declaration, the Agenda 21, the treaty on global warming (watered down by the USA, the world's greatest polluter) and the treaty on Biodiversity (with the US as the sole objector).

It's been said that the Rio Summit is a qualified failure, since it produced nothing but ambiguous statements of intentions, rather than a firm and committed schedule of performance. But like Human Rights in the Helsinki Declaration of 1975, it has provided the people of this world a rallying point for for revolutionary action.

"Green rights" may yet deter Man from raping his Mother Earth, may yet save this planet we all call our home.
June 1992

Part 4. The Pollution Of Manila Bay
JOSE ABAD SANTOS
ENGLISH 5
TITLE: "THE POLLUTION OF MANILA BAY"
THESIS: Manila Bay has been subject to pollution from so many sources but positive steps can be taken so that it can still be saved.
OUTLINE:
I. The bay has deteriorated in so many ways and this is easily seen in the bay's present condition.
A. Pollution has endangered the aquatic life in the area.
B. The water condition has deteriorated due to severe pollution.
C. The shoreline also has been subject to pollution.
II. The pollution in the area can be traced to several sources.
A. Untreated sewerage is a major source of pollution.
B. Spillage of fuel and chemical by-products is also a major source of pollution.

C. Rampant and uncontrolled garbage dumping is also a main source of pollution.

III. Possible steps to remedy the present condition can be taken.

A. A major clean-up of the area has to be to done.

B. The ecosystem of the area would have to be monitored.

C. Several control and check-up measures would have to be implemented.

IV. We can conclude that the bay has deteriorated in many ways due to pollution but it is still quite possible to save the area from being completely wasted.

THE POLLUTION OF MANILA BAY

The shores of Manila outstretch into a large body of water known as Manila Bay. At the start of the century this bay was still blessed with abundant aquatic life, it had clean shorelines and its waters were reasonably clear. This made it quite suitable for fishing and swimming in the early 1900's. However, because of the Filipinos' disregard for the preservation of nature, this bay had been subject to pollution from so many forms of toxic wastes. The damage is so extensive that the natural ecological balance of the bay is endangered. This bay used to be a haven for so many types of animal forms, but now almost all forms of aquatic life in the area seem to be threatened. Tropical fish used to be abundant in these waters as they should be near tropical shores. At present, they have all but vanished except for the more resilient but less attractive type of fish. The smallest of the fish are the weaker ones and they are the first to succumb to the toxins present in the bay. And without the small fish, the bigger fish would have no food source, they then have been forced out due to a scarcity in food supply. Other animal forms such as crustaceans (e.g. crabs and shrimps) have just about vanished from the area. There are, however, some mollusks such as the native "talaba" and "tahong" but these are quite dangerous for consumption because they sometimes carry the pollutants within their bodies.

Even the seagulls which once frequented the area have already disappeared due to the poisoning of the food they eat. This decline in animal life is directly linked to the deterioration of the water condition. From a once blue-green   color, it has gradually turned to a gray almost black color, especially near the basin area. The tell-tale sign of a rainbow colored film on the surface of the water is a clear indication that the bay has been subject to pollution by wastes of petroleum products. The surface of the water is also littered with all sorts of refuse from our people's urban dwellings.   The shoreline also has not been spared. The little sandy area that was left has been replaced by rocks and has been covered with mud coming from the inland rivers. The shore area would seem to be transformed into a display where all the pollutants of the people of Manila can be seen.

The condition of this bay and all its increments is quite grim. But what caused this condition? Well, this condition did not spring up overnight; it took years of gradual and effective destruction.   It all started when the people had to build their cities. Of course, sewerage systems had to be   built and these would certainly drain into the sea. Manila however, has never really had an effective way of treating sewerage. In fact, our favorite dumping ground for the sewerage, as well as other forms of garbage, was and is the ocean. Our bay also has the classic rainbow film on the surface of its waters; a clear sign of pollution from petroleum products and other chemicals.

Well, this might be traced to the upsurge of trade wherein our ports were the main point of entry and exit of so many international vessels. Through the years, marine vessels have grown in number as well as in size; and so did the amount of pollutants that they spill out into the bay. Chemical by-products from nearby factories also find their way into the bay by spilling into inland rivers, and also through the air as fumes coming from their exhaust pipes. Assorted garbage is also easily found on the surface and accumulating at the bottom of our basin. This would be due to rampant and unchecked dumping of garbage into the inland rivers such as Pasig, the *esteros* and other major canals. The garbage from these small bodies of water ultimately find their way into the bay area of Manila. The break waters along the bay seem to serve like a natural trap for the garbage and it is quite difficult for it to be drawn out into the open sea.

The conditions prevailing in our little bay would seem to be quite discouraging. It almost seems hopeless but it is not so.

Several steps can be taken to try to remedy these critical conditions. The first step might be to try to organize a major clean-up of the area. Accumulated surface garbage can be swept out with the use of nets and a group of small power boats. Garbage accumulated at the bottom can be dredged out but this is a very expensive process and can be done only a little at a time. A monitoring system to monitor the ecological balance of the area would have to be established. The levels of aquatic life could be checked and monitored so as to be able to determine steps to be taken to keep the ecosystem in harmony.

For example, if a build-up of a certain toxin was observed, steps can be taken so that the toxin could be neutralized to keep the ecosystem unharmed. With the area cleaned up hopefully aquatic plant and animal life can gradually be replenished. Of course all this would have to be done together with the implementation of control measures. Strict laws would have to be enforced against the indiscriminate dumping of waste material into our main inland waterways such as the Pasig River and the smaller *esteros* and canals. Also laws should be enforced with regards to spillage from freighters and tankers and other ships that might make use of our ports. Emissions from exhaust terminals of factories should also be checked because these pollutants also eventually find their way into the sea.

The problem that we have here is quite a different one. Through the years it has been allowed to grow so dangerously uncontrolled. Our bay has been poisoned in so many ways and the damage that has been done is quite extensive. We should realize however that if we are to fight this problem, positive steps toward its solution should be carried out as soon as possible. Time is of the essence here and if we are to wait too long... then all might be lost. The problem can be solved and if it is to be solved it has to be done now while it is still not too late.

ooooo

WHAT IT IS TO BE A COMMUNIST

Part 1. Romania

Bernie Villegas of the Opus Dei and the ConCom is advised to read the Constitution of Romania, promulgated in 1965, emphasizing "National Autonomy" and Economic Self-Sufficiency, and guaranteeing every citizen (1) Free Education complete with books and living allowances up to university level; (2) a Job Position commensurate with ability and education; (3) Free Medical Services; (4) Decent Living Conditions, including Adequate Housing at a maximum rent of 20% of his income.

President Ceasescu may live in the same kind of a house as the unskilled worker, but both pay in rent 20% of their income, $180 per month in the case of the president, $30 per month in the case of the worker. The housing industry is among their biggest, and has provided housing for every qualified   adult. Three out of four adults now live in new houses.

Medical Assistance is free; services by doctors are absolutely free. Medicines for contagious diseases are free; medicines are free for pregnant women, all children up to 18 years old, retarded people. Medicines are sold to working people with incomes at heavily subsidized prices, about 10% of prices paid in the western world. That's because Romanians make their own medicines.

Here in the Philippines, where we don't manufacture a single aspirin, we give the multinationals complete monopoly and allow them to charge us as much as 20 times what is charged in their own countries. At one time 250mg terramycin was selling at 6 centavos in Italy, while it was selling here at P1.20 per tablet; in another study, 250mg tetracycline sold at $1.038 in the States and $11.26 per bottle in the Philippines.

Education is absolutely free and obligatory, at least for 10 years of schooling, otherwise, there will be no job offered. From 1990 onward, everyone is obliged to have a university education. Today 70% of university students are on   scholarships, which mean not only tuition and books are free but also lodging, food and pocket money. The other 30% are given free tuition and books but no other, because their families belong to the highest category of income.

In 1946, there was an 80% literacy rate; two years later in 1948, the literacy rate was 99%. There are no persons in Romania with less than 7 years schooling.

School graduates are guaranteed jobs, and are obligated to work for the state for five years, during which they are sent to the provinces, where all communities (the size of our barrios) have electricity, schools with at least 5 university graduate teachers, one medical doctor, one highly educated administrator.

Listen to this, Bernie Villegas. In 1945, Romania was a backward agricultural country. Fortunately there was no one like Jimmy Ongpin and the IMF to tell the the Romanians that they must remain agricultural. So in 1949, a tractor factory was inaugurated, followed by factories making fertilizer and everything else the nation needed. Today Romania makes BAC 111 aircraft British design, makes nuclear plants of Canadian design, makes oil producing equipment to suck oil out of the Black Sea continental slope. Romania did this without foreign capital, without foreign advice either Russian or American, without foreign ambassadors presuming to lecture the natives on matters that are their own concern.

And to think that Romania has one half of our population, and they did it. Taiwan has 18 million people, less than half of ours, and they did it. Israel has only 6 million people, one ninth of ours, and they did it. South Africa has only 32.5 million people of which only 6.5 million are dominant whites, and they did it. South Korea has 42 million people, and they did it. All these nations achieved the status of an industrial state by deliberate state policy.

The Philippines has 54 million people, and they can not make a single ball pen, because they have such guys as Minister Jaime Ongpin, IMF proconsul Hubert Neiss and AmCham prexy Fred Whiting, to insist they must forever be dirt farmers and ersatz Americans.

The smallest administrative unit is the Commune, unlike that of the Soviets, and following ancient organizations much like our Barangays. There are 10,000 people in a a commune, and they elect their leaders directly as in olden times.

Every 30,000 to 40,000 electors elect an assemblyman who serves in a National Assembly which has about 500 members. The National Assembly elects a Council of State which in turn elects the national officials including the President.

To vote and have the right to be voted upon, one must be at least 18 years of age. If one had a criminal record, he cannot vote or be issued a passport for a length of time after serving his sentence, but his right to a living or education is unimpaired.

No one pays income tax on his regular salary, but theirs is a high tax on extra income like book royalties, from 20% to 80%; on property, 0.4% on house, 1% on cars.

But life in Romania is absolutely boring: no betamax follies, no nightclubs, no demonstrations, no Rene Espina and Sonny Osmena mixing it up on television, for that matter, no Inday Badiday seeing true, or Jimmy Ongpin snarling like James Cagney. Yeah man, Bernie, it is as if you were living in a seminary or the Opus Dei Youth Center.

Part 2. Eternal Russia

Ambassador Bosworth delivered another one of those speeches lecturing Cory on what to expect from her State Visit to the United States, and it irritated me to think that this stuff-shirt would feel free to do something he would not have dared to do, as Ambassador to Indonesia. I brooded for a while and thought, "What can I write to irritate Bosworth in return? Aha, I shall write about Russia which is considered The Evil Empire by Bosworth and the third rate actor he works for!"

The Many Faces Of Russia

There were 12 members of the mission headed by Filemon Rodriguez, and included myself, Tony Martel, Robby Delgado, and Joe the Immaculate Concepcion. We went to Russia in September 1974, even before diplomatic relations were established between our countries, so we had to get our visas in Tokyo. We then enplaned for Moscow 8,000 kilometers away over the vast stretches of Siberia.

The first impression we had of the Soviet Union was a voice over the plane intercom: "We are approaching Moscow. Taking photographs of the airport is forbidden." Imagine our surprise when we heard the same admonition when we came back to the Manila International Airport.

Jetting through seven time zones from Tokyo to Moscow can be a painful experience. Traveling east to west, we followed the sun, the daylight stretched out to 20 hours, and suddenly we got hungry at the wrong time, our toilet habits operated at the wrong time. (It is even worse going the other   way, from west to east, when night follows day every seven hours). When we landed in Moscow we were tired and eager to rest, if only to get back to the right time cycle.

The queue through the airport's health and immigration desks were no worse than those in other airports, but the officials didn't speak English and they scowled a lot. That's   the second impression we had in Moscow. People just did not smile. The impression lasted throughout our week's stay in Moscow. We smiled at people we met on the street or in the subway, but they would either look at us as if we were a little crazy, or turn around to see if we were smiling at somebody else.

Our third impression was the sight of row upon row of high rise apartments in Moscow, Leningrad and Baku. Never in our travels abroad had we ever seen so many apartment buildings, 15 to 20 building clusters all over the city, and   more being built all the time. Every Soviet citizen is guaranteed by law 15 square meters of living space plus kitchen, bathroom and corridor space for every apartment; he pays per month a total rent bill equivalent to 3 to 5 percent of his monthly income.

Night fell swiftly and all of a sudden, Moscow looked so different, so dark, so drab. We could not put our finger on it, till we realized it was because Moscow has no neon signs, no flashing lights glorifying toothpaste and headache pills. Gilbert K. Chesterton once said of city lights: "How beautiful if one cannot read!" It was really too bad that Moscow had no   neon signs, because we certainly could not read the Russian alphabet. The Russians use the Cyrillic alphabet; if I were to use it to spell out my family name, it would be written XEHAPEC (Henares).

There is real night life in Russia, no nightclubs, no hostesses, no call girls. Restaurants have floor shows consisting of folk dances and love songs. There are "dollar bars" for foreigners, mostly for hard drinks and you have to bring your own date. Of course there is always television, for which there are three stations in Moscow, mostly in Moscow, mostly exhibiting news programs, talk shows, sportcasts, Russian songs and dances, and absolutely no commercials.

In any case, Russian girls could not visit our hotel rooms because there were watchers on every floor. Foreign women, however, are not bothered by this technicality.

General Fabian Ver who had never been to Moscow at the time, warned us before we left: "Be careful, there are infrared cameras and hidden microphones in every room." We complained to President Marcos facetiously that if our privacy will thus be violated, we'd rather not go. And he answered: "That's easy to remedy. Keep under the bedsheets, and sing the national anthem."

Well, I have been bugged before, in my NEC office by the CIA, and I am a camera and electronic expert, and I can say without doubt that there was no camera nor mike in our hotel rooms in Russia.

This may come as a surprise to our American friends, but the Russians never tried the ideological approach and never cast aspersions on the free enterprise system. During our entire stay in Russia, we never heard any speeches or even the communist anthem "The Internationale", nor did we see any clenched fists of masses of red flags or revolutionary slogans. Statues of revolutionary heroes display not closed fists and heroic poses, but benign countenances and open palms stretched out in friendship.

One of the reasons I was in Moscow was to get in touch with radio amateurs who are very active in the single-side band frequencies, with many of whom Filipino amateurs formed friendships over the air. I asked my hosts to contact the radio club for me. No Dice. First was the alibi that they were having a DX contest and were too busy to receive me. But I was in Russia for two weeks, and after fruitless inquiries, I finally realized that the Soviet authorities did not want me to have an eye-ball QSO with Soviet radio amateurs.

Why did I not just pick up the telephone and call them up? For one thing, the Soviet telephone directory is in confusing Cyrillic script. For another, there is no telephone operator in the whole country. The telephone is absolutely automatic with every hotel room having a complete number all   its own, as if it were a house halfway across the city. And very few people who answer telephones ever speak English.

These are initial impressions we had of our Russian trip. Some impressions were later to be reinforced. Some were dispelled, such as the impression that Russians seldom smile. This may be true in Moscow, but not in Leningrad, and certainly not in Baku on the Caspian Sea where people go out of their way to smile, to introduce themselves, and make friends.

Maria The Miracle Worker

In going to the Soviet Union, a tourist puts himself in the hands of a state agency called the Intourist which charges for its services in advance. Each of us paid about US$700 for 14 days of first class accommodations or $50 per day. This included a single room with bath, three meals a day; transportation to and from and inside Moscow, Leningrad and   Baku by the Caspian Sea; tickets to the ballet, puppet show, circus and tourist tours; and the services of multi-lingual guides. In other European cities at that time, a tourist spent at least $100 a day for the same services.

For the most part, our hotel accommodations consisted of 2 to 3-room suites with television, reception room and enormous bathrooms. Meals consisted of all one can eat and drink of smoked sturgeon and tuna, soup, meat dish, caviar, wine, soft drinks, and occasionally champagne in the best restaurants. A bus was provided when all 12 of us went on tour, but individual cars were available when needed by each. We took a train from Moscow to Leningrad, a plane back to Moscow, to Baku and back to Moscow, all expenses paid. We were taken to the Bolshoi Ballet playing the Swan Lake, a Baku Ballet playing a romantic "Seven Beauties", a Leningrad circus, and numerous tours through the museums, parks, subways and historical spots in Moscow, Leningrad and Baku.

Of the guides, several come to mind: Natasha, the first and only smiling face we met in Moscow; Victor, the representative of the Chamber of Commerce, sensitive and sophisticated, struggling with his o's and r's; Suya of Baku who recalled her wonderful visit to the Philippines and kept singing "Let me go, let me go to Zamboanga,"; and Sonya of Leningrad, eloquent, poetic, philosophical, who moved us to tears over the Battle of Leningrad.

But the most unforgettable was Maria Samjatina, in her middle twenties, of German descent, married to an electronic engineer and aspiring chessmaster, and mother of a 5-year old child. An attractive woman with corn-silk hair, grey eyes and a Mona Lisa smile, always correct and proper, Maria was Mother Hen to us all. It was to her that we came with our problems, and in the absence of night life as we know it in Manila, she was the object of many innocent flirtations. But she remained cool, distant and serene like Mount Everest and one often wondered what raging storms swept her peak.

Taking care of a dozen of temperamental and comparatively undisciplined Filipinos is no joking matter. One was invariably missing when the bus was to be boarded. One kept losing his passport, his currency declaration, his traveler's checks. Another kept asking where the nearest bathroom was. And yet another kept disappearing into stores as if swallowed by Jonah's whale. But nothing seemed to faze Maria; nothing got lost that she did not find; no problem was too big for her to handle.

I lost a bag containing my movie camera and our all important set of conference reports in the lobby of the Leningrad Hotel. It was Maria who called up Leningrad from Moscow, deduced that the bag must have been mixed up with the luggage of a Japanese group leaving on a trip somewhere, traced their itinerary and located them in some distant station, and had my bag brought back to Moscow where I had already given it up as forever lost.

She got us tickets to ballets, concerts, puppet shows and the circus on short notice and saw to it that we got the best seats in the house.

Most of the Russians we met were sticklers for rules and regulations. At times we felt the entire governmental set-up was a jumble of bureaucratic redtape. Nobody wanted to take responsibility. Everybody passed the buck.

But Maria was an exception. Like a precocious child under a strict parent, she was constantly exploring the boundaries of her freedom, testing the limits of what she can or cannot do.

If we were late for a plane, she would somehow delay its departure so we could board it. If there were a line of people ahead of us, she would somehow stop the line and get us ahead. If the cloakroom attendant would not check in our bags (only coats and hats allowed), she would speak up in such an authoritative voice that the attendant would scurry to fetch our bags.

The Intourist agency kept our tickets for two weeks despite our daily follow-ups, only to return the tickets unacted upon a day before our departure. All we wanted was confirmation of our flights and the failure of Intourist was a frustrating experience that left us cursing in Filipino and Spanish.

Yet Maria saved us all. A visit to Japan Airlines, a phone call, and what was left undone for two weeks was accomplished in ten minutes.

We called her Maria the Miracle Worker, and vowed to write Brezhnev recommending that she be made president of Intourist: "What is impossible Maria made possible. As for the rest of the Intourist people, they make the possible absolutely impossible."

And so it went day by day, service and efficiency she afforded us. And even Romance... as on a mountain peak in Baku she stood in the moonlight like a goddess, with the lights of the city below flickering like candles to her divinity... or in a pine forest outside Moscow, she glided like Titania to our Oberon in a wonderful Midsummer Night's Dream.

Part 3. From Russia with Love

"How does our society compare with yours? was the persistent question Russians asked Filipinos as they spoke of their "perfect" social system.

If there is one word that describes what the Communist system means to the average Russian, it is security, literally security from the womb to the tomb.

Before a Russian is born, his mother is given maternity leave with full pay 2 months before and 2 months after birth. Prenatal care is free: monthly consultations for 3 months, twice a month for the next 3 months, and weekly for the last 2 months before delivery. If the delivery has been difficult, the mother may have as much as 4 months paid leave after delivery. Most mothers breastfeed their babies and are given time off twice a day to go home and feed the baby.

Trained nurses make daily visits to the baby's home for 10 to 15 days, weekly visits for the next 3 months, and monthly up to a year, during which the child gets all the injections he needs.

Working mothers may put their children in state nurseries (Yasli) from 8 AM to 7 PM, where doctors and childcare personnel take charge. From the age of 3 to 7 years, the child may be put into kindergarten classes. From 7 to 17 years, the child's education is compulsory by law, through 10 years of what is equivalent to grade school and high school, where teen-agers are given a heavy load of Math subjects, but not sex education.

At the age of 17, the Russian is ready to enter college. He is given an entrance examination. If he fails, he enters a professional school attached to a factory where he gets three years of technological education. If he passes, he enrolls in College, and is given books and materials free of charge and is given an allowance of $50 to $ 150 a month while in school. Every costing cited of course is as of 1974.

Every Russian is guaranteed a job by the Soviet Constitution. He earns from $100 a month (as a street cleaner) to $800 a month (as a factory manager). He works 5 days a week for 42 hours each week, gets overtime pay at twice his hourly rate, and takes one month's vacation (24 working days) a year plus unlimited sick leave. Hospitalization expenses for doctor's fees, nurses, medicines and food are absolutely free.

An average family with husband and wife working has an income of $600 per month, of which $20 goes for rent, $360 for food, for $12.50 for telephone and electricity, $36 for entertainment and miscellaneous, leaving them $171.50 disposable income. Beef tenderloin is $3.30 per kilo, chicken $4.00 per kilo; rent is $20 per month for 30 square meters living space plus kitchen, bathroom, gas and hot water; electricity is $6.60 per kilowatt hour and telephone $6.00 per month; shoes are $58.00 per pair.

A Russian may deposit his savings in a state bank at 3% interest rate per annum; he cannot borrow from the bank, only state companies can. But with his savings he can buy a condominium apartment for $400 per square meter, 50% down and   the rest for 20 years without any interest. He can also buy a   car and other personal things. But he cannot resell them at a profit; he must sell them back to state commission houses which resell them to others without profit. He may pass on his personal possessions, including his savings to his children without paying an inheritance tax.

A Russian girl may not marry until the age of 18, but she can have an abortion any time free of charge. There is no such thing as an illegitimate child in Russia.

If a Russian couple wants to get married, the partners fill up an application blank to do so and are given one month to think over their decision and to prepare for the wedding. They get married in the "*Dworez Brako Sotsyetani*" (marriage house) before a Soviet official and two witnesses. They get divorced anytime upon mutual consent and go to court to settle finances.

Every Soviet Citizen carries an identity card called "passport". It is issued to him at the age of 18 and contains: date of validity, name, birthplace, birthday, nationality (any of the 15 Soviet republics), employment, social position (peasant, worker, professional), army eligibility, children, marriage registration, blood type, and every new address. His parents' names are not in the passport.

He carries that identity card all his life till the day he dies, and when he does, he is given a free burial in the cemetery.

"How does our society compare with yours?" the Russians asked much too persistently, till I answered, "We have the free enterprise system and everyone is left to struggle in life as best he can. The brilliant ones succeed to riches, the poor ones lead a miserable existence. We worship God in our own way. Our government tries hard to tax the rich and give relief to the poor. We never pretend ours is the best system, and we are willing to learn and adopt the best in other societies, especially those in America." And left it at that.

ooooo

SUPREME COURT

Part 1. What kind of Supreme Court do we want?
What makes a great Supreme Court Justice?

Appeals Justice Nocon may believe that the best are those with experience as judges, because they are better capable of weighing both sides of the issue, more than practicing lawyers who are used to taking sides, to provocative advocacy rather than mature judgment.

Flerida Romero may argue: wouldn't judges in repetitious decisions tend to develop habits of thought and tunnel vision in their judgments, with more emphasis on the letter of the law than in its spirit?

Wouldn't practicing lawyers who take cases of clients with disparate and conflicting views, develop tolerance and have a better perspective of both sides of the issue at stake?

The greatest jurists are not necessarily from the bench or from the practice of law. Chief Justice Earl Warren was a politician, the Governor of California, whose landmark decisions on civil rights changed US history. The great Oliver Wendell Holmes was from the academe, a Harvard professor.

What kind of Supreme Court justices do we have? Six out of fifteen came from the ranks of the judiciary: Ameurfina Melencio Herrera, Carolina Griño Aquino, Edgardo Paras, Abdulwajid Bidin, Emilio Gancayco, Leo Medialdea.

Three were practicing lawyers: Chief Justice Marcelo Fernan, Florentino P. Feliciano, Teodoro Padilla. The latest retiree Abraham Sarmiento was also one.

Three like Oliver Wendell Holmes, were of the academe: Andres Narvasa, law dean of Sto. Tomas; Florenz Regalado whose bar exam grade is still unsurpassed, law dean of San Beda; Isagani Cruz, law dean of Lyceum. Irene Cortes, now retired, was law dean of UP.

And three, like Earl Warren, were from public service. Hugo Gutierrez was UP law professor who served in the SSS and Office of Solicitor General. Hilario Davide was assemblyman and Constitutional Commissioner. Recently appointed Flerida Romero was from the UP Law Center, and served in Malacañang.

What kind of Supreme Court do we want?

Dr. Hilarion M. Henares Jr.   **28**

When a majority of the Supreme Court decreed that there is no such thing as rebellion complexed with murder, condemned police check-points on our streets, frustrated PLDT's monopoly of cellular phones, and ordered BOI to return the petrochemical plant to Bataan -- when a significant minority voted for the right of Marcos to be buried in his own country, and condemned warrantless arrests based on continuing crimes -- the Supreme Court in effect challenged the status quo and conventional wisdom, and struck out toward new judicial frontiers, perhaps exercising what is pejoratively called "judicial legislation."

"The law is not an end in itself... but the means to serve what we think is right," said Justice Harlan Stone.

Because the law must reflect contemporary moral judgments, it cannot solely depend on precedents, or what was decided before. Viscount Philip Snowden: "All human progress has been made by ignoring precedents. If mankind had continued to be the slave of precedent we should still be living in caves."

Without changing the letter of the law, the US Supreme Court curbed police brutality with the Miranda Doctrine; advanced civil rights by ordering complete integration enforced by affirmative action; broke up business monopolies by new interpretations of "combinations and conspiracies in restraint of trade"; redefined human rights in the field of abortion, minorities, consumerism, child abuse, surrogate parenthood, environmental protection, dangerous drugs and cigarettes, even the limits of pornography.

"Under our constitutional system, courts stand against any winds that blow, as havens for those who might otherwise suffer because they are helpless, weak, outnumbered, or because they are non-conforming victims of prejudice and public excitement," wrote Justice Hugo L. Black.

The winds of change, the wave of the future in our Supreme Court may eventually mean:

o the final dismantling of the PLDT monopoly, like that of the AT&T in the USA, and the realization of a communication network linking us together and with the rest of the world.

o amnesty for all the rebels, the legalization of the Communist Party, and the beginning of true national reconciliation.

o the final removal of foreign bases, a state within our state that is an abomination to our national sovereignty, the fountain head of our colonial mentality.

o the repudiation of IMF conditionalities, the rejection of such exploitative investments as the Petroscam, and the return of the National Steel forcibly taken by Marcos and the technocrats back to the Jacintos who own it and who are determined to pursue, as the Cory technocrats are not, the final integration of the steel industry.

o and finally industrialization and the triumph of Filipino entrepreneurship over the IMF and multinational corporations.

Only then can our nation emerge from the candle-lit vaults of the Dark Ages, into the sunlit uplands of 21st century progress and enlightenment.

November 1991

Part 2. Supreme Court needs to define Treason

When ruffians mobbed Bertrand Russell in 1918 for his unpopular anti-war views, a friend pleaded with the police to intervene, to no avail.

"But he is eminent philosopher," the friend said, but the police did not care. "But he is famous all over the world," the friend insisted. The police shrugged.

"But he is the brother of an earl," the friend screamed desperately. The police rushed to the rescue.

Of course there is a different law for the rich and for the poor, "Laws are spider webs through which the big flies pass and the little ones get caught," said Honoré de Balzac (1799-1850), plagiarizing something Scythian philosopher Anacharsis said circa 600 BC.

Of course there is a different law for pro-Americans and for Filipino patriots, otherwise why do the police beat up demonstrators against the bases, but not those freaks who make a profession of treason, of selling us out to the CIA and the IMF.

State power applied in behalf of the rich and the powerful has always been challenged in the highest tribunals, resulting in landmark decisions that advanced the cause of a free society.

One of the first to be challenged in the USA is police brutality. "If police efficiency were an end in itself, the police would be free to put an accused on the rack. Police efficiency must yield to constitutional rights," said Judge John Minor Wisdom.

This resulted in the Miranda Doctrine by which no suspect may be detained or accused unless, as in every TV police drama, he is informed of his right to remain silent and have the benefit of counsel.

The civil rights movement was advanced when the US Supreme Court headed by Earl Warren rejected the old "separate but equal facilities" for the negro, in favor of complete integration of public facilities enforced by "affirmative action."

Anti-trust actions have steadily eroded the power of business monopolies. Under the Department of Justice, Bigness is Badness and the mere ability of corporations to commit monopolistic acts, even if unacted upon, is *prima facie evidence of intent.*

Under such jurisprudence, the telephone monopoly of AT&T was broken up, its international gateways shared by two other companies, its Mama Bell franchise areas split up into independent Baby Bells with mandatory interconnection -- the same way we would like to see the PLDT monopoly broken up in the Philippines.

Ever since the Articles of Confederation gave way to the US Constitution, the United States have been dealing with issues involving Federal Power versus States Rights, including the right of states to secede (resolved by the Civil War), jurisdiction over criminals, and control over interstate commerce.

And even now the best legal minds of America are engaged in great issues over pro-Choice and pro-Life positions on abortion; consumer rights and environmental protection versus the demands of Big Business; minority rights, sex harassment, child abuse, surrogate parenthood, and limits of pornography.

Here in the Philippines, the issues are mostly confined to State Power versus individual human rights; the interests of Multinationals and Big Business against the interest of the Filipino consumers and workers; the security needs of the US bases versus the constraints imposed by our Constitution.

On the issue of State Power versus Human Rights, there is a voting pattern emerging in the Supreme Court. Five of the Justices lean towards individual rights: Abraham Sarmiento (whose son was abused unto death during martial law), Isagani Cruz, Teodoro Padilla, Hugo Gutierrez (the most consistent in the defense of constitutional rights) and Andres Narvasa (who prosecuted Ninoy's killers).

On the other side of the issue, there are five conservative justices with concern for national security, law and order: Marcelo Fernan, Florenz Regalado, Leo Medialdea, Carolina Aquino and Ameurfina Herrera.

Five others are the swing votes, who may shift from one side to the other: Edgardo Paras, Emilio Gancayco, Abdulwajid Bidin, Florentino Feliciano, and Irene Cortes who just retired.

All other issues especially concerning multinationals and Big Business, the voting patterns are inconsistent.

Chief Justice Fernan is perceived to be a politician by inclination, and quite flexible. Florentino Feliciano is a corporate lawyer and Yaleman, familiar with the problems of Big Business, not too great on social issues, but usually abstains when the case involves the Sycip-Salazar law firm, of which he was once senior partner.

Hugo Gutierrez is known for his sympathies for the underdog and political dissenters, with a tendency to assert his independence from the administration. So is Abraham Sarmiento, whose eldest son was an anti-Marcos partisan tortured by the military, and released to die of his injuries.

Florenz Regalado is cerebral and academic, familiar with history and philosophy, usually cut and dry in his opinions. Gani Cruz is a Laurel appointee, practical and pragmatic, and his opinions are very well written.

Amor Herrera and Leo Medialdea use the trial judge approach with a deep and intuitive perception of the laws and the facts. Irene Cortes writes her opinion as if it were an article in the law journal.

Carol Aquino is distinguished by the fact that she and her husband have both been appointed into the Supreme Court, her husband having been the Chief Justice under Marcos. Edgardo Paras shows his background as academician and teacher.

The signs are there. Our Supreme Court Justices, unlike the President and her technocrats, unlike the Congress specially the Lower House, comparatively insulated as they are from pressure and influence of the IMF and the CIA -- have been developing lately a sense of nationalism so necessary to nation-building and may called upon to rule on the constitutionality of nuclear arms stored in the Philippines.

With the retirement of Justice Irene Cortes, and the 8 to 7 vote on the PLDT case lost to Express Telecom, Cortes' replacement is crucial to PLDT's motion for reconsideration.

PLDT's Emperor Tony Cojuangco, National Nephew, is very much concerned about this appointment. Among those being considered by President Aquino are:

o Raul Goco, thrice recommended by the Judicial Council, this time perhaps his time has come. He is a practicing lawyer and law dean of *Pamantasan ng Lungsod ng Maynila*. Considered a liberal.

o Jose Bengson Jr., corporate lawyer, political kingpin of Pangasinan, my cousin, considered very conservative.

o Jose Laureta, from the UP academe, corporate and human rights (BONIFACIO) lawyer, from the public service (PCGG and SEC where he was considered a liberal and non-conformist).

o Rodolfo Nocon, Presiding Justice of the Court of Appeals, may be the most senior of all being considered; Jose Melo.

o Vic Mendoza, Santiago Kapunan, Reynato Puno, once assistants Solicitor General, known as Estelito Mendoza's bright boys -- constructionists concerned with strict application of the letter of the law.

o Serafin Quiazon, close to the Lopezes, quite forward-looking, from the academe and law practice.

o Flerida Romero, from the UP Law Center, academician, serving in Malacañang close to the President, considered quite conservative.

Extraneous forces are again imposing their will on our nation. There is need to define what is meant by treason. A treacherous technocracy committed to the IMF and the CIA, and a spineless political satrapy so easily cowed to serve scalawags and carpetbaggers, have failed to protect, promote and defend the interests and aspirations of the Filipino people.

Where they failed, perhaps our Supreme Court can succeed, enforcing by affirmative action, as it did in the PLDT and Petroscam case, the patriotic ideals and nationalistic spirit of our Constitution.

December 22, 1990

Part 3. To hell with them, kill them all!

I wish I clipped the article by Former Supreme Court Justice Isagani Cruz in the Philippine Daily Inquirer a few Sundays ago when he wrote on capital punishment. Let me recall what he wrote. A former advocate of the death penalty, Gani Cruz now has changed his mind, and writes:

- that the death penalty is not a real deterrent to heinous crime,

- that revenge is not the province of the penal system,

- that the death penalty for the guilty can never bring the victims back to life or make up for the pain and loss of the surviving loved ones,

- that with a life term, there is always a possibility for rehabilitation even for the worst of criminals,

- and that death is too final and irreversible for those who may prove to be innocent in the long run.

These are the same arguments that my cousin ex-senator Rene Saguisag and myself used in our opposition to the death penalty. But I was wrong.

It is not altogether true that the death penalty is not a deterrent to heinous crime. Perhaps it is true for those who live lives of no consequence and therefore do not mind losing their own lives in expiation for their crimes. For sado-masochists who inflict suffering on others because they themselves find relief in their own suffering. For the criminally insane, the psychopath, the retrogressive, the suicidal, the stupid, the drug-addict. Perhaps it is true for these persons.

But it is not true for the rational, the logical, those who believe in divine retribution and ultimate salvation. Those driven to heinous crimes by temporary insanity, by the urgencies of survival, by desperation, by misguided sense of justice. For these people, death penalty certainly would be a deterrent to a heinous crime. To deter such persons is worth the effort, is worth the risk.

Of course the true deterrent is the certainty of being caught, the swift and inevitable application of justice and punishment. But even this is denied us.

Revenge? No, what we want above all is justice, justice for the victims and a punishment that fits the crime. An eye for an eye was an advancement in penology when a minor crime like stealing bread merited 20 years imprisonment, and killing the King's deer was punished by torture and death. It is no less appropriate today. More than any one, victims of heinous crimes deserve justice.

Majority of criminals aside from being fed and housed at great expense by the state, update and hone their criminal skills inside jails, pending their re-entry into society. Most are recidivists, unrepentant and hopelessly unsalvageable. Only a few are worth the overall effort and expense for rehabilitation. Better to reduce the prison population so that we can take better care of those left behind.

Death is final and inevitable whether through sickness, natural causes or state executions. I do not believe in letting thousands of the guilty go unpunished to save one hypothetical innocent, any more than a nation should go to war to rescue one guiltless prisoner. Shit, the state has an obligation to protect its citizens from madmen who rape little girls and bash their heads with a cement block, from policemen who commit heinous crimes on those they have sworn to protect, from fathers who rape their little children. To hell with them, kill them all.

October 18, 1996, ISYU

Part 4. Impeaching the Supreme Court

Knowingly rendering an unjust judgment

IF there is one entity considered sacred and inviolable, it is the Supreme Court, the last rampart in the defense of our constitution, our laws and ultimately our freedoms.

Never has the Supreme Court been subject to so much criticism: possession of Benzes under Memorandum Receipts, renovation of offices at P650,000 each, "Dear Raul" letters the anomaly of two contradictory Ayala decisions.

Now, for the first time there is an attempt to impeach two-thirds of the entire Supreme Court for:

o culpable violation of the Constitution on six counts.
o bribery, graft and corruption.

o high crime of knowingly rendering an unjust judgment.

o betrayal of public trust.

Former Ambassador Jose Alejandrino filed recently with the House of Representatives a verified complaint for impeachment naming as respondents ten of the fifteen Supreme Court Justices: Chief Justice Marcelo Fernan, and Associate Justices Carolina Aquino, Abdul Bidin, Irene Cortes, Isagani Cruz, Emilio Gancayco, Leo Medialdea, Andres Narvasa, Florenz Regalado, and Abraham Sarmiento.

The impeachment move is an offshoot of a damage suit filed in 1981 by Alejandrino against American Express (Amexco) for breach of card-membership contract, in which the trial court awarded Alejandrino in December 1982 P2 million in moral damages and P400,000 in exemplary damages with 12 percent interest from notice of judgment.

He was carrying a diplomatic passport when his Amexco credit card was unceremoniously seized at Bon Department Store in Seattle in September 1980 for alleged delinquency of account (for a measly $70), which was false, because his account was actually found to have a credit balance.

Considering that he was in the company of the Philippine Consul, he felt grievously hurt and humiliated, because he was made to appear as attempting to swindle the store with a use of a canceled credit card, the seizure of which at the instance of the Amexco Seattle Office, looked like he was using a diplomatic passport to facilitate the commission of a fraud.

Alejandrino felt that the dishonoring, leave alone the open seizure of his credit card in the USA, is a serious matter that is sure to destroy permanently his credit standing, the loss of which is incalculable and damaging to his personal honor.

Counting on his credit card, he brought only $6,000 in traveler's checks for his long trip. The seizure of his card threw him into a financial crisis, so much so that he had to cut his itinerary to other countries he wanted to see, thereby disrupting his travel plans.

Only by knowing the background can we appreciate the gross injustice committed against Alejandrino.

The judgment was affirmed *in toto* by the Court of Appeals on April 29, 1985. But on November 9, 1988, when the damages plus interest was already close to P4 million, the Supreme Court while agreeing that Amexco was guilty, reduced the damages to a measly P100,000 -- which is much less than a good executive earns in a month.

The unfairness of it all, reducing the damages from P4 million down to 2.5 percent of the total, to a measly miserly P100,000 ($4,700), small change which the Amexco spends in one cocktail party -- outraged Alejandrino and impelled him to move for the impeachment of the Court.

His arguments seem unassailable:

o Considering that the earlier decision of the trial court, affirmed by the Court of Appeals was already final and executory under BP 129 on May 22, 1985, what motivated the Supreme Court to set it aside, openly usurping legislative power in culpable violation of the Constitution?

o What motivated the Court to reduce the damages from P4 million to P100,000, which is patently ridiculous and unfair, after eight years of litigation during which the exchange rate toppled from P9 to P21.35 per dollar? Why did the Justices do this for a rich multinational corporation which obviously can afford much much more?

o Why did the Court allow the "*ponente*" (the author who penned the decision) to conceal his identity through a *per curiam* decision? Is it because of its patently unjust decision?

o Why did the Court render its judgment with "minute resolutions," which are unsigned by the Justices who adopted them, which give no reasons for its arbitrary decisions, which conceal the identity of the authors of the resolution, and which cannot be subject to inquiry by parties affected by them -- and are obviously unconstitutional?

This series will explore the legal recourse of an ordinary citizen against the highest tribunal of the land, and his chances of getting satisfaction for the injustice he feels is done to him.

Alejandrino denied constitutional rights?

IN November 1979, Jose M. Alejandrino contracted American Express Co. (Amexco), for a Credit Card, backed by a bank deposit in dollars, and for which Alejandrino undertook to pay an initial fee of $70 and other bills ``as and when presented."

The bill of January 1980 for the $70 dues was not received until May 1980, and was promptly paid by him to the

Amexco office in Hong Kong. For some reason, while the Alejandrino check was cashed, the payment was not credited to his account and no receipt was issued.

When Alejandrino presented his Amexco credit card to a store in Seattle in September 1980, it was seized from him on the grounds that he was delinquent.

He sued for damages before the Court of First Instance of Pasay City in March 1981, and was awarded in December 1982 P2 million in moral damages and P400,000 in exemplary damages plus 12 percent interest per annum from the notice of judgment till day of payment.

The amounts were determined following the guidelines in two cases against Pan American Airlines for not honoring the confirmed reservations of Vice President Fernando Lopez and poet Rafael Zulueta da Costa.

The Court of Appeals in a final resolution dated April 29, 1985, affirmed in toto the awards of the trial court.

Sycip Salazar, Amexco counsel, instead of filing a motion for reconsideration, filed a motion for an extension of 30 days within which to file a petition for review against the resolution of the Court of Appeals.

Alejandrino opposed the motion because under Section 39 of Batas Pambansa Blg. 129, the uniform appeal period from the final judgment of any court, is only 15 days from notice, not extendible by the Supreme Court. Since Amexco received the final resolution on May 7, 1985, the decision became final and executory on May 22, 1985.

Sycip Salazar's petition for review was filed on June 10, 1985, without waiting for the Court's resolution on its motion for extension.

Alejandrino filed a motion to dismiss the petition on statutory and constitutional grounds -- a motion denied by the First Division of the Supreme Court without giving any reason. Instead the Court ordered Alejandrino to comment on the petition within 10 days.

Again, Alejandrino filed a motion for reconsideration, and again it was denied though a minute resolution dated October 7, 1985, giving no reason for the decision and giving him a final 10 days period with which to comply under pain of waiver.

Having received a copy of the order on October 21, 1985, Alejandrino had until October 31 to file the required comment. Then suddenly, on October 28, three days before Alejandrino's comment was due, the First Division Supreme Court issued another minute resolution, without even a request from Amexco's counsel Sycip Salazar, motu propio dispensing with Alejandrino's comment and giving due course to Amexco's petition for review.

Alejandrino assailed this as highly irregular, and the First Division had the case re-raffled to the Second Division of the Supreme Court.

The Second Division sat on the case for a long time despite Alejandrino's motions for resolution. After the 12th motion, the Second Division tossed it to the Supreme Court en banc, which accepted it on September 25, 1988.

On November 9, 1988, the Court en banc rendered its decision. While it agreed with the trial court that Amexco was negligent in seizing Alejandrino's credit card, it held that the trial court's awards for damages were excessive and reduced them to P100,000.

Alejandrino filed a motion for reconsideration of said decision assigning grave errors therein, both as to findings of facts and of law, and assailing the Court for the use of an ancient, obsolete and non-analogous case (Alonzo vs. Villamor et al. 16 PHIL 315) which was decided in July 1910 on the basis of the old Code of Civil Procedure which has been superseded by the Rules of Court as of January 1, 1964, and in turn, modified insofar as they are inconsistent with the provisions of BP 129.

But again, this motion was denied through a minute resolution of January 12, 1989, without giving reasons, in culpable violation of Section 14, Article VIII of the present Constitution.

Alejandrino filed a motion to set aside said minute resolution on ground of unconstitutionality, pointing out that while the 1973 constitution allowed the use of minute resolutions to decide cases with finality, the 1987 Constitution eliminated such authority and required that no motion for reconsideration from the decision of a court shall be denied without giving the legal basis therefor.

Once again, this motion was denied through a minute resolution dated February 9, 1989.

Intriguing Questions on Alejandrino Case

The way the Amexco case was handled by the Supreme Court gives rise to many intriguing questions posed by Alejandrino:

1. The Court's decision of November 9, 1988, allowed the ponente to conceal his identity as writer of the opinion through a per curiam decision. Strange because the Amexco case had no political significance, being a simple case of action for civil damages for breach of contract.

Was the ponente afraid that an unjust decision will be recorded forever in Philippine jurisprudence, and did not want the public to know that he was responsible for such a judgment?

In the USA Supreme Court Justices often vie with each other for the honor of penning the decisions of the Court as the best way to get recognition. In the Amexco case, what motivated the ponente to hide his identity and thereby pass up the opportunity to shine as a legal luminary?

2. In his pleadings, Alejandrino continuously stressed that the government stood to benefit by over P1,300,000 in income tax from the financial awards, since the lower courts' judgment of P2,400,000 plus the accrued interest thereon at 12 percent per annum from December 17, 1982 to November 9, 1988, totaled almost P4 million.

He also pointed out that the said awards were not excessive based on the guidelines laid down by the Supreme Court in the landmark cases of Lopez vs. Pan American, and Zulueta vs. Pan American, and the fact that when the trial court rendered its decision in December 1982, the peso-dollar exchange rate was only P9 to $1, whereas when the Supreme Court rendered its decision on November 9, 1988, the exchange rate was down to P21.35 to $1, thereby reducing the awards by more than 60 percent.

Yet, after eight years of litigation, due to the dilatory tactics of Amexco's counsel, and the slow pace of the courts, the respondents ignored the above points and reduced the awards to P100,000, which is equivalent to $4,700 dollars, a paltry sum indeed.

There was negligence on the part of Amexco, the Supreme Court agreed, but to give Alejandrino just P100,000 and thereby save Amexco P3,838,000, foregoes taxes needed by a government so financially strapped that it has to go begging around the world for financial assistance!

What motivated them to be so generous to a giant American financial institution, to the point of depriving Alejandrino, a Filipino citizen, of nearly P4 million out of damages awarded to him by the lower courts, and the government of an income tax loss of more than P1.3 million?

3. Considering that the damages awards of the trial court as affirmed in toto by the Court of Appeals, were already final and executory under BP 129 on May 22, 1985, what motivated the Court to discard PB 129 and the Rule of Law by openly usurping legislative power in culpable violation of the Constitution?

4. What motivated the Court to face the possibility of public ridicule by citing an ancient, obsolete and non-analogous case to sustain their unjust and unconstitutional decision in the Amexco case?

5. Why did the Court close its eyes to serious irregularities committed by the First Division by entertaining a petition for review filed without leave of court and requiring Alejandrino to comment on said petition, and then dispensing with Alejandrino's comment and giving due course to the petition three days before the comment was due?

6. Why did the Court, in culpable violation of the Constitution, ignore and disregard Alejandrino's motion to set aside its minute resolution of January 12, 1989, for no reason at all, when said motion raised a very important constitutional question of whether the Supreme Court has the power under the 1987 Constitution to decide cases through minute resolutions as it did in the Amexco case in denying Alejandrino's motion for reconsideration of their decision of November 9, 1988?

Was it because they could not refute Alejandrino's arguments on the legal issues? Or was it to maintain the use of minute resolutions which are unsigned by the justices who adopt them, which give no reason for arbitrary actions therein, which conceal the identity of the authors of said resolutions, and cannot be subject to inquiry by the parties adversely affected by them, and which may have become the source of bribery, graft and corruption?

8. Would the two Divisions of the Court have given up the Amexco case if Alejandrino's side was not too meritorious to overrule?

9. What motivated the Court to risk impeachment for culpable violation of the Constitution; bribery, graft and corruption; knowingly rendering an unjust judgment; and betrayal of the public trust?

RES IPSA LOQUITUR. The facts speak for themselves.

Fiat Justitia is Mission Impossible

Not only Justice, but the perception of Justice, is essential to the survival of Society. Moral suffering caused by injustice is more permanent than physical suffering caused by body injuries that may be healed in time. The Romans said it for all time: Fiat Justitia etsi ruant coeli, Justice be done though the heavens fall!

More than anything else, the perception that Justice is impossible in the Aquino Administration will set the stage for its eventual downfall.

The failure after almost six years to convict the murderers of Ninoy who were certainly among those on the tarmac stairway with him (all equally guilty of conspiracy to murder) -- the failure to apprehend the assassins of Evelio Javier, Cesar Climaco, Lando Olalia, Lean Alejandro -- the whitewash of Emil Ong, Quisumbing, Juico and all the rest of the criminally incompetents in government -- the mounting criminality and human rights violations of the Armed Forces whom we depend on to uphold the majesty of the law and the protection of our freedoms -- all indicate an awesome lack of political will of the Cory administration to render justice unto its citizens.

We hope that the Alejandrino complaint against the Supreme Court, before whom so many Filipinos feel impotent, is not the last straw that will break the back of the present dispensation. For the enormity, the complexity, formidable stumbling blocks that lie ahead for this lone citizen who seeks only justice -- are enough to bring into fore the bitterness and frustration of a lost cause. And lost causes are the sparks of Revolution.

Just imagine Jose Alejandrino hurdling all these procedural steps in the Impeachment procedure:

o   An impeachment complaint may be filed by any Member of the House; or by any Filipino citizen, verified and endorsed by at least one Member of the House.

Alejandrino found that NONE of the 240 representatives of Congress would endorse his complaint, most begging off because ``My election is under protest in the Electoral Tribunal where three justices sit,'' and others, ``I am practicing law and cannot antagonize the Supreme Court.'' And so on, even as they concede that Alejandrino has a strong case going.

Here at the first step, Alejandrino is already stopped. Even if this is hurdled, the rest is Mission Impossible.

o   If the Speaker finds the complaint verified and endorsed, he includes it in the Order of Business of the House and it is referred to the Justice Committee chaired by Rep. Zarraga.

o If the Justice Committee finds the complaint sufficient in form and substance, it sends the complaint to the Supreme Court respondents with notice that they answer it within 10 days. No motion to dismiss is allowed to be filed against the complaint.

o   After receipt of pleadings and affidavits, Committee shall determine whether there are sufficient grounds for impeachment. If in the affirmative, Committee shall conduct public hearings. If in the negative, Committee orders the dismissal of the complaint and submits its report to the House in plenary session, which can overrule Committee by one-third vote.

o After the hearing and filing of memoranda, Committee decides to recommend impeachment or dismissal. Majority vote (18 votes) is required for any action taken. The Committee resolution and report is then submitted to the House.

Upon receipt of Committee resolution and report on the case, House shall calendar them for deliberation. If the Committee resolution contains finding of probable cause, it must be accompanied by Articles of Impeachment. If recommendation is dismissal, same may be overridden in the House by a one-third vote of all its Members.

o House Committee on Rules shall report the Committee resolution to the House in plenary. A one-third vote of all the

House Members is required to approve the Committee recommendation and report. Voting must be RECORDED VOTE, by roll call.

o If approved, Justice Committee shall draft the Articles of Impeachment which shall be endorsed to the Senate for trial. Two thirds vote of all the Senators is required for conviction. Otherwise, respondents will be absolved.

o The prosecution of the case at the Senate shall be handled by a panel of 11 Representatives elected by the House. The panel shall be the SOLE prosecutors at the Senate trial. The complainant himself is NOT allowed to participate in the prosecution of the case.

The labyrinthine procedure alone is insurmountable as far as an ordinary citizen is concerned.

No one dares challenge any Supreme Court Justice, much less a group of them acting in concert in what Alejandrino claims is an unjust judgment.

For Alejandrino, Fiat Justitia is Mission Impossible.

Conclusion.   Affirming People Power and Edsa Miracle

WHAT is the quantum of proof needed to convict in an impeachment case? Is it proof of guilt beyond reasonable doubt? Alejandrino submits that what is needed is mere preponderance of evidence to support moral certainty of guilt, even when the charges are criminal in nature, like bribery, graft and corruption and other high crimes, for the following reasons:

•   Impeachment is a disciplinary action and not a criminal prosecution, such that punishment cannot go beyond removal from office.

•   Guilt in the impeachment case need only to be justified on the principle of Res Ipsa Loquitur (The thing speaks for itself).

The present Supreme Court adopted the same view when it issued its Administrative Circular No. One, dated January 28, 1988. It provides that ``All judges are reminded that the Supreme Court has applied res ipsa loquitur in the removal of judges without any formal investigation whenever a decision on its face indicates gross incompetence or ignorance of the law or gross misconduct.''

Since only Congress can conduct impeachment proceedings against the Supreme Court, the misbehaving Justices like judges of the lower courts, must also be removable on the doctrine of res ipsa loquitur for culpable violation of the constitution, treason, bribery, graft and corruption, and betrayal of public trust in impeachment proceedings. What is sauce for the goose must also be sauce for the gander.

For an ordinary citizen like ex-Ambassador Alejandrino, there is no other recourse. Impeachment is a difficult process. The Justices of the Supreme Court have awesome powers and can easily rally fawning lawyers to their defense. They are protected by constitutional tenure of office. Their salaries cannot be reduced while in office.

The Court enjoys automatic appropriations. They are immune from Congressional investigations because of the principle of separation of powers. They cannot be hailed to the office of the Ombudsman unless first removed from office.

All these privileges are meant to shield the Supreme Court from the abuse of lesser men, from the assaults of tyrants and despots – and rightly so. For the Supreme Court is the nearest thing to God in a democracy, the fifteen Wise Men whose wisdom and experience entitle them to be the Final Arbiter at the Last Judgment.

But suppose they are, as the rest of us, less than God-like. Like the Supreme Court Justice who tried to blackmail Carmelino Alvendia and the Philacor to fork over two million pesos to guarantee that Dante Santos does not go to jail for unfair trade practice.

Who then is to protect us from our protectors? If we are abused by the very persons we depend on to protect our rights, to uphold the full majesty of the law, to render justice to every man – to whom do we turn?

The very provisions in the Constitution that protects the Supreme Court from the abuse of our enemies, also protects them from wrath of the people they betray.

It behooves us to assume as much as we can, that the Supreme Court will always be supreme in wisdom, thought and deed.

And yet the opportunities for graft and corruption are greater in the Supreme Court than in the Bureau of Customs or the Bureau of Internal Revenue, because of the awesome powers of the Justices. For the Supreme Court has the final say in the dispensation and administration of justice under the law.

There is no appeal from their abuse of authority, or from the so-called ``judicial discretion.'' The only way to remove erring Justices is to expose them in public, and hopefully, with sufficient public clamor, force them to resign.

It is ironic that under the Marcos regime, Supreme Court Justices opted to resign en masse over the bar scandal in the Ericta affair, which compared to many scandals attending the present Supreme Court, is a minor anomaly.

But rarely in our ``democratic times,'' do our public officials resign out of delicadeza – with the singular exception of Senator Orly Mercado who just resigned his position of Majority Floor Leader, to protest a nasty rumor. According the Alejandrino, today the motto seems to be ``Morir antes de dimitir.''

Is delicadeza indeed dead? The only other way to force their resignation is through impeachment. Unfortunately, this process is cumbersome, expensive and often frustrating, unless the members of Congress themselves are ready to deal with it with objectivity, selflessness and courage.

The media can play a large role in making impeachment work if it is courageous, independent and unrelenting in its quest for good government.

Above all what we need is an affirmation of people power and the miracle of Edsa.

September 31 to August 4, 1989

ooooo

CONSTITUTIONAL COMMISSION

Part 1. Our Patriots In The Concom

A ConCom Commissioner, called Uncle Tom because of his dark complexion and his habit of greeting American agent Dick Holmes, "Yes, massa!", protested that so-called nationalists in the ConCom have no monopoly on Patriotism. "We love our country too," he exclaimed.

He is right. Although all nationalists must necessarily be patriots, not all patriots are nationalists. Some people assume that nationalism and patriotism are identical and interchangeable. They are wrong, there is a lot of difference between the two.

Patriotism is LOVE for the Philippines; Nationalism is FAITH in the Filipino. Patriotism is an EMOTION. Nationalism is an intellectual concept, the IDEA that we are all Filipinos, of common culture and race, that we must promote and protect and defend our interests against the interest of other nations, in the same way Americans promote, protect and defend their own interests against the Japanese and the Soviets.

President Manuel Roxas was a patriot; but he felt that the interests of the Filipino will be best served if Americans are given parity rights to exploit Philippine natural resources. He was a patriot, but certainly not a nationalist as Claro M. Recto was. For Recto believed that the Filipino is   perfectly capable of developing his own resources and build a prosperous industrial nation without dependence on the Americans.

Jimmy Ongpin is a patriot who loves the Philippines, but he feels Filipinos cannot be trusted enough to be honest, so he wants to pay $500,000 to the Swiss SGS to watch and check the value of imports coming into this country, something nationalist Bobby Tañada will not do. Jimmy loves the Filipinos, but he does not think Filipinos have the talent to develop the country or mount a real industrialization, therefore he wants foreign investment to do the job, and the Filipinos to concentrate on being dirt farmers -- something   nationalist Renato Constantino will never accept.

Take Commissioner Christian Monsod, the unabashed nemesis of the "nationalists" in the ConCom. He is a graduate of Wharton, an American business college with a scholastic standing somewhere between Harvard and the Far Eastern University; he worked for a time as a minor functionary in the IMF/World Bank and in the Meralco Securities. "I know my business!" he exclaimed in a shouting match with nationalist Alejandro Lichauco, and he does. He headed and directed the destinies of two extinct financial companies, GenBank and FilCapital, and is determined to do the same to the economy of the Philippines. He considers himself a true patriot "with the tranquil and steady dedication of a lifetime" (to hear him quote Adlai Stevenson) when he advocates, as Jimmy Ongpin and the American Chamber of Commerce do, Free Trade and Open Economy for the Philippines.

Christian Monsod is assisted in his endeavors by an alopecic misogamic messianic gynander who heads an economic research agency giving out economic predictions that never come true. His agency is supported by the contributions of American multinationals and a neo-Fascist organization called Hans Seidel Stiftung, the financing arm of the Christlich Soziale Union of Bavaria, West Germany. This is a political party headed by Franz Joseph Strauss, a neo-Fascist politician who was fired from Adenaur's cabinet when he conducted Nazi-like raids on newspaper offices like those of Der Spiegel magazine, and allegedly accepted kickbacks on military supply contracts. Like Hitler, Strauss is a patriot too.

Christian's demolition team is called The Four Horsemen of the Apocalypse, because the four, having control over the Committee on the Economy and the National Patrimony, tend to ride roughshod over any proposal to make Filipino citizens the chief determinants and the principal beneficiaries of economic development. The other two are respected lawyers representing the interests of American multinationals: Jose "Peps" Bengson and Ricardo "Small Dick" Romulo.

The group is supported by the Loyalist Opposition headed by a public relations expert, Blas Ople. Blas, if one recalls, masterminded the campaign of Marcos for the presidency, with his masterful "Seven Pillars of Wisdom" and "The Bravest are the Tenderest" slogans reinforced by a picture of Marcos throwing a child up into an overhead electric fan. As Labor Minister, Blas forbade strikes in certain industries operated by American multinationals.

Today, Blas Ople has been bitten by the Presidential Bug, and is kowtowing to the Americans to get support for his bid. He spends his time operating a word processor churning out press releases designed to make it appear he is doing all the work at the ConCom. Giving out his releases in specially   prepared envelops, he manages to get headlines and TV coverage for his vaguely worded polysyllabic profundities. Blas Ople is a patriot too, and a pompous ass to boot.

With such patriots, the nation need not concern itself with traitors.

August 28, 1986

Part 2. Raising The Quality Of Debate In The Concom

Dear Sylvia Mayuga, lovable Sylvia, it was nice of you to take up the cudgels for Christian Monsod who is really taking the flack that should be properly be directed to Bernie Villegas, the head of the ConCom Committee on the National Economy and the Patrimony.

It was nice of you, Sylvia, to call for the return of the boycotting nationalists "back to the halls of constitutional debate", urging them, as Christian often does, to raise the quality of debate between "absolute protectionists" and "enlightened compromisers".

In the first place, Sylvia, there has never been a proper debate between the so-called Nationalists and the so-called Pro-American Bloc. By omission or deliberate design, not a single nationalist economist was appointed into the Constitution Commission, not Alejandro Lichauco, not Renato Constantino, not myself, not Joseph Lim, nor Mariano Miranda.

As a result, the so-called Pro-American Bloc, the free market economists like Bernardo Villegas and Christian Monsod, and lawyers Jose Bengson Jr. and Ricardo Romulo (who have many American clients) -- the famous Four Horseman of the Apocalypse -- had a strangehold on the Committee on the National Economy and Patrimony. Only they had the "expertise", the technical jargon that can be wielded to impress rather than to enlighten the uninitiated.

Oh yes, the nationalist economists were allowed to appear before the Committee, to express and argue their views, but such views never got to the plenary session where it counted. Instead, the Four Horsemen filtered, distorted and compromised the nationalist views to reflect their own prejudices, and that was what the Commission voted upon.

In other words, Sylvia, in the debate about the economic provisions, Christian et al. were not only the debaters, they were the judges of the debate. In the absence of any economic experts within their ranks, the nationalist bloc urgently moved that the Commission itself, in view of the importance of the subject, constitute itself into committee and conduct impartial hearings, so that the entire body may hear a REAL DEBATE between economists of the same rank, let's say, between Villegas and Lichauco, or between Christian and myself.

But no, with unseemly haste, the economic provisions drafted by the Four Horsemen, further obfuscated by Blas Ople were voted upon by Commissioners who probably did not understand the implications of what they were voting on.

In the second place, lovely Sylvia, the terms that were put into your pen by Christian, "absolute protectionists" versus "enlightened compromisers", "monopolists disguised as nationalists, hard-nosed businessmen out to confuse the issues... nationalists-come-lately and infant zealots" hardly contribute to a serious and high level debate on the basic issues involved. They imply that the Nationalist Bloc is uncompromising and motivated by greed, while the Pro-American Bloc is enlightened, open-minded, and righteous.

Bernie Villegas can indulge in patronizing proposals, as you did, Sylvia, "to include readings in Philippine economic history" in front of people who do not know what he is talking about, but he never dared to face me in open debate. When he faced a knowledgeable Alejandro Lichauco in the Monday Kapihan in the Manila Hotel, as was revealed on television on Channel 4, he looked pathetic.

Now why not have Christian Monsod and Bernie Villegas conduct a high level intelligent debate with Alejandro Lichauco and myself, before the entire Constitutional Commission?

You know, Sylvia, lovely Sylvia, there is a basic difference between the debating posture of a defender of the status-quo (the Pro-American Bloc), and that of one who challenges the status quo (the Nationalist Bloc).

The defender urges Sobriety, Moderation, Compromise, Non-Emotional Involvement, and Sweet Reasonableness, because he is squatting on the status-quo and time is on his side and any deadlock or delay is Victory for his side.

The challenger starts with a defeat situation, he must equalize the debate by appealing to the Emotion, as did Voltaire, Samuel Adams, Plaridel and Rizal, when they challenged the intolerable status-quo, because Emotion moves people while Sobriety does not. He must demand more than he expects to get, he must raise his voice and cry to high heaven. A nationalist must say to the American imperialist, "Get out of my house first, let me in, and then let's reason out our differences."

But the fact that you must recognize, Sylvia, is that the nationalists are supported by the broadest coalition of consumer, labor, business, political and cause-oriented groups ever assembled. The pro-Americans have no one except the American Chamber of Commerce, the CRC, and ten U.P. professors who never had to compete in the market-place... and you.

August 29, 1986

Part 3. Keeping Henares Quiet About Americans

Someone found a way to keep Henares quiet about Americans on TV, by asking him to host the show, "ConCom and You". We taped the first broadcast on the Bases Question, with guests, ex-MP Enrique "Ike" Belo and BAYAN secretary general Lean Alejandro in a debate unsurpassed for eloquence.

Our problem has always been the paucity of convincing speakers for the "pro-American" side. We are impressed with Ike Belo for his sincerity, eloquence and forthrightness: "I am proud to be pro-American up to a point... I want the bases retained... Future generations must make their own choice."

Contrast him with ConCommissioners Peps Bengson and Nap Rama in past TV programs, who take no position except to give Cory all possible options; or Greg Tingson with his "Mother America right or wrong!" and often quoted "Let the Bases stay for a hundred years!"

Lean Alejandro is an old hand in debates about the Bases, but has never had the opportunity to take center stage because there are just too many speakers invited at the same time. I think it is a pretty good idea to limit the guests to two knowledgeable antagonists, and not necessarily from the ConCom.

Tune in on Channel 4, tonight Friday 10:30 to 11:30 PM, and see an wonderful debate on the Bases Question between Ike the eloquent elder statesman, and Lean the passionate youth leader, with Larry in a quiet and unaccustomed role as host. And tune in again every Friday thereafter.

You, Central Bank Governor Jobo Fernandez, when I say something that wounds you, you cry Ouch. When I say something nice about you, you do not bother to say Thanks... or do you feel as Beth Day says, that it is not enough to make up for what was printed in the front page?

This E.I.R story about Hank Greenberg's Gang of Four is simply fantastic. I keep telling Jobo that he is in bad company. When I wrote the story of Benguet Corporation -- and Herb Allen, ugly Kirpatovsky, William Groves and the Bahamas deal, I suspected that the Mafia was involved somehow.

My suspicions grew when Jimmy Ongpin began to plaster down his hair with pomade just like George Raft, and to snarl like James Cagney, "Ya lousy rat!" as he pushed half a grapefruit into the face of his gang moll, in the movie "Public Enemy Number One".

Today, NEDA minister Solita Monsod, who dared to contradict Jimmy by advocating "selective repudiation" of our external debt, simply refuses to be within arm's length and boarding-house reach of Jimmy Ongpin, especially when he is having grapefruit for breakfast.

And take a good look at Cesar Zalamea, the guy who shoots down Dumbo, Bambi and Bugs Bunny. Look at the flat face, pug nose, the fat jowls, a mouth that extends from ear to ear, and lopsided smile. Put a cigar into his kisser, by golly and he looks like Edward G. Robinson, playing the title role in "Little Caesar" (rent it in Video Sonix at Forbes).

And the last in Hank Greenberg's Gang of Four, as reported in the July 25 1986 Executive Intelligence Review, is ex-Prime Minister Cesar Virata. The closest I can place him is Mortimer Snerd, the brother of Charlie McCarthy; both are dummies of Edgar Bergen, father of Candice. Charlie is the smart aleck and sounds like Jobo Fernandez. Mortimer is the slow poke, who, like Virata, says, "Uh... uh... I don't get it." Bergen of course is Uncle Sam.

The Claro M. Recto Foundation, organized by the friends and followers of the Great Nationalist, on its 25th Anniversary, issued several statements that merit the attention of the nation.

First, it expelled Ferdinand Marcos, one of the charter members, for acts inimical to the objectives of the organization.

Second, it distanced itself away from Recto's only living son, ex-MP Rafael Recto, by reaffirming its acceptance of his irrevocable resignation dated October 7, 1980. The organization has been feuding with Raffy because of his refusal to turn over the Recto memorabilia deeded to it by the family.

Third, it expressed support for the Cory government for its efforts to return the country back the rule of law, a ratified constitution, the norms of morality and justice, and the spirit of democratic pluralism.

Fourth, it expressed profound appreciation for the invaluable services of Justice J.B.L. Reyes, and Senators Lorenzo Tañada and Jose Diokno, in upholding the ideas and ideals of Claro M. Recto, and in graciously passing the torch of leadership to a younger generation of Recto admirers.

Above all, it reiterated its adherence to Filipino Nationalism as a unifying force in the building of the nation, expressing support for the propagation of a national language, exaltation of national heroes, and economic nationalism.

The document was signed by Oscar Lopez, chairman; Hilarion M. Henares Jr, vice chairman; Antonio Quintos, treasurer; Galileo Brion, secretary; and Trustees, Alejandro P. Roces, Wigberto Tañada, Rosalinda Orosa, Alfredo M. Santos, Jose L. Gamboa, Pablo M. Malvar, Jose O. Desiderio, Jr., and Antonio U. Miranda (honorary chairman).

September 5, 1986

Part 4. The Right To Life Of The Unborn

Tonight Sunday on Channel 4 from 9:30 to 10:30 in the evening, tune in on "ConCom and You" with yours truly, Larry Henares as host, on the subject: "Right to Life of the Unborn vs. Right of Choice of Women who bear them". Guests are Auxiliary Bishop of Manila, Monsignor Teodoro Bacani, and the Protestant Pastor of Ellinwood Malate Church, Reverend Cirilo Rigos -- both

ConCommissioners -- and two feminists from the cause-oriented organization Gabriela, Ms. Fe Mangahas and Ms. Larraine Sarmiento. Watch the women beleaguer the Bishop, with the Pastor right in the line of fire. What a debate!

My wife Cecilia with whom I can never win an argument, never fails to remind me that biologically speaking, the female is much more important than the male of the species. And by way of proof, she postulates two hypothetical situations: a world of women where there is only one man; and a world of men with only one woman.

If all the women in the world died except one, she says, the human race will be back to the status of Adam and Eve; and with the woman producing once every nine months, it will take the human race thousands of years to get back to the population it has today.

On the other hand, she says, if all men in the world died except one, the human race will hardly skip a beat. One male can ejaculate at least 50 million sperms in one sexual act, and has the potential of being able to impregnate one whole country of women after only one orgasm. Given the ability of our scientists to collect, freeze, store and distribute male sperms, it is possible for one lucky man to repopulate the entire earth in a few years.

But suppose the lucky man happens to be a Jesuit priest or a celibate numerary of the O.... my wife Cecilia stares at me with a devastating look that means I not only lose the argument, but I am out of the *kulambo* for the night.

Since the women are the most critical factor in the matter of sex and population, they are the most vocal, most concerned and most involved in the debates regarding The Right to Life of the Unborn Vs. The Right of Choice of the Women who bear them.

I was traipsing around the ConCom trying to catch the attention of Christian, Bernie and Dick Holmes, when I was pounced upon by a group of women from Kilusang Singalong, led by schoolmates of my wife in Sta. Scholastica and including Pich Ocampo Unson, Dora Badillo Ledda, Erlinda Perez Paez, Tessie Rosales Pajarillo, Charing de Venecia, Teresing Fernandez, and Tillie Momponbanua.

ConCom delegate Ambrosio Padilla, who is described by one of the Four Horsemen as a refugee from the 12th Century, dropped by and was collared by the women too, and the two of us got a lecture on the precise moment the Unborn becomes a Human Being. It is the contention of Pich et al. that such moment comes when the sperm impregnates the egg and becomes a viable being. Any abortion of the foetus therefore is an act of murder.

It was a little disconcerting, when we taped the next show of the "ConCom and You", to find the Right to Life of the Foetus defended by a man, no less than my favorite Bishop, ConCom delegate Teodoro Bacani, against the assault of two very assertive women Fe Mangahas and Larraine Sarmiento who are Catholic mothers and feminists, described by the same one of the Four Horsemen as "female chauvinist sows".

The other member of the panel, Rev. Cirilo Rigos, was expected to come to the rescue of the Bishop, but he didn't. Instead he suggested that the ConCom leave the question to the Congress, since there seems to be too wide a divergence as to when the Human Being comes into being -- at the moment of conception, at the moment of birth, or any moment in-between.

Fe and Larraine on the other hand insisted on the right of women to control the disposition of their own bodies. As long as the foetus is in her womb, consistent with the advice of doctors, priests and husbands, the woman reserves the right to make the final decision. Suppose the pregnancy is the result of rape or incest? Suppose the foetus is defective and will lead to the birth of a mongoloid? Suppose the mother feels incapable financially or emotionally, to carry the foetus to birth?

I asked questions to help the Bishop: Does complete control over one's body mean that the law will condone sexual activity outside of marriage? or suicide? or drug addiction? But the Bishop needed no help; after all he never had to face a nagging wife, he was not cowed by the two feminists.

Bishop Bacani spread out illustrations of foetuses aborted, a horrible sight like those of the gas chambers of Dachau and Austerlitz. I almost puked and fainted, and summoned only enough strength to call for commercials....

The last 5 minutes had to be retaped because the tape got garbled... which prompted me to challenge the right to life of our director Nori Sagun, but before we aborted her...

Hey, what am I telling you all this for? See for yourself tonight, Channel 4 at 9:30 PM, "ConCom and You"!

September 14, 1986

Part 5.　Military Bases, With The Help Of A Long Spoon

Now there is that joke about Mike the Irishmen and his wife Maggie. Mike was an Irishman from the tip of his tongue to the pit of his stomach -- which means that he was given to drinking whisky and carousing with the boys every night after dinner. At midnight, he usually staggered home and headed straight for the kitchen sink, where in a fit of drunken nausea, he threw up his evening's meal.

His wife Maggie kept nagging him: "Mike, one of these days, you will throw up your guts!" And Mike would answer, "Impossible, impossible."

Well one night, Maggie was disemboweling a freshly killed chicken which she dressed and placed in the refrigerator. And feeling too tired to clean up, she left the entrails of the chicken in the kitchen sink.

As usual, Mike staggered home at midnight and headed straight for the kitchen sink where he regurgitated his evening repast. Silence. Then a scream, "Maggie!"

Maggie called out, "What happened, Mike?"

Mike answered: "It happened, Maggie, exactly the way you said it would happen! I threw up my guts. But by the grace of God, and with the help of a long spoon, I got 'em all back in!"

The story reminds me of the joke that is perpetually being played on us by a bunch of American wise guys and their little brown brothers who keep nagging us: "One of these days, if Americans are not around to protect you, the communists will come and take you over."

We Filipinos are being goaded into a state of mind wherein we can very well, by the grace of God and with help of along spoon, swallow hook, line and sinker, the unwholesome and lethal aspects of foreign occupation of our national territory, the indignities of racial discrimination, the dangerous delights of the honky-tonk with its drugs and venereal diseases, and the searing promise of a nuclear holocaust.

All these years, we have been systematically subjected to a mass psychological treatment that makes us react like laboratory rats in the manner of Pavlov's conditioned reflex. Whenever some American says, "Hoy, the communists are about to take you over!" gongs clang in the cranium, glands secrete their juices and suddenly, "O judgment, thou art fled to brutish beasts and men have lost their reason!"... and predictably, we are subdued into a mute hypnotic stupor, to endure once more the colonial injustices, extraterritorial privileges and unequal treaties that need desperately to be corrected if we are to proceed with our nation building.

It is primarily for this reason that I advocate the insertion in the new Constitution of a provision prohibiting military bases and nuclear weapons in our territory. And decry the constant repetition of a stupid lie that suspends our disbelief, and insults our intelligence -- that without　　American soldiers in our territory armed with atomic bombs, the Philippines will fall like a domino to the Communists as did Vietnam and Cambodia.

According to the Nazi propaganda minister Goebbels, any lie, if it's monstrous enough and if it's repeated constantly, becomes a truth. And this we Filipinos have accepted as Goebbels' Truth and Gospel Truth: that there is no alternative between American Imperialism and International Communism, and that we must choose between the two evils.

This ignores the evidence of what we read about and know:

-- that such countries as Yugoslavia, India, Indonesia, Sri Lanka and Burma can exist and prosper while being unaligned and neutral in the cold war between the superpowers;

-- that such countries as Indonesia, Singapore and Malaysia may contain the Communist threat on their own initiative without having American bases within their national territories;

-- that such nations as Vietnam and Cuba may succumb to communism even with the existence of American military bases on their soil, and even with American armed intervention;

--- that most nations especially in Europe have allowed Communist parties to participate in elections and get beaten in the market place of ideas;

--- that the Communist Bloc is no monolith; that the Soviet Union and Mainland China may disagree with each other more violently than they do with the Imperial United States;

--- that no nation in the world except the Philippines would lend itself to being a pawn in superpower geopolitics without sufficient guarantee of American retaliation in case of attack;

--- that the external threat of Communist invasion in our part of the world across the China Sea is pure myth, the product of the fevered imagination of our colonial mentality; that the best proof of this is the inability or unwillingness of Mainland China to invade the Taiwan stronghold in the Quemoy Islands within sight of its own shores;

--- and that internal threat of Communism is a function of our own response to socio-economic problems, and well within our own capacity to contain, as we did in the 1950s and the 1970s.

Anyone who believes otherwise in spite of massive evidence to the contrary, is an intellectual cretin and an incurable colonial.

This cretinization of our cerebral cortex invites further injury to compound the insult: the massive interference of the Americans and especially the CIA in our internal affairs; the surrender of our foreign policy and recently our economic policy to the dictation of the IMF, the American Embassy and the American multinational corporations; racial discrimination in the bases and within American corporations; the loss of loyalty of Filipinos to the Filipino nation; and our humiliating acceptance of the role of running dogs and cannon fodder for American Imperialism.

September 17, 1986

Part 6. Loyalty To RP Ends Where Loyalty To USA Begins

The indefatigable Manuel L. Quezon, parting ways with Nacionalista leader Sergio Osmena Sr., exclaimed: "My loyalty to my party ends where my loyalty to my country begins."

By the same token, the Four Horsemen of the Apocalypse (Christian Monsod, Bernie Villegas, Ricardo Romulo and Peps Bengson) who have been professing their loyalty to the Philippines when their professional and financial connections to American Multinationals and the IMF were exposed a few weeks ago, can now proclaim: "Our loyalty to the Philippines ends where our loyalty to the United States begins."

In the ConCom, whenever the interests of the Filipinos conflict with those of the Almighty Americans, the Four Horsemen under the hypnotic spell of CIA Agent Dick Holmes, who is always present in the peanut gallery, and who probably acts as their Control as in the James Bond movies, cast their votes to protect and defend American interests.

These four cowboys who treat the rest of us Filipinos as savage Indians, insignificant and disposable, voted:

(1) to allow Americans and foreigners to own 100% of Catholic and religious schools, and 40% of other private educational institutions, in spite of the fact that almost all our schools today are already Filipinized;

(2) to keep American English as our official language, on par with Filipino, in order to perpetuate the cultural enslavement and colonial mentality of our people;

(3) to omit "ecological consciousness" as a goal of Education, so that American multinationals can continue to disembowel our mountains, convert our lands to desert waste, and poison Filipinos with noxious waste.

(4) to omit a phrase in the provisions on Science and Technology, that would promote "National Self-Reliance" in the transfer of technology, so that the American multinationals can continue to keep us a nation of dirt farmers and beggars, forever dependent on Americans.

(5) to omit one of the proposed provisions that the Philippines should be a signatory to the Patent and Copyright Unions only under conditions of "full reciprocity of benefits", so that American drug monopolists can continue to charge the Filipino people 14 to 20 times the price they charge in other countries, so that we shall spend millions for Betamax Raids on small Filipino businessmen for the benefit of Frank Knight.

(6) to constitutionally prohibit the Philippines from protecting its industries the way Japan and the United States

does, so that the Philippines will forever have an agricultural subsistence economy, and be a dumping ground for surplus American goods and a happy hunting ground for Multinationals;

(7) to allow Americans to own 40% of public utilities, with management contracts for 100% control, especially in communications companies, so that the American CIA can monitor all messages going in and out of the country, something that no nation in the whole world will allow;

(8) to maneuver the ConCom into rejecting provisions prohibiting military bases and nuclear weapons, for the sole purpose of eroding the bargaining position of President Cory Aquino as she goes on a Working Visit to Washington DC, all in spite of urgent requests from government to postpone any voting till Cory arrives from the States.

The Four Horsemen are probably hopeless. Their colonial mentality is congenital, they have been crawling on their bellies since birth, and somehow never learned to rise from their knees in the presence of Americans.

But those who help them are something else -- Napoleon Rama, Soc Rodrigo, Bishop Bacani, Alberto Jamir, Crispin de Castro, Greg Tingson and the rest of the Esperanza Group.

"Take it easy on the Americans, Larry, we need them!" my one-time hero Nap Rama keeps saying. For what, Nap, for what? They don't bring capital, they borrow 88% of the capital they use here! They bring in 12% of the capital and take out 95% of the profits, they take out $6.50 for every $1.00 they bring in! They sell us outmoded army equipment with 3-days ammunition, just so they can control our Armed Forces! We need Americans like we need a hole in the head, Nap!

When ConCommisioner Greg Tingson said in open session, "Why we even send our daughters to the United States so they can marry Americans and breed beautiful children!" he insults Christian Monsod who looks as if he descended from the aborigines. But Greg really believes what he says, for he was adopted by an American soldier, and many of his daughters did marry Americans.

My former teacher and fellow senatorial aspirant, Soc Rodrigo may be sincere when he says that he represents the 70% who are consumers against the greedy producers, just as he was sincere when he represented the 88% who are Catholics and who will be offended if forced to read the Noli and Fili of Rizal. But I cannot understand why he does not speak up for the 100% who will be incinerated if the U.S. bases provoke nuclear war. Nor can I understand why Bishop Bacani so solicitous of the unborn, does not care enough for those annihilated by war.

And there is Commissioner Crispin de Castro, looking every bit the general that he is, raring to go to war like Dr. Strangelove and General Bullmoose, to save the world for democracy and multinational corporations.

September 19, 1986

Part 7. Four Fours Most Foul

Tomorrow the ConCom winds up its work, and each commissioner will sign about 100 copies of the printed constitution.

In Chinese the word signifying the number Four, sounds very much like the word signifying Death. In Fokien, both are pronounced like the Spanish SI; in Mandarin, both sound like the Pangasinan SE.

It is the curse of the Constitutional Commission that it is plagued by deathly groups of four, as a matter of fact, four groups of four most foul, all dedicated to the United States:

There is the Four Horsemen of the Apocalypse, standing astride the Committee on the Economy and Patrimony, riding roughshod over any pro-Filipino proposal.

Then we have the Gang of Four, the opposition loyal to the Americans, remnants of the discredited Marcos KBL.

Then the Four of Methuselah, mostly in their seventies in age, and way back in the Dark Ages in their thinking.

Lastly there is the Four Clerical Errors, who invoke the Lord to justify their support of American policies.

The Four Horsemen are of course quite known to all: (1) the Alopecic Misogamic Gynander, (2) the Raging Bull,(3) Dickie Peter, and (4) the Little Brown Jug-Ears.

The Gang of Four is headed by (1) Blast Opel the Great Inebriate, with members (2) Acid Rain, (3) Rusty Brain, and the Storm Trooper.

The Four of Methuselah are venerable. Two of them were 1971 Constitutional delegates; two were veteran senators; two were jailed by Marcos, and two are greencard holders or possibly American citizens. The head is (1) Tiny Joe, also head of the Esperanza Group, with members, (2) Puwit (poet) who is the phone pal of Phil Kaplan, (3) Rip Van Winkle who is a refugee from the 12th century, and (4) Nardong Putik from Cavite who is ironically a former assistant of Claro M. Recto. Appointed for their wisdom and experience, they proved to be a throwback to the colonial past.

The Four Clerical Errors are of course (1) Torquemada (of the Spanish Inquisition) whose sermons like those of Father Damaso are directed against the Filipino *filibusteros*; (2) Billy Graham, (3) Jerry Falwell and (4) Our Lady of Zeroes, a lay woman who contributes nothing but always votes with the Inquisition. Rasputin does not belong to this group; neither does the wonderful Nun But the Bleeding Heart, who was born with a silver spoon and and a heart dedicated to the cause of the urban poor. The Clerical Errors were appointed as the conscience of the nation, and turned out to be frontally lobotomized.

The sympathizers of the Four Fours most Foul, are the rest of the Esperanza Group: Napoleon II, General Bullmoose, Popeye, The Sword of Islam, E.T. the law dean, and the Sacristan Judge.

And ranged against the Four Fours Most Foul, are the Magnificent Dozen who managed to uphold Filipino interests against all odds, whose names now belongs to history: (1) Jose "Sengseng" Suarez; (2) Minda Luz Quesa; (3) Jaime Tadeo; (4) Ponciano "Pons" Bennagen; (5) Wilfrido Villacorta; (6) Rene Sarmiento; (7) Ed Garcia; (8) Chito Gascon; (9) Felicitas Aquino; (10) Sister Cristina Tan; (11) Rosario Braid; and (12) Adolfo Azcuna. Plus the wonderful Lino Brocka who resigned in protest.

The nationalist sympathizers deserve mention: Hilario Davide, Jose Nolledo, Father Joaquin Bernas, Vicente Foz, Lugum Uka, Yusup Abubakar, Chief Justice Roberto Concepcion.

Nardong Putik took ailing Celing Palma's place as presiding officer and was observed by a reporter to have taken instructions from Napoleon II and Little Brown Jug-Ears: "We expect you to give no quarter to the nationalists!" *Talagang walang awa sa bayan*, said the reporter.

Tiny Joe, leader of the Four of Methuselah and the entire Esperanza Group,is leaving soon for New York where his family resides, and was given a *despedida* at the Nielson Towers, the control tower by which American fighters and bombers were guided into landing on the Makati runways during the last war. There is no truth to the rumor that Tiny Joe was given a plaque for outstanding service to the USA, and the rest of the evening was spent by the Esperanza Group singing God Bless America and The Star Spangled Banner.

Don't forget to watch "ConCom and You" tonight, 10:30 to 11:30, Channel 4, with guests The Fighting Monsignor from Magallanes Nico Bautista, and the Pastor from Ellinwood Cirilo Rigos, with myself as host, on Church and State Relations.

October 14, 1986

ooooo

CORAZON AQUINO, THE EARLY YEARS
(arranged chronologically)

Part 1. Towards A Progressive, Just And Equitable Society

 Ms. Cory C. Aquino   January 5, 1985
25 Times Street, Quezon City
Dear Cory,
PLEASE read and consider the enclosed for your policy speech on the 6 January. In case the other is not in your style. At least read the beginning and the end of the speech.

It is based on the various Declarations of the Opposition especially Ninoy's and the Convenors' Group, as well as the Unido and the Liberal Party -- all of which are remarkably uniform in their economic prescriptions.

I know you are educated in the Liberal Arts, and I composed this in your style, using only quotes for the economic prescriptions, complete with footnotes, so that you don't slip out of character and sound like an economist.

This speech is only 25 minutes long, but it covers everything, clearly, logically, and in simple language, with quotes from Ninoy and W.H. Auden.

I took the liberty to do this because the group assigned to it suddenly became secretive and uncommunicative, and I panicked at the thought that they may write something that is not compatible with the Declarations of the Opposition.

Onward to Victory,
Hilarion M. Henares Jr.
****

Towards A Progressive, Just And Equitable Society by Corazon C. Aquino

delivered before the Makati Business Club, the Bishop-Businessmen's Conference and the Management Association of the Philippines, on January 6, 1985, Manila Intercontinental Hotel

We are a nation in crisis. We are a nation state of 52 million people, with an economy whose production structure is so weak that it suffers in comparison with that of Singapore with only 2.5 million population, or that of Taiwan with only 18 million people to support.

President Marcos's technocrats have so mismanaged the economy, and presidential cronies and relatives have so misappropriated the resources of the nation, that the Philippines has become a basket case in a high growth area, registering a negative rate of growth while its neighbors are   succeeding in warding off the effects of the world recession.

From Taiwan we import computers and even toys and flashlights, while to Singapore we export laborers our economy cannot employ. We cannot even make a single hammer or a pair of pliers or a simple screwdriver, which we import from nations once more underdeveloped than ours, namely India, Pakistan and Mainland China.

Mismanagement, Powerlessness

Marcos's mismanagement of our economy has caused such an engulfing poverty that a majority of our people live lives no higher than that of scavenging animals, our once prosperous nation now reduced to a garbage heap whose inhabitants must do violence to each other in order to survive.

But the most searing expression of this poverty is the prostitution to which children, boys and girls as young as 8 years old, are being compelled by the poverty of their parents, on such a scale that is unimaginable elsewhere in the world.

In the 1950s, we had the highest rate of growth in this part of the world. We were the envy of Taiwan then the backwater refuge of the defeated Kuomintang armies. We were the envy of Korea then suffering the throes of a civil war.

Today, Taiwan and Korea export ships, whole factories, computers, while the Philippines as depicted in the television spots aired by Mr. Cendaña, is back to the production of buntal hats, shellcraft, ipil-ipil, and mail order brides.

In the 1950s, our agriculture could at least function without fertilizer. Today, without imported fertilizer our entire agricultural system ceases to function. Out of the 30 original varieties of rice that can grow without chemical inputs, only 2 varieties are left because of genetic erosion.

If for any reason whatever (such as war, a worldwide depression or a collapse in the international banking system), we are suddenly isolated from sources of industrial imports and foreign loans, our country would be thrown into chaos and 52 million people will literally claw at each other for food.

All modes of economic activity, from the operation of traffic lights, hospitals and funeral parlors, to the working of farms and factories will cease, and we will be transported overnight into a dark and violent age.

This is true measure of the nation's underdevelopment and powerlessness, brought about by Marcos's economic policies during the years of the Martial Law.

Uniform Stand Of United Opposition

The United Opposition has in many instances proposed solutions to this economic problem, solutions that are remarkably uniform in their approach and objectives.

In the Declaration of Common Principles of the Allied Opposition signed by Lorenzo Tañada, Eva Kalaw, Cesar Climaco, the two Laurel brothers, among others, and presented by Ninoy Aquino to the Solarz Committee on June 23, 1983, two months before he was killed, the pursuit of the following was urged:

"1. The Filipino people must be the sole determinant of the nation's political, economic and cultural life and the principal beneficiary of the national patrimony. All forms of foreign domination, exploitation and interference in the country must be eliminated.

"6. The ownership of the principal means of production must be diffused and income equitably distributed to promote development, alleviate poverty and insure the rational utilization of resources."

The Declaration of Unity of the Convenors' Group, signed by Jose Diokno, Teofisto Guingona, Eva Kalaw, Doy Laurel, myself, Jimmy Ongpin, Lorenzo Tañada and the representatives of Jovito Salonga, Rafael Salas, Butz Aquino, and Raul Manglapus, also reiterates the above objectives exactly in the same words, in paragraph 3 and 4, with the following elaborations, among others:

"3.1 The freedom of the nation from any form of economic, cultural, and political domination or interference by the government of any foreign power or any international institution or group will be safeguarded.

"3.2 A self-determined and autonomous course of economic, social and political development will be pursued to provide a higher income for all, expand the domestic market, foster profitable foreign trade, establish appropriate basic industires, develop effective technology, encourage the use of Filipino creativity and resources and in the distribution of the fruits of development.

"3.3 All economic and financial agreements, entered into, assumed or guaranteed by the Marcos regime will be subjected to public review to ensure that the welfare of our people has not been sacrificed to foreign or private domestic economic or financial interests.

"4.4 An effective land reform program truly beneficial to the underprivileged will be vigorously and honestly pursued.

"4.5 Industrial and agricultural monopolies prejudicial to the national interest will be abolished.

"8.3 Ill-gotten wealth, property and assets shall be confiscated or sequestered for the direct benefit of the entire body politic and all special privileges given individuals close to the Marcos regime shall be immediately terminated. Properties illegally taken by the Marcos regime from private individuals shall be returned to their owners."

The UNIDO Development Program, drafted by its June 12, 1985 National Conference, also states that "The economy must be freed from the control of the privileged few as well as from domination of foreign interests." And it formulated its programs on the Policy of Self Reliance "which does not mean closing our country to all external factors or influence. It essentially means gaining control of, as well as mobilizing, all available resources to accelerate our development before bringing in resources from outside. It means that our development should be based not on external demand but on our people's most urgent needs." The same policy of Self Reliance is expressed in the Declaration of Unity of the Convenors' Group and the Liberal Party Vision and Program of Government (Salonga wing).

Economic Development, Self Reliance

It is interesting to note the difference in the expressions used when talking about our economy. President Marcos speaks of Economic Recovery, the IMF speaks of Structural Adjustment in our economy, and we of the United Opposition speak of Economic Development, as if we are really talking about different things. Perhaps we are. Recovery means bringing the economy back to what it was before; Structural Adjustment means making the economy different from what it used to be; and Development means moving the economy forward toward something better than what we had before. We of the United Opposition stand four-square on Economic Development, based on a policy of Self-Reliance and a Balanced Industrial Development.

"The experience of most developing nations has shown that if the question of what is to be produced is left entirely to the forces of the market and external factors are allowed full play, external values tend to become dominant and production is geared towards luxurious and superfluous commodities, generally for the consumption of privileged sectors. The pressing needs of the people remain unsatisfied."

1.   Indeed, we find that in the Philippines, we produce soft drinks and shampoo while we import yellow corn, sorghum and soybean cake that represent 53% of the cost of the pork we eat, 60% of the chicken, and 80% of the cost of the eggs we eat. And we import the simple tools we need to produce what we need.

We are determined therefore that our economic activities shall primarily directed to the production of food and other items essential to our survival, and the production of fertilizer and other industrial inputs needed for farm modernization and mechanization. We are equally determined that as soon as warranted by our capital, foreign exchange and technological capabilities, "our industrial development shall include the setting up of machine tool industries, base metal industries, basic chemicals, and such industries that will provide forward and backward linkages to complete the integration of our economy from the primarily agricultural and extractive phase to the processing stage, maximizing our capacity to produce industrial products for import substitution and for export."

2.   "The restructuring of industry, after the basic needs of our people are fulfilled, should combine protection and selective development of industries which can produce the most comparative advantage for export, while discouraging those industries which would depend on external inputs of raw materials or supplies for their operations, continuously draining the economy of foreign reserves."

3.   "A major cause of balance-of-trade deficits is the unlimited importation of luxuries and non-essential goods. We should cut down imports to the barest minimum, to the most essential needs."

Rural Mobilization, Wage Policy

4.   We shall give the highest priority to a vigorous rural mobilization program, based on "floor price support to guarantee an adequate income to the farmers, encouragement of products that will not require too much imported seeds, fertilizers and other inputs, improved rural credit system, selective application of foreign technology in food processing and other agri-business, encouragement of indigenous technology and organic fertilization of our farms."

5.   We shall pour resources for the development of small entrepreneurs, "not only as a job creation program, but to broaden the base of the middle class, a substantive requirement in breaking the traditional colonial structure of our society."

6.   We shall pursue a program to preserve, to develop and   protect our natural resources, especially our forests, seas, rivers, and lakes, and prevent pollution of our environment.

7.   We shall pursue a program to "lessen our dependence on   imported fuel and relying on indigenous sources of energy especially for use in the rural areas. We shall review the present cost and pricing structure of power generation with a view to decreasing and ultimately eliminating the layer upon layer of taxes and levies imposed on the consuming public."

8.   "It has been bruited about, and with some amount of pride, that our country's major competitive advantage is cheap labor. This policy is not only inconsistent with our public statements that the Philippines has the highest literacy rate in Asia (except Japan) and has a large reserve of manpower

resource highly skilled in management and production, it is also an affront to the dignity and pride of the Filipino people. But beyond national pride, it is a short-sighted national policy that also perpetuates our present state of colonialism. Low wages do not provide incentive for increased production, it also does not create a domestic market bases to support our industrial activities."

We commit ourselves to reversing this policy or practice of controlling wages by upgrading the quality of education, formalizing a realistic industrialization program, undertaking a massive retaining program, and instituting a wage differential policy.

Foreign Investment, Debt Service

9.   Above all, "we must restore and strengthen the constitutional and legal safeguards of economic nationalism. Present policies which have opened the country to unlimited foreign exploitation must be reviewed, and the capability of Filipinos to assume the dominant role in the economy duly strengthened. While foreign investments may be needed at this stage of our underdevelopment, we must properly delineate activities open to foreign capital so as to ensure that these supplement, rather than supplant, local capital and initiative."

10.   "The most severe constriction on economic development is the burden of servicing our foreign debt. As much as we condemn the practice of some hospitals of asking dying emergency patients for proof of their capacity to pay future bills before any form of medical treatment, we should reject the current rescheduling program for subordinating economic survival to the repayment of our debts."

Interest payments on our debt service alone exceed 40% of our merchandise exports. The opportunity cost of these payments represent imports that could have been used to maintain domestic employment. We hope to be able to send representatives to our creditors to renegotiate our debts better than a corrupt Marcos Government without any credibility, proposing as other nations have done with success:

"(a) a cap on the interest rate paid on foreign debt to protect the country from increases in interest rates caused by monetary and fiscal policies of other countries.

"(b) Foreign debt service should not exceed a fixed portion, say 10 percent of exports, to protect our exports from protectionist policies of countries whose banks are financially exposed to the Philippines, to give high priority to domestic employment and economic growth, to shelter domestic policy from IMF's standardized prescriptions and monetarist assumptions   that differ from Philippine realities.

"(c) A moratorium interest and principal payments on commercial debt, especially those guaranteed by the government; and selective repudiation, especially for projects which had   demonstrably overpriced equipment or which were infeasible from the beginning."

Make Work Program, Human Justice

11.   We are disappointed at the failure of the Marcos government to protect and build on the production base that the country has built during the last thirty years. Billions of dollars worth of assets have been allowed to rust in idleness, hundreds of thousands of trained workers were retrenched and   thrown out of work, and worst of all, the entrepreneurs so gifted with initiative, imagination, talent for organization, and ability and willingness to take risks, have been mocked, betrayed and pushed into bankruptcy by policies designed to satisfy the requirements of extraneous interests.

We are determined on a course of action to stop the hemorrhage on our resources, to bolster our people's will to overcome our economic difficulties, to end our economic recession and get our industries going again, as once said and put into practice by President Alan Garcia Perez of Peru.

We shall at the earliest opportunity stimulate domestic demand by engaging in a make-work program that will satisfy a desperate need of our people and at the same time minimize inflation. We are referring to a massive low cost housing program, on a scale that will have significant multiplier effects on 56 other industries, from steel, wood and glass to real estate and construction. This is the kind of program that has comparatively little imported inputs, the kind of a program that has been the keystone of the development of many socialist countries.

If only the Marcos government had concentrated on truly low cost housing on a massive scale, employing local labor and materials, instead of building monuments to vanity, extravagance, and conspicuous consumption such as the Cultural Center Complex, 5-star hotels and Agoo's Marcos Mountainhead, perhaps the Philippines would have weathered the economic crisis as did our neighbors in Southeast Asia.

My friends, what I am saying today are actually quotes and paraphrases from those who have long studied our economic problems and proposed solutions alternative to those followed by Marcos's bankrupt and discredited regime. I actually quote from the proposed courses of action by the United Opposition, by the Convenor's Group, the UNIDO program of government, and from a recent study by the U.P. School of Economics.

Ninoy Aquino once said that Economic Development is not a game of chance where the prize goes to the strongest, the luckiest, the brightest, or the greediest. For him an Economic Development Program is a scenario for change, a grand design for the advancement of the Filipino people, especially those whom Father Ben Villote called "the poor and the hungry among us, the friendless, the cheated and the beaten."

And as a housewife, mother, widow of one whose mission I am committed to pursue, and I hope, the first woman president of our country, I cry out the same sentiments expressed by poet W.H. Auden, who wrote: "Clear from the head the masses of impressive rubbish,/ Rally the lost and trembling forces of the will,/ Gather them up and let them loose upon the earth,/ Till they construct at last a human justice."

That is the essence of my message to you who are the creators of wealth and the hope of our nation.

I thank you.

Note: Quotations indicated in the text:
DECLARATION OF COMMON PRINCIPLES OF THE ALLIED OPPOSITION, June 12, 1983, by Lorenzo M. Tanada, Eva Estrada Kalaw, Antonio Olmedo, Valentino Legaspi, Cesar Climaco, Luis Mario General, J.B. Laurel Jr., Abraham Sarmiento, Rogaciano Mercado, Homobono Adaza, Wilson Gamboa, Salvador Princesa, Salvador Laurel; presented by Benigno S. Aquino to the Solarz Committee on June 23, 1983.

The DECLARATION OF UNITY (Convenors' Group) December 26, 1984, by Jose W. Diokno, Teofisto Guingona, Eva Estrada Kalaw, Salvador H. Laurel, Ramon Mitra Jr., Ambrosio Padilla, Aquilino Pimentel Jr., Corazon C. Aquino, Jaime V. Ongpin, Lorenzo M. Tanada; and the representatives of Agapito "Butz" Aquino, Raul S. Manglapus, Rafael Salas, and Jovito Salonga.

TOWARD A JUST SOCIETY, UNIDO National Conference (Platform), June 12, 1985, as approved by the Conference.

The LIBERAL PARTY VISION AND PROGRAM OF GOVERNMENT, Platform October 5, 1985, as approved by the Executive Committee (Salonga Wing).

Footnotes Follow:

1. Toward a Just Society, UNIDO National Conference, Platform approved June 12, 1985, Section on "Sustained Economic Growth", More Rational Structure of Production, page 9

2. IBID: Balanced Industrial Development, page 9

3. IBID: Protection and Selective Development of Industries, page 9, 10

4. IBID: Curtailing Imports of Non-Essentials, page 10

5. IBID: Rural Mobilization, page 10

6. IBID: Small and Medium Industries Promotion and Entrepreneurial Development, page 10

7. IBID: Development and Protection of Natural Resources page 10, 11

8. IBID: Energy, page 11

9. IBID: Fair and Just Wage Policy, page 11. 12

10. IBID: Reversing the Neo Colonial Status of the Economy, page 13

11. Towards Recovery and Sustainable Growth, U.P. School of Economics, September 1985,

12. An Alternative Program, A. Servicing and Rescheduling of Foreign Debt, pages 26 to 28

January 5, 1985

Part 2. Replay Of The Great Betrayal

It's uncanny how history repeats itself. It is like the instant replay of the Betamax videotape machine; one can almost predict what is going to happen next.

America The Bountiful

In 1946, the Philippines just suffered through three years of a cruel Japanese occupation and military dictatorship. In 1986, the Philippines just underwent 14 years of Marcos martial law and military dictatorship.

In 1946, the Philippines was bankrupt, its productive assets destroyed in the war, its economy in ruins because of Japanese rapacity and greed. In 1986, the Philippine economy suffered a recession, its economy further deteriorated due to import liberalization, high interest rates, devaluation and other excremental conditions of the IMF, as well as due to the rapacity and greed of Marcos and his cronies.

In 1946, the Philippines had a new leader who begged for aid from the United States, and promised to "follow in the wake of America", America the beautiful, America the bountiful. And he got his aid -- War Damage Payments and War Surplus at 2 cents on the dollar; Back Pay at half the price and Veterans Benefits at one-twentieth what Chinese and Polish volunteers in the U.S. Army were paid; and an annual sugar quota subject to yearly Congressional approval. For these niggardly benefits which lasted only three years till the next foreign exchange crisis in 1949, the Philippines amended its constitution to give Americans Parity Rights till 1974, and gave Americans free use of the Bases for 99 years.

To Test Cory's Will And Resolve

In 1986, the Philippines also has a new leader who is asking the United States and the IMF for "massive aid" in the wake of the world recession, the IMF liquidation of our industries, and Marcos' plunder of our national wealth. The United States which has not yet paid for its "rent" for the bases, through its State Secretary Shultz, has rebuked Foreign Minister Salvador Laurel in Bali for asking for "infinite aid" when the American capacity to give aid is finite.

At the same time, Shultz is asking for something that the Philippines is not prepared to do: issue a passport for Marcos, his wife and their staff for use in going to any third country. US Undersecretary Armacost in his turn and AmCham Prexy Fred Whiting (both of whom supported Marcos throughout the Martial Law period) are trying to get Minister Bobbit Sanchez fired for remarks uttered against American multinational corporations. Getting Bobbit fired will serve notice to all the rest of Cory's cabinet that they stymie Americans at the risk of losing their jobs.

Also the IMF took its cue and demanded that the Aquino government impose additional taxes on the Filipino people (specifically the gasoline tax), and also applied pressure on the administration to pay the Ex-Im bank loan for the useless and overpriced Bataan nuclear plant.

All these are necessary to test the will and resolve of the Aquino government, preparatory to making more and more demands. In the meantime, after having supported Marcos almost to the very end, the American government (as distinguished from the American press and people) is frantically trying to get credit for giving Marcos "the final shove" that drove him out of power.

Pregnant And Barefooted

The United States it would seem is positioning itself for an opening gambit to gain advantages in the negotiations that will inevitably follow. What does she really want, and what is she prepared to give in return?

The standard American offer is a large amount, payable in yearly installments subject to approval by the American Congress. This is the same bovine ordure they gave us for the unconditional use of our bases: $900 million payable every year at the rate of $180 million a year subject to annual Congressional approval. In this way, they can get additional concessions every year, merely by withholding promised payments. This is the same bovine ordure they gave us when they made the Philippine sugar quota subject to annual Congressional approval while getting irrevocable parity rights for twenty eight years, then claiming a vested right to continue parity rights beyond 1974.

They keep us on short leash, in other words, perpetually "pregnant and barefooted", poor and manageable.

And what do Americans want in exchange for their yearly dole-out? First, Americans want all the extraterritorial privileges given by their old friend Ferdinand Marcos, reconfirmed, expanded, and kept permanently on the books, among which are:

Foreign Exploitation Of Natural Resources

(1) A constitutional rider that authorizes "service contracts" by which wholly foreign owned corporations may exploit our natural resources in contravention of the constitutional provision reserving that right to Filipino citizens and corporations owned 60% by Filipinos;

(2) various decrees that authorized service contracts with foreign entities in petroleum exploration, mining of minerals, development of geothermal resources, and exploitation of lands of the public domain;

(3) PD 194 which abrogated the Rice and Corn Nationalization Law by opening up the rice and corn industry to foreigners;

(4) PD 1942 which exempted from land reform, new rice and corn lands to further encourage the corporate farming program of local and foreign corporations;

(5) decrees which nullified the Supreme Court resolution of the Quasha case, by allowing Americans to own residential real estate, and to keep on owning our productive lands through the fiction of free donation and lease-back, even after Parity rights ended.

(6) PD 704 which allows foreigners to fish in Philippine waters, a special gift to Japanese corporations.

Pressure And Bribery

(7) a series of decrees raising the minimum paid up capital of banks, allowing concentration of economic power in universal banks and American participation therein to the extent of 40%;

(8) PD 714 which emasculated the Retail Trade Nationalization Law, and redefined "retail trade" to allow Americans to keep their monopolies;

(9) the open skies policy with respect to foreign airlines, which grants privileges to foreign carriers without reciprocal concessions to our own;

(10) PD 92 and PD 151 which allows the NEDA to suspend nationality requirements existing in Philippine statutes in cases where foreign investment is deemed vital to national interest;

(11) a decree (?) that gives American citizens of Filipino descent all the rights of Filipino citizens, except the right to vote and the obligation to serve in the armed forces.

These and many more were done by Marcos under foreign pressure and monetary inducements (bribery through secret commissions and kickbacks) in order to deprive the Filipinos of their right to be the chief determinants and principal beneficiaries of their country's economic development, and to negate the constitutional mandate of preserving the national patrimony for the benefit of Filipinos.

Probably the reason Armacost hailed the appointment of Minister Jaime Ongpin and his team is that the Americans can now be reasonably sure that the extraterritorial colonial privileges they extracted from Marcos, will be theirs to enjoy for many years to come.

Dirt Farmers And Mail Order Brides

Second, Americans want continuation of IMF policies to keep the Philippines agricultural, frustrate our efforts to industrialize and above all, perpetuate American control of our colonial type of plantation economy. From the dismantling of Filipino monopolies but not those of Americans, to import liberalization, to privatization, to devaluation and floating the peso, to non-reciprocated Free Trade and Open Economy -- the ultimate purpose is to confine Filipinos, as the IMF expressed it, to "export oriented, agriculture based, small scale, labor intensive, rurally dispersed industries" so that only the most menial jobs are assigned to Filipinos in the international division of labor. Such as being dirt farmers, makers of shellcraft, weavers of hats, growers of ipil-ipil, exporters of unskilled labor and mail-order brides.

Third, the Americans want an extension of the Bases Agreement beyond 1991, on the same yearly dole-out basis, at a slightly higher rate but still a lot less than in the Spanish and Turkish Treaties, still on the bas of annual Congressional approval, and of course, without any real Filipino authority over the bases, and without an "automatic retaliation" clause in case of nuclear attack.

Under no circumstances, under threat of the kind of destabilization that Americans applied on Marcos, will the Aquino government be allowed to ask the Americans to move their bases elsewhere. Lately American officials in Washington indicate that a private understanding has already been reached in this regard, although negotiation will officially start in 1988, subject to ratification by the people. This is the reason why the CIA (and Mr. Kaplan's) activities in this country are intensifying.

Protuberances Of The American Ischia

Fourth, the Americans want no less than a complete revamp of our Constitution to do away with any provision that will limit the exploitation of our natural resources and operation of public utilities to Filipino citizens and to corporations owned 60% by Filipinos, or any provision inserted that will give Filipinos some advantage in retail trade or basic industries. Nor will the Americans want any provision that will make Nationalist Industrialization or Economic Protectionism a national policy for economic development.

Americans want to insert a constitutional provision for reciprocal "National Treatment" that will give the Americans parity rights in all business activities, a provision for "Dual Citizenship" for Filipinos who want to be American citizens and Americans wanting to be Filipino citizens.

They also want to be sure there will be no provision renouncing war as an instrument of national policy, or adopting a policy of neutralization for our nation and immediate area, or forbidding the storage of nuclear weapons within the country, just to make sure that we Filipinos are available as cannon fodder and magnet for enemy attack.

That is why Americans and their surrogates totally ignore the Constitution drafted by the elected members of Constitutional Convention just after martial law was lifted, a draft that is nationalistic and democratic. That is why Americans support the appointment, not election of those who will draft the next constitution. So expect an attempt by Americans and little brown brothers to exert all influence to   pack the Constitutional Commission with those whose loyalty is primarily to Mother America.   For the ConCom, the likes of Renato Constantino, Alejandro Lichauco, Alejandro Roces, Roland Olalia, Hernando Abaya, Charito Planas, Jose Diokno, Lorenzo Tañada and other nationalists need not apply.

What the Americans and their surrogates expect to do is to present the Filipino people with two painful alternatives: ratify a Colonial Constitution, or continue with a Revolutionary Government. Either way, the Americans can keep us poor and manageable.

This is a big replay of the Great Betrayal that was foisted upon us in 1946 when we gave the Americans unconditional use of military bases on our soil, and amended our constitution to grant them parity rights.

If we Filipinos fall for the same con game, we might as well resign from the human race, and concentrate on doing what we seem to have been born and bred to do... and that is to osculate the fleshy protuberances of the American *ischia*.

January 31, 1986

Part 3. How To Appoint Cabinet Members
When Cory Aquino was proclaimed President in the morning of February 25 in the Club Filipino, she announced her first appointees: Juan Ponce Enrile for the Ministry of Defense, Fidel V. Ramos, full general and Chief of Staff of the New Armed Forces, and Salvador Laurel, Prime Minister designate.

Cory also announced that she was forming task forces in the field of Foreign Affairs, Finance, Education, and other vital areas, primarily to advise her on basic policies and to help her select the best men to implement the policies.

Cory, contrary to what Marcos partisans said during the campaign, is a very bright woman. She was a consistent valedictorian and honor student. She was good in both mathematics and languages when most are good in one or the other but not both. Such intelligence is on a higher level, like that of Leonardo da Vinci who was a superb artist and a mechanical genius at the same time. Cory had an impressive college degree, something Ninoy did not have. Cory certainly knew what she was doing.

What bright hopes and great expectations Cory kindled that day of the People's Revolution! We imagined all the brilliant minds suppressed during the Marcos regime suddenly liberated in the light of Cory's policy of "Consultation, not Dictation".

At one point in her campaign, Cory said that she will be opposite of what Marcos had become, and her new administration will depend on those who opposed Marcos "from the very beginning", like Senator Lorenzo Tañada.

People had visions of a task force on Legal Matters, headed by no less than Cecilia Palma, assisted by Jovito Salonga, Lorenzo Tañada, Jose Diokno, Homobono Adaza and constitutional lawyer Father Joaquin Bernas S.J. suggesting the legal framework by which the government may operate.

A task force on Education headed by ex-Secretary of Education Alejandro Roces, assisted by ex UP president Emmanuel Soriano, Francisco "Soc" Rodrigo, Edgardo Angara, Renato Constantino, and Ateneo president Father Joaquin Bernas S.J. suggesting an educational system that will make Filipinos proud to be Filipinos, and prepare them for the great task of nation-building.

A task force on Finance headed by Jaime Ongpin, assisted by Jose Concepcion, Aurelio Periquet, Alejandro Lichauco, Bernie Villegas, Teopisto Guingona, Solita Monsod, Randolph David, and Father Joaquin Bernas S.J. suggesting an eclectic approach toward achieving a balanced agro-industrial economic development. I would have been proud to serve in such a group.

A task force on Human Rights headed by Joker Arroyo assisted by Rene Saguisay, Juan T. David, Juan Ponce Enrile and Father Joaquin Bernas S.J.... a task force on Foreign Affairs headed by Emmanuel Pelaez assisted by Leticia Shahani, Jose Ingles, Raul Manglapus, Heherson Alvarez, and Father Joaquin Bernas S.J... a task force on Public Health headed by Dr. Constantino Manahan, Ambrosio Tangco, Carlos Sevilla, Victor Reyes and the rest of the wonderful doctors who gave their all for Cory, plus the indefatigable critics of drug monopolies, Professors Clemente and Bautista, and of course, Father Joaquin Bernas S.J...

A task force on Public Information headed by MP Orly Mercado, assisted by Teddyboy Locsin, Raul Contreras, Eddie Zialcita, Lupita Aquino Kashiwara, Max Soliven, June Keithley, Louie Beltran, Jose Burgos, Cornelio de Guzman, Letty Magsanoc, Vicente Foz and Father Joaquin Bernas S.J....

Then Cory could have floated 3 or 4 names for every important position, asking people to comment on their qualifications. It was important to determine not only that the appointee be competent, but that the people's impression of him is one of being trustworthy and credible. Persons facing estafa or other serious charges in court should be asked to dispose of their cases immediately, since appointment to a high office in effect is pre-judgment and would constitute undue pressure on the courts.

Alas, in the wake of Marcos's flight, a hasty news conference in the Mondragon building revealed that there were no task forces, no list of candidates for the appointive positions for consultation with the people. In a surprise announcement, Cory revealed her choices, leaving the Filipino people stunned, confused, and disappointed. The air was rife with unanswered questions:

Why he, why she? Who is he, who is she? But the guy is a crook! What happened to those who are better qualified? But the guy will only continue the discredited policies of Marcos! But he is a communist, an American boy, an oligarch, a *peninsulare*, an *insulare*! He is not even recognized among his peers in his own field! How come, the guy does not even have a college degree. The man is a balimbing, what happened to those who fought the longest and the hardest? Why were we not consulted about it?

But then the confusion continued. Day after day, surprises came. And the more surprises the more disappointments. Criticisms abound: a hodge-podge of college cronies... a bunch of hungry politicians... power-grabbing, self-righteous, sanctimonious pin-pricks... with no direction, no policy, no shared vision, no Grand Design.

To be fair, Cory's cabinet have some of the best, many good ones, and some quite obviously bad choices. She could have done better.

March 29, 1986

Part 4. Formula For Economic Recovery

The Clerico-Imperialist free market economists will have to learn that Economic Development is not a game of chance wherein victory goes to the strongest, the greediest and the whitest of skin. Nor does it consist of blithesome forecasts of economic performance that should best be left to fortune tellers and *manghuhulas*. To the leaders of this nation, economic development should be a scenario for change, a deliberately orchestrated magnum opus to make Filipinos the chief determinants and principal beneficiaries of this country's economic progress; to set up an economy that is self-reliant, self-sustaining and self-sufficient in the production of the basic needs of the Filipino people.

The Philippines is undergoing an economic crisis like that of 1949, but is in a better position to survive. Firstly, there are billions of dollars worth of existing equipment, taken over by the banks as non-operating assets and left to rust in idleness. Secondly, there a millions of workers trained to man those machines, now retrenched or laid off. Thirdly, there are the entrepreneurs, the men with vision, initiative, imagination and talent for imagination. These are the risk-takers who combine men, money, machines and materials in productive and profitable relationship, and who have lost their nerve and self-confidence, driven to bankruptcy by the spate of devaluations, spiraling interest rates and other factors totally outside their control.

The government should put the three ingredients together in a critical mass sufficient to achieve a self-sustaining chain reaction of economic activity. How? The government having guaranteed the dollar loans on non-performing assets, should cut its losses, bite the bullet and give back those assets to those who know how to operate them, at prices commensurate with attendant risks and market conditions. These entrepreneurs should be encouraged to compete with each other without the burden of foreign competition, and without foreign exchange risks (asset sales must be in pesos). Former crony-owned enterprises should be sold to the highest bidders.

Additionally, the government should embark on a massive low-cost housing program, since housing produce a commodity with an almost infinite demand with respect to supply (as such, recession proof); is low in import requirements (hence, little drain on our foreign exchange); is labor intensive rather than capital intensive; and has multiplier effects on 56 different industries from real estate to such construction materials as cement, wood, steel, aluminum, etc.

All these must be done all at the same time, because a National Economy can not operate in bits and pieces; all parts must produce for each other, providing sources of materials, markets, and a common pool of trained workers and management talent. Above all, we need an economic leadership that is not secretive, introverted, fossil-minded, colonial, sanctimonious, bigoted and *pikon*, but one who is eloquent, inspiring, nationalistic, open-minded, pleasant in disposition, firm in conviction yet flexible in approach, progressive without being radical, traditional without being conservative, passionate without being fanatic, coldly analytical while being provocative, who can raise bright hopes and great expectations as President Franklin Delano Roosevelt did at the height of the Great Depression, when he said, "There is nothing to fear but fear itself!"

The guy I mean is certainly not the guy up there now.
April 6, 1986

Part 5. Enrile Out, Adaza In San Miguel Board

There's a lot of bets going in the business community on the prediction that Homobono Adaza and Teddyboy Locsin will be in the San Miguel board; and Ramon del Rosario Jr. and Raul Roco will be out of it. Wanna bet?

A friend of mine who was there, swears this is true and will bet anyone P1,000 that on June 5th it will be borne out by a San Miguel press announcement. The story has been denied by all the principals involved. On the other hand, this friend is a good Catholic and goes to confession and communion often. So it may be a fair wager. Anyone who wants to take up the bet, must send his P1,000.00 or part of it to Business Writer Ray Lagonsin of Daily Inquirer, before midnight of June 3. Get a receipt. The information will be verified on June 5th during the San Miguel stockholders' meeting.

Last Thursday night (May 28), through the intermediation of President Cory Aquino, the PCGG and the SSS forged a secret agreement with the Soriano group, with regard to the composition of the San Miguel board.

Minister Enrile is out, and so are Maria Clara Lobregat and Oscar Santos who claim to represent the coconut farmers. Roberto Coyuito of the Manila Stock Exchange and Boboy Virata from a Bankers' Trust, who were nominated by the government are also out because of the objections of the Soriano group.

To represent the government are Ramon Diaz, Raul Daza and Mary Bautista of the PCGG; Jose Calderon and Teddyboy Locsin who are perceived to be nominees of Peping C., and Homobono   Adaza who is Cory's personal choice.

To represent the Soriano group are Andres III and his two brothers, Carlos and Eduardo; Antonio Roxas, Benny Toda, Nono Ibazeta, Ernest Kahn, and Antonio Prieto. Little Blue Boy Ramon del Rosario Jr. who masterminded the ill-fated Neptunia sale, is out of the board and will go back to Asian Bank.

The PCGG, having sequestered the 33.1 million shares purportedly owned by Danding Cojuangco and/or the coconut farmers, is now in possession of almost 60% majority stock in San Miguel Corporation, and is in a position to make the agreement stick.

Out of the 15 board seats, Soriano gets 8, the government gets 6, and the minority stockholders get one. This means that Soriano group will run the corporation under the watchful eye of the PCGG which will oversee any major transaction. Is this privatization?

On June 4th is scheduled a stockholder's meeting where the lone representative of the minority will be elected, and the secret agreement between Soriano and PCGG will then be finally divulged to the press. Minister Juan Ponce Enrile is lobbying hard to be this minority director.

The proceeds of any subsequent sale of the 33.1 million shares will not be held in escrow by the United Coconut Planter's Bank under Ponce Enrile. It will be held directly by the PCGG who will take charge of the distribution to the 1.4 million coconut farmers, if any. This means the the PCGG, not   UCPB of Enrile and Danny Ursua, will represent the coconut farmers.

This is still part of the story my friend swears is true. He is also willing to bet another P1,000 on this one.

Ramon del Rosario Jr., the Little Boy Blue who packaged the Neptunia-Soriano deal and expected to be the President of San Miguel, is in the doghouse and will not even be in the San Miguel Board.

Raymond, as he is called by Herb Allen, has been to see President Cory Aquino four or five times, in an effort to save the Neptunia-Soriano deal from being junked, and to complain about "vilification campaign waged by anti-Soriano forces which have been trying to penetrate the food and beverage conglomerate through the back door."

Little Boy Blue was referring to a group composed of the wife of a cabinet Minister and Ambassador businessman, and an official of the Manila Stock Exchange, who accused LBB of using his connections with President Cory, as a post-election favor, to get the San Miguel presidency. At the same time Ramon Diaz and Raul Daza of the PCGG indignantly denounced the deal as anomalous and immoral, and moved to cancel the sale and sequester the controversial shares.

Nonetheless, as a sign of good faith, LBB volunteered to the President that after the negotiations will have been successfully concluded, he will no longer seek the presidency. Cory offered him any government post he wanted, but he declined any position that might make him stand close to Jobo Fernandez, who is a six-footer. He declined because he preferred to be in private business.

Ramon (or Raymond) del Rosario Junior is the spitting image of his father Ambassador Ramon (or Raymond, as the old foreign Jaycees call him) del Rosario Senior. Only Junior is smaller than his father, and was said to have been born a blue baby. That is why he is called Little Boy Blue, and is often serenaded with a little ditty, "Five foot two, skin of blue, slanting eyes and glasses too. Has anybody seen Raymond?"

Like every little guy, Little Boy Blue has a Napoleonic complex and is often seen with his arms akimbo barking at his immediate subordinate who shall remain unnamed. Asian Bank where he is president, is often called Lilliput, because all executives there reportedly have to be smaller than he is.

Now, the Napoleonic ambition of Little Boy Blue is to be the president of the biggest corporation of the Philippines, the San Miguel Corporation. And in pursuance of this, he packaged the whole Neptunia/Soriano deal, by which a wholly owned corporation of San Miguel, Neptunia, would buy the majority stockholdings of Danding Cojuangco and/or the 1.4 million coconut farmers. These holdings which amounted to 32% of the outstanding shares plus some 18% under Soriano control, would have been enough to insure absolute control of San Miguel by Andres Soriano III. LBB's prize would have been the presidency.

What causes LBB sleepless nights was that the Neptunia deal did not pull through because the PCGG branded it unfair, anomalous and immoral. The deal cooked up by LBB was rejected because by its terms, the stockholders of San Miguel sold a money maker in Hong Kong and with the proceeds bought the shares of Danding/farmers at more than three times its worth.

The shares bought was not put into Treasury Stock or distributed among the rightful owners, but used to augment the voting power of Soriano who had only 18% control. The public that controlled 35% and the government that controlled 24%, cried foul. The deal of LBB just collapsed, and LBB is in the doghouse with Soriano.

So much so that not only did LBB lose the presidency of San Miguel, but he is not even on the board. He is going to go back to Lilliput, the Asian Bank.

Little Boy Blue, if you recall, was a member of the powerful Jesuit Mafia, also known as Cory's Seven Dwarfs, of which Jimmy Ongpin is Grumpy and LBB is Sleepy because of his Chinese eyes. Sleepy or not, LLB has been staying awake lately trying to figure our how to disengage himself from Grumpy and rebuild his sagging image. To which we can only say, Good Luck.

June 3, 1986

Part 6. The Second Generation Bloodsuckers

For twenty years, Marcos and his wife sucked the blood of this nation, and their apologists keep saying, "Well there will come a point they will be satiated, *bubusog na iyan*, but they are much preferable than those who are still lean and hungry." Oh yeah? Those two bloodsuckers gave birth to a second generation of bloodsuckers who had a running start building a pyramid of plunder and privilege.... son Bongbong Marcos, and sons-in-law Greggy "Greedy" Araneta and Tommy "*Tomo*" (I take!) Manotoc.

Marcos and Imelda were so selfish that they did not share their loot with their children. Instead they taught the kids to steal their own wealth. The KKK, the Human Development Corporation, the Technology Resource Center were the milking cows of the second generation bloodsuckers.

Bongbong Marcos, being the heir apparent, was given the first crack in the disposition of government favors. Bongbong chose to create his own kingdom in the Ilocos. He controlled the distribution and sales of all commodities entering his Ilocoslovakia from Taiwan and Hong Kong and other foreign sources. This he did with his control of the Shipping Port and International Airport at Laoag City, and through control of highway checkpoints and cold storage facilities.

In addition, while Ver and Ongpin were operating the Binondo Central Bank, Bongbong had his own Laoag Central Bank, shipping dollars out of the Laoag Airport to Hong Kong and Taiwan, dollars that were sent in by 3,000,000 Ilocano migrants from the United States and all over the world. Bongbong even went to the extent of taking over the Olongapo Central Bank where dollars from American servicemen enter the country.

Not satisfied with this, Bongbong set up several enterprises designed to control the economic life of Ilokoslovakia, such as Northern Food Corporation based in Sarrat, Ilocos Norte for the processing of tomato paste and mango puree, strawberry mash, papaya, *guyabano*, guava, etc. Over P90 million were coughed up by the KKK, HSDC and TRC to insure the completion of the processing plant, with the blessing and support of Ambassador Stephen Bosworth.

The National Food Corporation is ostensibly owned by Bongbong's La Salle buddies: Alejandro "Sandy" Daza, Flavio Gutierrez, Eusebio Tan, Jose Mari Buñag, Emeterio Manibog, Tadeo Hilado, Victor Lazatin, Armand Ongsioko -- who gave only P1,000 each to become the majority owners -- they were in effect the second generation cronies. The big questions are: why is this corporation not sequestered by the PCGG? And who's running it today?

The trouble is that the farmers who gave their produce to the corporation have not been paid January 1985, more than a year ago! The plant can run 24 hours a day but only for 120 days per year, the rest of the time is spent in critical maintenance.

In the meantime, Bongbong's interest in the Makati financial world was purportedly advanced by Rolly Gapud of the Security Bank, by Ralph Nubla of Philippine Bank of Communication, Lucio Tan of Allied Bank, and through Kokoy of the PCIB. Many in the banking circles suspect that the above were fronting for Bongbong.

Bongbong in effect was doing to the Ilocos what his father was doing to the Philippines, a sort of on-the-job training preparatory taking over the entire Philippines.

On the other hand, there is Greggy Araneta who as soon as he married Irene, went on a rampage of plunder as the biggest business pirate in town. He got the PNB, the DBP and Land Bank to finance his operations.

During the 1984 bank runs, he suddenly became a one-share director of Manilabank; then branched out to a monopoly importation of car parts for Ford, Toyota and Isuzu; and importation of luxury items in competition with Glecy Tantoco of Rustan, supplying her competitors. Then Greggy moved into the purchase of Pantranco North, took over the *ampao* banks of Disini, and bought into a bank in Hawaii.

Imee was a bit envious of Irene. She was the second wife of Tommy after all, and did not have the kind of wedding Irene had, or the large mansion that Greggy brought Irene to live in. Poor Tommy Manotoc, he was not interested in anything except golf and basketball, and did not have the penchant for larceny that Greggy and Bongbong had.

Imee started to nag her parents. If Irene has a Forbes Park mansion, then she must have her own in Dasmariñas Village, a P40 million mansion located in grounds covering 8 residential lots. If Bongbong has Security Bank, and Greggy the Disini banks, then by God and Jobo, she must have Banco Filipino -- which was a bit too big to swallow. If Greggy had a monopoly of car parts importation, then Tommy must have his very own monopoly of fruits and sardines. Tommy even went on to purchase coconut and sugar lands in an attempt to cut in on Danding's territorial imperative.

Greggy, Tommy and Bongbong were La Sallites, and had their own *barkada*, their own second generation cronies. But I think we should not list some of them down, since their connections with the second generation bloodsuckers have been prematurely aborted by the February Revolution. They still have a long and useful life ahead of them, so we will let them off for now.

June 13, 1986

Part 7. Benguet And The American Gangsters

We should really know the history of the companies that we always read about in the front pages. Let's start with Benguet Corporation, Jimmy Ongpin's mother company.

Benguet Consolidated, with all its changes of name, was organized by Judge John W. Hausserman (The Gold King) at the outset of the American Occupation. Hausserman was never really a judge, but apparently American yokels called every lawyer a judge in those days. The law firm he founded eventually became De Witt, Perkins, Brady & Ponce Enrile, the latter being the father of Minister Juan Ponce Enrile who together with brother-in-law Leonardo Siguion Reyna (the silent partner of Armida) inherited the firm eventually.

An interesting sidelight, with some data from Domini Torrevilla Suarez and an absent-minded lawyer, was the court battle over Benguet shares between the firm's law partner Eugene Perkins and his wife Sarah Idonah Slade Perkins who married in 1914 and were divorced in the 1930s after an affair where one of them was caught with erotic love letters from a third party. It was a bitter vendetta of many long years that ended sometime in 1956-60 when both spouses finally died within four years of each other. The fight, we are sure, continued out of this world, with the heavenly angels forced to take sides.

In their hatred for each other and determination to keep their property from each other's clutches, they gave whatever they had to charity and completely forgot their own daughter, Dora who did not inherit a cent. Mrs. Idonah Perkins was an irascible old woman who changed her lawyers like she did her stockings, among them Mauro Baradi, Claro Recto, Gibbs & Gibbs, and Ferdinand Marcos who was, our informant says, her lawyer for 3 days. According to our informant, Marcos never had the nerve to ask for a fee until he was already President in 1966, whereupon he demanded P250,000 as his compensation, knowing that the executors of Mrs. Perkin's will would not dare refuse to pay. On the record, however, a Supreme Court decision penned by Justice Enrique Fernando, gave Marcos the amount in 1968.

Old man Alfonso Ponce Enrile, one of the best lawyers of his time, used to tell the neophyte lawyers on his staff to study only two cases in his file: the Perkins case and the Cu Unjieng estafa case involving falsified "quedans". In doing so, he said, they would be introduced thoroughly into all the intricacies of corporate law.

Another footnote. Throughout the pain and humiliation of the Cu Unjieng court case and its aftermath, this Cu Unjieng had a beautiful wife who stood by him for years on end. Unlike the Perkins couple, Cu Unjieng and his wife loved each other with such devotion that only recently they died within a day of each other. I mention this because I remember what my own mother once said, as the Cu Unjiengs must have learned to their eternal glory: "To gain riches is a beggar's dream. But to find love, ah, that is the dream of kings!"

Hausserman owned most of Benguet shares, but it seemed that during the war he sold the shares to clients of Herbert Allen and his associates, although he remained nominal owner till the end of his days.

In the heady days of the late 1950s, there came into Manila a character named Kirpatovksy who brought with him excellent credentials as a good friend of Senator George Smathers of Florida, a fun-loving man who "was to John Kennedy what Ernie Maceda was to Ferdinand Marcos".

Kirpatovsky, remember the name. He was Jewish, barely 5 feet 3 inches, ugly as sin but always surrounded by beautiful girls, had a beautiful mansion in Biscayne Bay and an 80 foot cabin cruiser, with reported interests in casinos in the Bahamas and elsewhere. Old man Alfonso Ponce Enrile whose firm was asked to represent Kirpatovsky, assigned a junior partner to do the job, because he just could not stand the sight of Kirpatovsky, and referred to him as an s.o.b.

According to informed sources, Kirpatovsky was a big shot in the real Mafia, a Sicilian Brotherhood of Gangsters that has come to be known as the Mob in the American underworld. He was a Jewish electronic expert who reportedly was able to rig up a wireless network that gave the Mafia bookies advance information as to who won the horse races all over the country about three minutes before the telegraph companies could transmit it. Thus the Mob was able to accept sucker bets knowing full well who already won the race. Because of this, Kirpatovsky reached high up in the American Mafia.

Well, Kirpatovsky acquired a block of Benguet shares and was set to challenge Herbert Allen and his associates in a proxy fight to control Benguet Consolidated. Why? because, according to the scuttlebutt, Benguet was listed in the New York Stock Exchange, and the Mafia needed a company listing to launder the money earned illegally through gambling, prostitution and drugs.

Herb Allen in his proxy fight was represented by lawyers Honorio Poblador and Antonio Carrascoso. Eventually Kirpatovsky lost the proxy fight, but apparently he won his objective anyway because in 1968, Herbert Allen and his associates merged Benguet Consolidated with the Grand Bahamas Port Authority which owned resort hotels and gambling casinos in the island just across where Kirpatovsky lived.

It was reported then that a Wallace Groves owned 20 million Benguet shares while Herb Allen had only 2 or 3 million shares. Herb Allen was representing Wallace Groves and all the stock holders, and was largely instrumental in consummating the Benguet-Bahamas merger. The merged company was then operated as Resort International, Inc.

Now Wallace Groves had a huge mansion in Freeport, was a close friend of the Bahamas Prime Minister Lynden O. Pindling, and had casino concessions in the Grand Bahamas. He reportedly made his money in Canada under shadowy circumstances. And he is reputedly a friend of good old Kirpatovsky. He was probably the leader of the Baywater boys exposed by Salonga as having been involved in Mafia and the Bahamas deal.

And the stage was set for the infamous XYZ affair, starring now PCGG commissioner Jovito Salonga, President Marcos, and Marcos crony Jose Yao Campos.

June 14, 1986

Part 8. Another Sucker Play On PLDT Shares?

Remember in 1976 when the price of Oriental Petroleum shares was manipulated from one centavo per share, to 3, to 8, to 25 centavos per share, only to fall in a few days to 8 centavos per share?? When the sucker play was over, many people lost fortunes, and a group led by Imelda Marcos and Geronimo Velasco were richer by millions. This group simply fooled the public by buying and selling among themselves at increasingly higher prices, until the investing public was caught up in the fever of speculative buying. Then the group simply unloaded its shares at the highest price and left the public with a lot of shares to sell and no buyers. Bingo!

Well, don't look now, but blue chip PLDT shares which at the beginning of the year was P35 to P40 per share, suddenly started to move upwards after the February Revolution to P50, upwards still to P105 last Wednesday (June 11th). On the Makati and Manila Exchanges, T.J. Wolff & Co. along with Jimmy Ongpin's brother and father are said to be active. In the New York Stock Exchange, guess who is promoting the PLDT stocks? They say, Herb Allen and associates, former boss of Jimmy Ongpin. Interesting, no? Read on.

At first, the price rise was attributed by Ongpin's friends to the regained confidence in the Cory Administration. When the price broke the P50 barrier and continued to climb steeply, the stockbrokers expected a downward "correction" and advised their clients to start selling. Imagine their surprise when the price continued to rise inexorably, so they ate their words and advised their client to buy again and contribute further to the market speculation.

Actually there is really no reason why the PLDT stock should go up. Alfonso Yuchengco, the kingpin of PLDT after the revolution, unloaded his shares through his niece Vivien Yuchengco-Locsin, wife of Information Minister Teddyboy Locsin. And many of his friends followed suit. A week later, the PCGG sequestered the PLDT; and reporters speculated that Yuchengco and his friends were given advance information of the sequestration through a phone call from a government official.   PCGG Commissioner Ramon Diaz who was Yuchengco's lawyer felt alluded to, and offered to resign, but his resignation was not accepted. Mon Diaz is known to be a man of integrity and could not have possibly done the deed.

While there was much furor over the unloading of the Yuchengco shares and those of his friends, the price of the PLDT shares fell only for a few days and quickly reasserted its strength. As a matter of fact, its phenomenal rise started on the day of PLDT sequestration, and continued to rise even when the National Telecommunications Commission (NTC) started to monitor PLDT's return on investment to be sure it is still within the legal limit of 12% on investment, a maximum rate allowed to protect the public against excessive monopoly profits. On the other hand, the last quarter's profits were "fantastic".

The PLDT monopoly firm has spent some P14 billion in its expansion program and needs P2 billion more to complete its program.   And it still continues to pay the amortizations on sizeable foreign loans.

Not that it does any good. The PLDT continues to give its long suffering clients the lousiest service in the world. Dial tones disappear mysteriously off the line; the phone on the other end fails to ring, or the wrong number answers; the voice of the American woman says "The number you dial..." cuts in even when the number you call actually exists. It is a measure of PLDT colonial mentality that it is easier to call New York than Pasig. Still the PLDT shares continue their price rise.

There is no reason for the phenomenal price rise since (1) the Yuchengco smart money has left the firm, (2) the firm is being sequestered, (3) the firm is saddled with foreign debt, and (4) the firm is not making any spectacular profits over the long run.

What the hell is happening? A group of skeptical and suspicious stockbrokers are saying that the heavy buying at the Manila and Makati stock exchanges are being orchestrated by Wolff & Co. with the active participation of the brother and father of Jaime Ongpin. Reporters inquiring about the heavy buying phenomenon were given the run-around by the Ongpins who simply said, ?We are just following the price escalation in New York."

True enough, in New York, there was a flurry of activity in PLDT shares, of which little is known in the New York Stock Exchange, resulting in ever spiraling price. Stock analysts with their charts and inside information, simply cannot find any fundamental reason why the stock should zoom upward. They figured that the New York buys would soon end their buying spree. But contrary to all expectations, the buying spree continued.

Local stockbrokers began calling their contacts in New York to find out what was going on. It was discovered that "a group of Filipino cronies led by Marcos broker Bernstein are selling PLDT shares to Americans suspected of being connected to the American Mafia." The crony group is unloading its shares in New York instead of in Manila. But why the price rise?

Reports from the New York bourse say that "a group of Jews closely connected with the Herb Allen's investment group are buying in." Herb Allen you remember is the architect of the Benguet Bahamas deal that involved the American Mafia which wanted to use Benguet to launder their casino, drug and prostitution money. So there is Allen in New York and T.J. Wolff in Manila. But why the speculative fever?

At first it was suggested that the PLDT has elicited the interest of multinational companies in New York; and the Chinese-Filipino community in Manila are buying in to be part of the action. The Americans, it is said, are sacrosanct to the Cory technocrats, so that any company, including the PLDT, with substantial American interest, is not subject to harassment as much as purely Filipino companies are.

Then again, the sale of the Yuchengco shares (which has no conflict of interest with his ambassadorial job) fires the speculation that a new anointed group is about to take over PLDT, that this is a corporate maneuver to install a new management nice to the powers-that-be.

Then again, this may be the usual stockbroker/banker's ploy to play arbitrage, that is, trafficking in PLDT stocks for the purpose of deriving profit from the price differences of the stock in New York and Manila. Or it could be an arrangement to facilitate heavy block transactions in which one forces the price to go up in one market, and buy low in the other, just like Marcos cronies used to do in the bad old days.

Meanwhile activity continues to mount on the buying and selling of PLDT shares. Its market price after breaking the P50 barrier, has broken the P100 barrier as well, and is quoted at P105 per share last Wednesday (June 11).

Then again, according to Irving Ackermann, the first quarter profits of PLDT is said to be fantastic. The profits the last 12 months was P45/share or $2.25 per share while the shares in New York are selling at about $5.00 per share, a price-earnings ratio of only 2.2 times. It should go up more to at least 5 times or $11.25 or P225 per share.

But wiseacres among the stockbrokers are cautioning their favored clients not to take a position at this point in time, warning that there may be a sucker play in the offing, just like in the 1976 Oriental Petroleum scandal, when the price of Oriental shares zoomed to 25 centavos in a single week and dropped disastrously to 8 centavos in a few days.

Okay suckers, if there is really such a play being concocted, beware. The stocks will zoom up so fast you may be tempted to join the merry go round. It will be easy for you to buy today and sell tomorrow at tremendous profit to yourself. But the odds are against you. The big boys are buying and selling from each other at constantly spiraling prices, till the public gets caught up by the fever and buys and sells too in enormous quantities.

Then BOOM! the big boys suddenly unload, they sell all their shares at the artificially high price, and buy no more. The suckers will be left holding the bag, a bag full of PLDT shares nobody wants to buy. The prices will plummet to hell, and there will be weeping and gnashing of teeth. There will be no joy in Suckerland, because you, sucker, will have been creamed. You just struck out. And you deserve it.

June 17, 1986

Part 9. The Travails Of Sylvia Lichauco

There is one way of destroying the reputation of innocents, and that is imputing "guilt by association", a technique that was developed by Joe MCarthy in the 1950s and honed to perfection by the CIA.

The pejorative term "McCarthyist" was derived, not from Eugene McCarthy the unsuccessful candidate for the U.S. presidency, but from an abominable character Senator Joseph McCarthy who accused everyone of being a communist including

President Eisenhower. His favorite weapon is imputing 'guilt by association". If Charlie Chaplin sympathizes with the poor in the same way Communists do, then Charlie must be a communist and must be thrown out of the United States, and he was. In the same way, such great American writers as John Steinbeck (Grapes of Wrath, Of Mice and Men) and Lillian Hellman (The Children's Hour, Pentimento) were hounded and persecuted because they had friends who were suspected communists.

Congressman Leonardo Perez as the chairman of the House Anti-Filipino Activities was also employing McCarthyist tactics, from which he developed his endearing qualities as a Marcos hatchetman. Marcos himself was not above employing such tactics when he categorically accused Ninoy Aquino and Rene Saguisag as communists. The CIA and the NICA/NBI did the same thing on our greatest nationalists -- on Claro M. Recto, Amado Hernandez, Renato Constantino, Hernando Abaya, Lorenzo Tañada and Jose Diokno.

Today we employ such tactics on those who at one time or another enjoyed the patronage of Marcos, even if they were also victims of his rapacity and the great recession, like Ricardo Silverio and Rodolfo Cuenca. But we never do it to the American friends of Marcos in the Embassy and the American Chamber who have, it would seem, a permanent residency on our pantheon of heroes.

I am going to tell you about Sylvia Lichauco -- broke, sick at heart, alone -- whose reputation as a Filipina and a businesswoman has been put in jeopardy by the McCarthyist tactics of an American paper San Francisco Examiner, simply by imputing guilt by association with the deposed President Marcos.

Sylvia Lichauco and her Jamestown Company were involved in the "212 Stockton Project", a 10 story project in Union Square that was to have been built by the GSIS in San Francisco.

Whatever the merits of the project, the Examiner chose to impugn Sylvia Lichauco by creating the impression that the project was part of Marcos's personal wealth, that Sylvia and her company were fronts for the Marcos family, that because of illegal campaign contributions to Mayor Feinstein, the project was given special exemptions not otherwise extended to others.

Of course, the building in question is not part of Marcos's ill-gotten wealth; it is registered in the name of the GSIS. But Marcos's name appears 66 times in three articles to give the impression that the building was part of the Marcos real estate empire.

The paper even portrayed pictorially the links of Sylvia Lichauco to President Marcos, citing among others Myra Sulit, cousin of Imelda, Patricia Araneta and her brother Greggy Araneta, the President's son-in-law. Now Myra Sulit, identified as Sylvia's assistant at Jamestown, is a 24 year old woman who worked only part-time for a limited period and earned a total of $650 from the Jamestown Company. Patricia Araneta is a friend from way back in school. Neither she or her brother Greggy had anything to do with the project. These three references were inserted simply to imply guilt by association.

Yet the Examiner knew that Sylvia had far more extensive connections with the Cory Aquino government, such as a cousin Ching Escaler, presidential Appointment Secretary; a cousin Vic Sison, General Manager of Manila Hotel; a cousin Ernesto Lichauco who is married to the sister of Ninoy Aquino; and the many relatives in the de Leon, Arevalo, Lichauco clans who poured their talents and resources in the campaign to get rid of Mr. Marcos. No mention is made of that.

Instead the insinuation is made that Sylvia Lichauco was involved in the looting of the Philippine economy of billions of dollars by Marcos and his associates. Although nothing was said specifically by the Examiner, the article was written to suggest that it is true.

After stating that the Marcoses had "secretly bought more than $350 million worth of New York real estate, acting through a Netherlands Antilles shell corporation," the authors continued, "Public records indicate that Filipinos who wanted to use Netherland Antilles corporations to quietly buy real estate in the Bay Area turned to either the San Francisco la firm of Graham and James -- or increasingly, after 1981, to Realtor Sylvia Lichauco." Read it well, it never says Sylvia had anything to do with Marcos, which is the truth. But the bar-sinisters make it appear that it is so.

The rest of the articles suggest that because of campaign contributions, Sylvia's project was exempted from regulations which upon closer scrutiny either (1) do not exist, (2) came into effect after the project approval, or (3) are waived by a plethora of agencies for good reason.

Sylvia Lichauco is a member of a very distinguished family, whose roots go back several generations to a Chinese immigrant christened Tomas Ly-Chau-Co; Lola Grande who made the family fortune; Faustino of the Hong Kong revolutionary Junta who earned and lost millions as cattle king; and Marcial, Sylvia's father who was our Ambassador to the Court of St. James in the 1960s.

Sylvia's parents were unique in that they cared for the human race; they adopted all sorts of orphans and sent them to school, even rescued an abandoned baby from a garbage can. Of all her siblings, it was Sylvia who cared most, she who took care of her brothers and sisters and mother, and even her nephews, my own children. She was not the prettiest, but by far she was acknowledged to be the most brilliant and the most caring.

One day, Sylvia got married to the scion of one of the richest families in the Philippines. She bore her husband a beautiful daughter, after which they were separated, and she had to go to work to support herself and her daughter. So she worked in San Francisco as a real estate developer along with her brother. So many years of sweat, tears and loneliness, so much grit and determination, above all a lot of loving and caring, have gone into the making of Sylvia Lichauco.

She deserves to be treated like a human being.
June 19, 1986

Part 10. Minister Enrile And The Juvenile Delinquent
The United Coconut Planters' Bank (UCPB) stockholders' meeting was confusion, pandemonium, bewilderment. Fifteen thousand "coconut farmers" showed up, thirty seven nominees were presented by four contending groups; there was scrambling for microphones that were intermittently cut off; the PCGG headed by Raul Daza and Ramon Diaz voted 94% of the shares they sequestered from the farmers; Enrile, Ursua, Lobregat and the rest of the UCPB board walked out en masse, with murmurs of *"Inyo na yan! Kayo na mag-aaway!"*

What the heck is going on? What is the purpose of all this bloodletting? why the mob, too many characters working at cross purposes? Is it worth de-stabilizing the UCPB, the Army, the country?

We recall that the UCPB came into being out of the Philippine Bank of Commerce, the only private Filipino bank after the war, owned by the old Cojuangco brothers along with their children, the cousins Ramon (who later controlled the PLDT), Eduardo (who later became the coconut king), and Pedro (brother of Cory and Peping). Jobo Fernandez was the Vice-President of that bank, surprised?

The three Cojuangco branches broke up, with Monching remaining in the Philippine Bank of Commerce which was absorbed by another bank; with Danding and Cory's branch setting up a new bank, the First United Bank (jokingly called the Second Disunited by Ninoy). Imagine Cory and Danding in the same business.

In the time of Marcos, Danding bought out Cory's branch, then reincorporated the First United into the United Coconut Planters' Bank (UCPB) with Enrile as Chairman, first as a P100 million, then a P500 million Universal Bank, all with the copra levy collected from the coconut farmers.

And so on Monday June 30th, destiny turned a full circle, and the UCPB fell into the hands of the Cory Cojuangco government. Its aftermath threatens a major bank run, a split in the armed forces and the possibility of a military coup d'etat.

Defense Minister Ponce Enrile is hopping mad. He has been accused of conspiring to take over the Danding Cojuangco financial empire to finance his political ambitions. He has been accused of toeing the McCarthyist CIA line that there are communists in the top echelon of government, of accepting the support of Marcos loyalists determined to de-stabilize the government, of irresponsible threats to mount a counter revolution (a coup? "Ask my boys!"), of challenging the leadership of the President too early in the game ("Me run for the Presidency? I was only joking!"), of using the military to strong arm his opponents, to protect all sorts of illegal loggers and other undesirable characters.

Now that is not fair. Enrile is not like that at all, when he is not mad, that is. Really. I was with him almost every step of the way, in his war-room during the February Revolution. A prominent politician candidate came and proposed, with implacable logic, that since the political situation was murky, Enrile should constitute a "civilian junta" embracing all political factions. Enrile never hesitated, saying "The power is not in this room, it is out there in Edsa. How long do you think we will last if we do not give them Cory Aquino?"

Whatever political situation exists today is the work of Enrile. On the second day of the Revolution, he was the first to articulate what should be done. He rejected outright any reversal by the Batasan of its proclamation of Marcos victory, "We will only inherit an intransigent law body." He knew that the first thing on the agenda was to dismantle the Marcos power structure as fast as possible, "We must set up a Revolutionary Government, answerable only to the people." Those were his words, not those of Father Kinik Bernas SJ.   Enrile's perceptions of our concerns were valid and clear.

Enrile is no American boy. When those *&%$#"! Americans were trying to get credit for the Revolution, even only as gas attendants fueling the helicopters, Enrile contemptuously and unequivocally asserted, "This is our revolution.   The Americans had absolutely nothing to do with it. I ought to know, I started it." or words to that effect.

On the other hand, *anak ng kalabao*, put yourself in Enrile's place. The Light-A-Fire Movement declared itself out of existence, so business has declined lately at the Philippine Match and the Panomatch. The 1.4 million farmers entrusted you with 33 million shares of San Miguel, which were just sold for 4 times what they are worth; and PCGG cancels the sale. Then without any by-your-leave, without even the courtesy of informing you or consulting with you, the PCGG sequesters and votes those shares held in your trust, and you are unceremoniously and pointedly denied one itsy bitsy board seat in San Miguel. Instead you find sitting in your stead Teddyboy Locsin Jr., with his baby face, beady unblinking eyes and ill-fitting blue suit.

And so you say Ouch! and give out with the primal scream, and make noises like Charley and Joseph McCarthy, threaten a coup d'etat (which you would never threaten to do. if you really intend to do it) -- but what you really want to do is to send unmistakable signals to Cory's bright boys, please to lay off, stop humiliating me in public, shit I am on your side.

But do those nerds get the message? The message batters its way into the impregnable barrier of their skulls, only to fall defunct, void and useless into the soles of their feet.

Then came the UCPB stockholders' meeting. The PCGG sequesters 94% of the votes by special powers granted by Malacañang, humiliates you by offering you the chairmanship under its sufferance, forces you to refuse the nomination, and when the dust of battle clears, you see sitting in your stead the same baby faced brat, Teddyboy Locsin Jr., with the same beady unblinking eyes and ill-fitting blue suit.

Anak ng kalabao, if you were Minister Juan Ponce Enrile, how will you react?? The famous Enrile temper, so long held in check reaches critical mass and triggers a self sustaining chain reaction. You scream, "If they have to humiliate me, why can't they send Bono Adaza or Pepe Diokno or Jovy Salonga to do the hatchet job? Why do they add insult to injury by sending in a snooty faced juvenile delinquent who can not even shave properly? If he needs all those board seats to be able to pay alimony to Vivian, why do it at my expense??"

Well, Minister Juan Ponce Enrile, the play is not ended. One of these days, just when you see the sun shine bright and birds sing their songs of joy, you may enter your office and see.... sitting in your place as the new Minister of Defense of the Revolutionary Republic... one familiar baby-faced brat with beady unblinking eyes, and again and forever, with the same ill-fitting blue suit.

July 3, 1986

Part 11. Resurrection Of Two Great Newspapers

The loss of Manila Times chief editor Titong Roces, and the scandal over the investment of Marcos crony Geronimo Velasco (which was returned) were bad enough for the newly reborn Times.

Then came the third shock that threatened the very existence of the Times. The Times managing editor Vergel Santos who used to be the assistant of Gus Villanueva at the People's Journal, was not comfortable with Alejandro "Anding" Roces who took the place of Titong. Vergel quarreled with

Anding on front page layout; Vergel wanted it to stay a 7-column, while Anding insisted on changing it to an 8-column so that when folded lengthwise, there will be a clear 4-column on each side.

They quarreled about missed deadlines and delayed printing and late newsstand deliveries, even about the quality of typewriters used by reporters. Vergel wanted to indicate in the editorial box that Titong Roces was still editor on leave, and did not want to recognize Anding as his superior, his editor in chief. "I'll prove to you that I am the chief editor," Anding said, "You are fired." And that is how the Manila Times strike started.

The entire staff walked out with Vergel Santos, together with all the stuff needed to put out the 16-paged paper the next day. "You're all alone now, Anding, and you won't have a paper tomorrow," one of the boys jeered.

"I'd rather be alone than be in bad company," muttered Anding, "and I'll put out that paper tomorrow." His cousin Don Ramon said that under the circumstances, he will be happy to see a 4-paged edition with an explanation of what happened.

Anding called his former student, Joe Quirino who was playing mahjong and reluctant to leave because he was losing. When Anding explained, Joe said, "I'll be there." And so he was, with two others Hernando Abaya and Napoleon Rama. All four of them stayed up that night, writing stories culled from radio broadcasts in local stations and that of Clark Field, typesetting, and making paste-ups, and at midnight they had a 16-paged edition, with a final insulting touch, a 1-inch column notice that said "The Manila Times staff walked out last night."

The strike was on, but the Manila Times took it in its stride, including a picket line that included even Deputy Minister of Social Services Karina David. When a military hero of the revolution showed up to grab some headlines on the picket line, Anding Roces beckoned him aside and said, "Listen asshole, you may be a hero now but not when I start exposing your record of human rights violations -- rape of young girls, tortures of suspects, salvaging of innocents, need I say more?" The hero left the picket line.

Well, all's well that ends well, because the strikers led by Vergel Santos finally found their niche in the new Manila Chronicle, published by no less than Joaquin "Chino" Roces himself, and printed by the Manila Times printing presses.

Chino Roces finally decided that the time has come to recapture the old glory. He is not happy about the appropriation of the name "Manila Times" by his elder brother, but he is determined to show that he still has the stuff to put out a great paper. So Chino joined up with the Lopezes to resuscitate the old "Manila Chronicle".

The Lopez family, former Vice President Fernando Lopez and the two scions of his late brother, Eugenio Jr. (Henie) and Oscar are putting together their old the newspaper, radio and television empire (ABS-CBN network). There were wild rumors that the Chronicle was pirating Max Soliven and Art Borjal from the Philippine Inquirer, and has Raul Manglapus and Jose Mari Velez as columnists and TV hosts on Channel 2 which will revert back to the Lopezes in July. As much as P100,000 per month are being offered to the top talents, according to newsmen, but publishers say only P25,000 a month are being offered.

But the momentum just wasn't there. After a publicity campaign in newspaper ads and TV commercials about the Chronicle's debut on June 12, the first issue was a disappointment, in the words on its competitors, a dud. The printing ended at 7 AM instead of 11 PM the night before, and by the time it hit the stands, all other papers were already sold out. The expected big guns in the editorial page were not there. The promise was a big splash. The reality was a little drip.

But do not count Chino out, he did it before and he will do it again. By the second day he solved his problem, that paper came out in time.

But his greatest problem as well as those of other papers is the lack of reporters and columnists of the caliber of Yeyeng Soliongco, Celso Cabrera, Ernesto Granada -- all deceased -- and Chitang Nakpil of the pre-Marcos Chronicle; and Max Soliven (too expensive now and he wants to be associate publisher), Alfredo Roces (in Australia), J.V. Cruz (in Hades) in the pre-Marcos Manila Times.

Everyone blames Information Minister Teddyboy Locsin for not handling the press as Cendaña did before him. But Teddyboy is right when he said the reporters in the Marcos era are used to being spoon-fed and coddled. Teddyboy is right when he dared them to be like the newsmen of old, digging up their own scoops, and independent stories. But Teddyboy was wrong when he assumes these newsmen can rise up to the challenge. They have to be re-taught and re-trained.

And that is the problem of editors today, including the two Roces cousins gearing for a circulation war between Manila Times (150,000 printed a day) and Manila Chronicle (40,000?), which has come to be known as the Second War of the Roces.

July 10, 1986

Part 12. Ben David Waging War On Teddyboy

Everyone makes war on Sir Galahad Teddyboy Locsin, but to no avail.

Last April Information Minister Teddyboy Locsin Jr. was involved in an embarrassing incident on the PAL plane where he attempted upgrade his airline ticket to first class status. In this particular trip, he found his way to Washington D.C. where he called on the State Department without even informing the Philippine Embassy in Washington. This diplomatic snafu is attributed by his subordinates to an incurable colonial mentality, an occupational disease to which any Filipino studying in Harvard is invariably exposed to. Attempts to cure the same disease in the Katzenjammer Kids of the economy proved utterly futile.

Teddyboy then snubbed a dinner prepared by the lily white hands of Edith, the gracious wife of the Ambassador, to the embarrassment of Ambassador Pelaez and his diplomatic guests. The good ambassador who was Vice President and Foreign Secretary while Teddyboy was still playing with his baby rattle, found himself begging Teddyboy to please help in getting funds for the Embassy, to allow the Ambassador at least to advance the funds from his pockets. But Teddyboy was adamant, his advice was to keep expenses within the funds available. Pelaez was inconsolable -- what will happen to the state visit of Cory in September? will it be in good hands?

In the Embassy, there are still remnants of the past administration -- a follower of Blas Ople (a de la Rosa) and a follower of Kokoy (Tony Villanueva) -- and Teddyboy was appalled to find out why they are still there: the embassy does not have enough money to send them home! So, what is the PAL for?

In the Embassy, Teddyboy met with one of his subordinates, Ben David, erstwhile Bulletin columnist, now Information Officer in our Washington Embassy with the rank of Ambassador. Ben who has been in Washington D.C. for more than two months without having been paid his salary, complained that he has not been given any funds to carry on his mission. He informed Teddyboy that something has to be done to counter the public perception of the Cory Administration in Washington.

The image of Cory administration is absolutely shot, according to Ben -- unstable, without direction specifically in the economic field, not firm enough in dealing with subversives, the PCGG and Minister Bobbit Sanchez giving the Americans sleepless nights.

This according to the Embassy staff needs a press campaign to offset these perceptions and give Cory a better image if she is to be effective when she gets to Washington in September.

"Would you believe that the boy does not want to issue press releases because he sees them as an intrusion into press freedom? Where the hell did he go to school?" one of the Embassy staffmen wrote, answering his own question with, 'He went to the same schools that the most useless of the other cabinet members went to -- Ateneo and Harvard. There must be something about the two schools that cancel each other out, and leave the student with an empty coconut shell for a head."

Wrote the same correspondent: "There is a total lack of administrative ability in the boy that I even doubt if he had managed a sari-sari store at any time in his life. Ben David is back in Manila to see Cory. He is waging a war on Teddyboy."

Sorry to tell you this, Ben, but if Minister Johnny Ponce Enrile cannot tackle Teddyboy Locsin Jr., neither can you. You don't fault the boy because Budget Minister Bert Romulo cannot release funds for the Washington Embassy. And if you have seen him lately on television, fully shaven without his five o'clock shadow, his blue suit retailored and spic and span, his usually unloosened tie and untuckered shirt all neatly in place, his beady eyes glowing with a beatific smile blessed with the touch of angels... you will know that no one except maybe Bedan Raul

Contreras or Teddy Benigno of Agence France can move Teddyboy out of Malacañang.

This column did not intend to give the impression that the Sta. Clara Plywood went into bankruptcy solely because Don Ramon Roces sold out his shares. Like every other business Sta. Clara was caught in the maelstrom of economic recession.

Sta. Clara was organized by late Ramon Arevalo (godfather of my wife), a brilliant man who was the First Filipino Contractor (Ateneo and Universiy of London) to compete with American firms like AG&P. He built the Legislative Building, the Post Office, the Metropolitan Theater and most of the landmarks of pre-war Manila. He sired three children who managed to be the *summa, magna cum laude* of their class -- Renato "Ning" Arevalo who headed Sta. Clara, Maria Clara "Ateta" A. Gana, and Father Catalino "Nono" Arevalo S.J., considered the best Jesuit theologian in the Curia in Rome.

In 1970, on its 50th anniversary, Sta. Clara was at the height of prosperity, with hardly enough capacity to fill up the orders of its distributor in the States, the U.S. Plywood Corporation. So it borrowed from the DBP cheap dollars to carry out a major expansion of its plants in Davao, Cotabato (Guinoog), and Zamboanga City. And then came the oil shock and recession that started in 1972 and ended in the economic disaster of the 1980s. The U.S. Plywood stopped buying, leaving Sta. Clara with no market to sell to. A series of devaluations and rising interest rates skyrocketed the value of the dollar loan beyond its capacity to pay. The firm was doomed due to factors totally outside its control.

I wish I could tell you more about the travails of Ning Arevalo and Sta. Clara... about Chairman Rafael Sison (on loan from the World Bank) and the DBP... about the indignant Alice Reyes, not the dancer but the beautiful and competent Governor of DBP... about Mr. Diploma and Ramon Gana and the continuing attempts to keep the firm alive... but that is another story.

July 21, 1986

Part 13. Jose Mari Reaches Out To The People

"Amado Pineda, speaking English on Channel 7, sounds like a clown. Amado Pineda, speaking Pilipino on Radyo Ng

Bayan, sounds like a Nobel Prize scientist. On his TV program Straight From the Shoulder, His Immenseness Luis Cardinal Beltran was asked to shift to Pilipino so that more Filipinos can understand what is being said; and Louie did. A few moments later, a foreigner called up and said that he did not understand, so please shift back to English; and Louie did. Now if I were Louie, I would have told the foreigner to get himself a Filipino interpreter, because it is the Filipino people that must be informed, concerned and involved in the affairs of the nation."

So said Jose Mari Gonzalez, in the 60s a movie superstar, in the 70s a radio amateur and successful businessman, today the OIC of the Bureau of Broadcasting, the head of Radyo Ng Bayan.

The total circulation among all the newspapers have never been more than 1.2 million copies. That's a readership of about 6% of Filipino families. Television commands an audience of 18% of Filipino families. But radio commands an audience of over 82% of Filipino families, with 95% having at least one radio, and 77% having at least 2 radios. By far, the most efficient way to communicate with the Filipino people is through radio. And the best way to be understood is to speak in *Wikang Pilipino*.

Even Channel Seven's 7 o'clock News is now in Pilipino. "That's Entertainment" with a star cast of mestizos and *insulares* speaking perfect Pilipino is now Number One in the charts. The Number One Station Channel 13 communicates almost 100% in Pilipino. And Jose Mari's government stations, formerly Voice of the Philippines, now renamed Radyo Ng Bayan, broadcasts mostly in Pilipino, with a full 50,000 watts of radiated power that reaches all the way to Brunei and Japan on a good day.

Jose Mari's Radyo Ng Bayan certainly concentrates on the news of the day. Early at 6 AM, a 30 minute newscast, followed by a 5 minute update every hour on the hour, then a 15 minute newscast at noontime, continuing the 5 minute update every hour, and then capping it with a full newscast at 6 PM. Then another cycle from 6 PM to 6 AM, to complete a 24 hour broadcasting.

Manned by enthusiastic, though not necessarily knowledgeable, announcers and commenters, with phoned-in comments by the public as well as letters mailed all the way from Filipinos in Tawi Tawi, Sabah and Brunei, the Radio Ng Bayan originates from the Media Center in Bohol Avenue, and propagates 100% public service, as it seldom did before the February Revolution.

Lately I heard broadcasts by Roger Lagasca, Bert Cruz, and Malou Liwanag, exposing El Nido Resort in Bacuit Bay, Northern Palawan, as a nest of Japanese gold traders, treasure hunters and smugglers of quail eggs, lapulapu, shrimp and prawn fries, and logs, with an ill-disguised accusations of bribery against three cabinet members, and attempts to bribe the broadcast people themselves. I myself have been attacked for having gone there to investigate for myself, and my findings indicate that the three ministers have been unfairly maligned.

Minister Mitra is being accused of having a good time at the resort, when in truth he went there after a Tourist Convention to check on its facilities, as MP of Palawan. Minister Maceda is being accused of having a good time there too and allowing the Japanese to exploit our natural resources, when in truth he has never been there and it was his predecessor Rudy del Rosario who declared the area a marine sanctuary (I saw no Japanese Yakusa, at least in the resort itself). Minister Ponce Enrile is being accused of having a good time there and providing a military escort for the Japanese, when in truth he has never been there either, and the only military men I saw were Navy underwater experts charged with protecting the marine sanctuary.

Jose Mari sent a team there to investigate these charges, and promised to give us any details for publication here. Notwithstanding rare lapses in reporting, the enthusiastic no-holds-barred news commentaries from Radyo Ng Bayan has elicited many good comments from the listeners. Its attacks on various ministers for various sins of omission and commission, have made the station credible even to Marcos loyalists. Complaints are immediately attended to, and problems are solved through the cooperation of various ministries.

July 24, 1986

Part 14. Will Teddyboy Do An Angara On Johnny E.??

I should not really make fun of Teddyboy Locsin Jr. His papa is one of my favorite Ateneans, we both come from the same province (*Te kay, taga Bacolod kami nga duha*), and we were both together in the Cory Media Bureau writing news-items against Marcos so libelous, not even Inquirer would print them. When I complained to Cory about what Jimmy Ongpin and the Jesuit Mafia were doing to the speeches I drafted for her, it was Teddyboy Locsin whom Cory assigned to me as a liaison with her, and peacemaker with the abrasive Jimmy.

Well, a mutual friend called up, laughing like nobody's business at my column on Teddyboy as Enrile's nemesis, and saying, "I don't think you are kidding at all. Did you see the TV news on the Manila Hotel fracas? Guess who was negotiating with Tolentino on behalf of the Cory government? Teddyboy Locsin Jr. and General Ileto! Guess who was not there?"

Without waiting for my answer, our friend continued, "Listen to something else. Enrile's lawyer friends, the PECABAR (Cayetano, Bautista, Picazo & Reyes Law Offices), are still under retainer with UCPB, especially since the senior partners are still there. Tony Picazo is a board member and Eleazar Reyes is the corporate secretary. But guess whose law firm will take over from PECABAR?"

Not Teddyboy! "Oh, yes!" But why? "Well, Larry, everybody is afraid of Enrile, even more than they are scared of Danding. Enrile has two things Danding never had: the Army and the support of the American spooks. With those two plus Danding's wealth, Enrile can be Emperor of the Philippines. Well, nobody wants to tackle Enrile so they are sending Sir Galahad Teddyboy to slay the dragon."

"Of Teddyboy it has been said: Like Galahad, his strength is the strength of ten because his heart is pure. Besides, he is dispensable; if he disappears, nobody, not even Vivian will miss him."

Are you saying Teddyboy is a lawyer? "Ateneo Law School. Hoy, *alaga ni Edong Angara si Teddyboy*. Teddyboy was in ACCRA four years before he went to Harvard. Jose Concepcion of ACCRA used to be UCPB corporate secretary before Eleazar Reyes of PECABAR was. Concepcion's assistants were Binky Herrera and Vicky de los Reyes of ACCRA. Guess what Teddyboy organized? The law firm of Herrera, Laurel, de los Reyes, Roxas & Teehankee. They may soon take over from PECABAR."

Hey, I said, I know those people. They are a bright bunch of kids, friends of my children. Florentino "Binky" Herrera Jr. is the great grandson of Aguinaldo, the son of Justice Ameurfina Herrera, and Number 12 in the bar exam. Roberto "Bobby" Laurel is the son of Lorna and Sotero, and my favorite godchild. Victoria "Vicky" de los Reyes is the niece of Pacita Phillips. Manuel "Manny" Roxas is the grandson of President Roxas. Enrique "Iking" Teehankee is a bar topnotcher and is the nephew of the Chief Justice.

Quite a powerhouse of young lawyers, I exclaimed, they just moved to their new offices in the Laurel Building near the Makati Sports. I was told Teddyboy helped organized it before he joined the government, and he says he will leave the Ministry of Information on July 15th... Oh my God, don't tell me Teddyboy will do another Angara on Enrile???

One will recall that Enrile and Edong Angara, longtime law partners and close friends, suddenly parted ways; and Danding of UCPB chose to stay with Angara's ACCRA rather than PECABAR. There was weeping and gnashing of teeth.

"Yes," said my friend, "There will be blood and gore all over the floor, and me without my spoon! There is a 10 to one bet, Teddyboy will soon be fertilizer, figuratively speaking of course. "Yeah? Fertilizer is expensive, Teddyboy will be more valuable than he ever was as Minister of Information."

You guys out there will never know whether my friend is joking or not. Teddyboy knows I am. Really I am kidding, and that's no kidding.

There seems to be an emerging rivalry between Finance Minister Jaime Ongpin and CB Governor Jobo Fernandez on one hand, and NEDA Minister Solita Monsod and Trade Minister Jose Concepcion on the other.... as to who has more of an influence on President Cory Aquino. Most of the bets are on Winnie Monsod, since she is a woman, and feels more at home with the President than the two MBA's from Harvard.

Introverted and aristocratic Ongpin is used to pompous ex-cathedra statements that irritate everyone and convince no one. Jobo Fernandez cannot back up Ongpin effectively because of his contrived and convoluted Oxford accent which no one understands nor appreciates. Winnie on the other hand, is an extremely argumentative female who browbeats her husband

Christian all the time, and has no trouble putting Ongpin and Fernandez in their place.

Winnie who is an economist from the U.P. School of Economics has shown that she knows more about her subject than the two Business Administration graduates of Ateneo and Harvard, enough anyway to make up for her partner Joe Concepcion who is an Agriculture graduate (with a penchant for industrialization) from Araneta University.

The most reliable bell-weather of Cory's confidence is Cesar Buenaventura who seems to be distancing himself from the Katzenjammer Kids of the economy, "Hans" Ongpin and "Fritz" Fernandez, and edging closer to "Winnie the Poo" and the Immaculate Concepcion.

This is hard to believe but a former official of the Philippine National Bank reportedly disclosed that one of the reasons the Century Bank of California failed is that top Filipino officials were collecting salaries from $150,000 to $300,000 per month. From five government officials alone, the salaries amounted to $1.5 million per month!

The Century Bank, one will recall, is a bank in Los Angeles, purchased by the Social Security System (SSS), the Land Bank of the Philippines, the Government Service Insurance System (GSIS), the Development Bank of the Philippines (DBP), and the Philippine National Bank (PNB). This means that those involved in the management were Cesar Zalamea, Gilberto Teodoro, Basilio Estanislao, Roman Cruz Jr., and Panfilo O. Domingo. Will someone enlighten us about this?

"Stamp out graft and corruption in government" reads the lapel pin worn by many government officials. Big joke. The lapel wearer strides into businessman's office and within hearing of many employees, demands, *"Magkano ba ang amin diyan?"* What used to be done within the secret confines of air-conditioned offices, are now done openly and without shame, "because we had to pay something to get this position."

In the old regime, to facilitate matters in one particular office, one has had to pay P20,000 to P30,000 payable after the transaction is completed. Today the price has doubled to P40,000, payable up front, before the papers are even processed. Surprising no doublecross has yet occurred.

Nowadays, it is the government grafter who does not trust the businessman he extorts from.

Whether it is the threat of sequestration, or the frustrating effort to secure payment for services already rendered, or the nerve-wracking anticipation of an approved contract, the businessman today is ever wary of the inevitable "squeeze play" that seems to be standard procedure in most offices. Times are hard indeed.

That and the difficulty of getting working capital at reasonable rates of interest, the minimal rates for savings deposits and the proposed 20% tax rate on interests earned, the shrinking domestic market due to import liberalization and the 20% sales tax on goods sold, as well as the constantly scowling and snarling countenance of one Minister that seems to augur ill for the economy -- simply erodes any serious attempt to get our economy going.

Part 15.   Giving Cory Unsolicited Advice For Her Wastebasket

When President Cory Aquino went on television to say that her pet peeve is he who gives unsolicited advice, that although she listens politely, her mind is impenetrably closed... I was crestfallen. For it was not long before, that I was in her office giving her unsolicited advice; and I was sure it was her gentle way of telling me that the only advice worthy of solicitation was that of Jimmy Ongpin and Jobo Fernandez.

I was inconsolable even when Raul Contreras, Bono Adaza, Doy Laurel, Rene Espina and a host of others were proudly and perversely proclaiming that they were the ones being referred to by Cory. Indeed, it did not even help when it was proven beyond all shadow of doubt that for sheer volume and frequency of unsolicited advice to Cory, no one, absolutely no one, can beat David Sycip.

Well, David Sycip goes merrily on his way, writing voluminous articles, complete with qualifications and quantifications, on everything from the bases to the external debt, and ever careful not to offend proconsuls Bosworth, Kaplan and Fred Whiting, totally oblivious to the fact that being unsolicited, his advice is being relegated to the wastebasket.

Well, Dave is not the only one capable of giving unsolicited advice. In view of the presidential speech delivered before the chambers of commerce, giving unsolicited advice to businessmen who have their own minds impenetrably   closed, in view of businessmen giving in turn unsolicited advice to Cory about Jimmy, Jobo, Bobbit and Nene... well, let's all join David and have fun giving unsolicited advice to all who would not listen.

Mrs. President, the key word here is Entrepreneurship, the entrepreneur being the businessman you are really appealing to, the one with the ability and willingness to take risks, the one with initiative, imagination and talent for organization, the one who puts together men, money, machines, materials together in productive and profitable relationship.

CB Governor Jobo Fernandez is not an entrepreneur; he is a banker. He takes care of money that is not his own, and he never takes risks, he lends money secured by real estate and paid for with a fixed interest rate.

Finance Minister Jimmy Ongpin is not an entrepreneur, he is a professional manager, a *bantay*, a *katiwala*, and he never risks his own money. He gets a salary and a bonus, and he can leave anytime to join another firm.

NEDA Minister Solita Monsod is not an entrepreneur either, she is an economics professor. What she knows she learns from books and seminars, and from picking the brains of her poor husband who is not an entrepreneur either but a banker.

The only one in your cabinet who is a real entrepreneur is Trade Minister Joe the Immaculate Concepcion. Together with his twin, he built an industrial empire. Listen to him, Mrs. President, he is the only one who knows what makes a entrepreneur take risks and invest in the economy.

If Joe the Immaculate Concepcion can only shake off the influence of Christian Monsod, and get over his fear of Stephen Bosworth and Fred Whiting, he can tell you what you really need to know.

First, he will tell you that entrepreneurs do not respond to the kind of witty speeches Teddyboy or Father Bernas makes. They only respond to the possibility of a Big Profit with the Least Risk. Offer them that and they will invest in our economy no matter how many Bobbits and KMUs, or how many Nenes, Jimmys or Jobos there are to irritate them.

A Big Profit with the Least Risk comes with a guaranteed market. Tell them they must compete, but only among themselves in the Philippine market without the burden of unfair foreign competition. This means having to reject the import liberalization plan and other excremental conditions of the IMF.

Second, protect the entrepreneurs as much as possible from risk factors outside of their control, such as IMF-dictated devaluation, exchange risks, dumping, smuggling, and spiraling interest rates. This can be done by judicious policy without the dictates of extraneous forces. In Latin America, this is called the policy of "*Concordata*".

Third, force the government to live within its means; this means no government deficits of P25 billion to be financed by U.S. credits. This means you may have to reduce the armed forces from 250,000 men back to what it was before martial law, 50,000 men. In 1922, Austria fired 100,000 government employees; in 1923-24, Germany fired 230,000 government employees, to get their economy going again. Resources employed to support government employees are a total waste; they do not create consumable wealth, they are strictly overhead.

Fourth, prime-pump the economy, not by financing Winnie's infrastructure projects, but by going into a massive housing program which have multiplier effects on the rest of the economy:(1)housing industry uses local materials, is least import dependent and exerts little pressure on our dollar reserves; (2)it is labor intensive and will relieve our unemployment problem; (3) it is not capital intensive and is easily set up; (4) it will enhance real estate values, increase the value of bank collaterals and create needed credit; (5) it will stimulate 68 other industries, such as the steel, aluminum, wood, glass, paint, construction, etcetera; (6) it is recession-proof, the demand for housing rarely gets satisfied by the supply, such that this industry is the engine of growth in most socialist economies, from Singapore to Sweden to the Soviet Union.

How much will the housing program cost? Making 20,000 dwellings at P100,000 per dwelling, you will spend only P24 billion a year, a little less than your annual deficit of P25 billion.

Won't you rather have 240,000 dwellings and a robust economy than a bunch of useless grasping bureaucrats and 200,000 unneeded soldiers with guns pointing at you?

There it is, Mrs. President, just a little unsolicited advice to chuck into the wastebasket.

July 26, 1986

Part 16. Give Cory A Break, Johnny E.!

Johnny, one of these days, by the grace of God and Rene Cayetano, you will be the president of the Philippines. And if you have Bono Adaza as vice president and Defense Minister, Ding Lichauco in the NEDA, and Joe the Immaculate Concepcion as Finance Minister -- barring earthquakes, floods and a CIA plot to assassinate you -- if you can somehow extirpate the shameful obeisance to Uncle Sam, the self-destructive double-allegiance that corrodes our pride and dignity as a nation -- what a great president you will make!

But that is 6 years away, Johnny, so give Cory a break, will you? Give her a chance to be President of all the Filipinos, even those who did not vote for her, even those who are up in the hills shooting at our soldiers. For that is what the Presidency is all about, Johnny: Unity, Reconciliation, Consensus, the consent and cooperation of the governed. That is the Historical Necessity. That is the Final Imperative, the key to our Survival as a nation.

There is a difference between the motivations of the male and the female. Without pretending to know what motivates the tomboys and the effeminate, who seem to infest some sectors of our government -- I will say this much: In the animal kingdom, the male seeks power for power's sake, for the pleasure of having a harem of females all to himself; the female fights to the death for one sublime purpose, the care and protection of her young.

It is God's design that in this crucial period of our history when we are torn asunder by treason, disunity and differences in ideology, we have a woman President who looks upon the entire nation as her family.

To President Cory, the Communist insurgents are Filipinos too, and so are the Muslim Separatists, the Marcos Abandonados, the Nationalists -- no less than the likes of

Ricardo Romulo and Blas Ople, Nene Pimentel and Joker Arroyo. To her, Steve Bosworth, Phil Kaplan, the CIA boys (Norbert Garrett and John Ettinger), the AmCham boys (Fred Whiting and William Quasha) are guests in this country, not the governors-general; nor are they part of the family, they are an extraneous force with imperatives of their own.

Those who are outside the pale -- the Communists, Separatists, the *Abandonados* -- are not enemies, Johnny, they are brothers gone astray, they are prodigal sons that must be welcomed back to the heart. We need to talk to them, address their concerns, solve their problems, redress their grievances. We must bridge our differences and strengthen the ties that bind us together. And that is what Cory Aquino is trying to do.

Those insurgents in the mountains are not paid to defend foreign interests; they do not receive salaries or consultant's fees, or legal retainers, nor are they looking forward to high paying salaries in non-devaluable dollars. No Johnny, they are risking their lives for something they believe in, and we should have more respect for them than those assholes who promote American interests for 30 pieces of silver.

Our greatest problem is to ensure the survival of our people and our nation. If it means legalizing the Communist Party and allowing them to peddle their ideology in the marketplace of ideas, as they do in Europe and in most countries of the world, then we should do so, with confidence that our way of life will prove superior and more acceptable to our people. You believe in this, Johnny, you said so.

I know, I know, those buggers in the cabinet have it in for you. They accuse you of sabotaging Cory and de-stabilizing the government. Many suffered a lot during the Marcos regime and they accuse you of criminal complicity at worst, or negligence at best. Joker Arroyo, Rene Saguisag, Bobbit Sanchez, Pepe Diokno and many of their people were human rights lawyers fighting military abuses; to them there is a lot of difference between abuses by the military, backed by public resources and the full force of government and the Americans, and those of the insurgents who are fighting alone and unaided.

It does nobody any good for you to lose your temper. It makes people nervous, and makes you look menacing, erratic, and imperious, which you are not. It makes your enemies happy that they can get your goat so easily and force you to do things that you will regret afterwards. Above all, it drives a wedge between you and our lady president. Believe me, in this country, Johnny, you cannot win against a woman, unless she is a screaming banshee, which Cory is not.

Lean to laugh at yourself, Johnny. A sense of self-deprecating humor is a shield against pride and self-pity, and is good for the soul. And learn to laugh at your enemies. Believe me, your enemies will find it a lot more intolerable to be laughed at, than to be hated.

Take a lesson from Homobono Adaza who laughs at his enemies. Both of you have the same tormentor, Nene Pimentel. Nene was asked why does he not hit Bono the way he hits you, and he answered, "When I get into a fight with Bono, he enjoys it and I don't!" Apparently Johnny, when Nene gets into a fight with you, he enjoys it, and you don't.

Part 17. Hail Bingo Full Of Grace

For many of us it started with the movie Red Shoes starring a young ballerina named Moira Shearer, and/or Walt Disney's Fantasia where crocodiles and hippos cavort to the music "Invitation to a Dance".

"Oh everything is beautiful at the ballet," sang three dancers in the Broadway musical A Chorus Line. And indeed it is. The ballet is one of the most beautiful of the performing arts -- it is all there, the colors of a master painting, the tri-dimensions of a master sculpture, above all, the fluidity, the motion, the magical music that bring to life graceful swans, lovely princesses and children with dreams of Christmas.

We may damn her to hell for many things, but we should be at least thankful to Madame Imelda Marcos for ushering in, almost against our will, a cultural renaissance in our country. She built the Cultural Center Complex, gave us a national symphony, and Alice Reyes' Ballet Philippines with its own CCP School of Dance.

But it was characteristic of Imelda that ignoring many other dance groups, some of whom are well-known and recognized all over the world, she gave the Ballet Philippines her patronage and favors.

The Ballet Philippines enjoyed for 17 years free use of the CCP's equipment and facilities, including a rehearsal hall, the Main Theater, the Little Theater, storage space for costumes, office spaces, even a little gift shop; an annual subsidy for its performances especially with international artists; exclusive use of new works produced annually by the League of Filipino Composers; half-rates at the Philippine Airlines; and the full support of the First Lady and important government officials for its fund raising campaigns.

How about the other dance groups? The Filipinescas Ballet of Leonor Orosa Goquingco, which pioneered in and brought the attention of the world to our Philippine Dance forms, and raised it to a creative concert level... Julie Borromeo and her Dance Art Studios who gave the world Tina and Cecile Santos, and choreographed the production numbers of musical plays so delightful to watch... Tony Fabella and Eddie Elejar of Manila Metropolis Ballet... Inday Gaston Manosa of Hariraya Ballet... Basilio and Felicitas L. Radaic of Dance Theater of the Philippines... Eric V. Cruz and Vella Damian of Dance Concert Company... Gener Caringal of Dance Repertory.

Shouldn't these groups be given an equal chance to compete? Surely, the Ballet Philippines after a decade and a half of practical monopoly of Madame Marcos' favors and patronage, should be strong enough to withstand equal competition with other groups in the interest of equity and democratization.

The Ballet Philippines' CCP School of Dance, essentially a private enterprise, should not be accorded rent-free facilities in the CCP. The CCP Rehearsal Hall should be open to all, and not for one school's exclusive use. A liberated CCP should be left open and free to admit all deserving companies, including Ballet Philippines, on equal footing and with equal encouragement. After all, what was our Revolution all about?

The newly installed boss of the CCP, Bing Escoda Roxas, my *comadre*, godmother of my youngest boy, my childhood friend whose wedding gown was personally brought to the States by my own dear little mother, fellow supporter of Cory, beautiful wonderful woman, Hail Bingo full of grace --- aw come on, Bing-bang-bong, what else can I say to convince you to start on the right foot and democratize our Ballet Arts?

In my piece about the Bedans, I mentioned that only San Beda can claim Ninoy as an alumnus, since it was in San Beda where Ninoy got his grade school and high school diplomas; Ninoy never got a college diploma. San Beda has something in common with Sta. Scholastica where President Cory Aquino was graduated. Both colleges are run by the same religious order, the Benedictines. Are you surprised then that despite the Jesuit Mafia and Opus Dei, it is the Benedictine Bedans that Cory specially likes?

The Benedictine Order was founded by Saint Benedict in 529 AD at Monte Cassino in Italy, the very first of the religious orders that survive to this day. Compared to the Benedictines, the Jesuits (founded 1540) and the Opus Dei (founded 1928) are upstarts.   Born in the Dark Ages, the Benedictine Order originated the vows of poverty, chastity and obedience; propagated the Gregorian Chants; and gave sanctuary to people sick of the constant upheavals that happened after the death of the Roman Empire. Their monks cleared forests, drained marshes, and developed agriculture; kept the spirit of learning alive by teaching Latin and copying the old Latin classics laboriously by hand; and preserved the treasures of Science and Literature, for the coming age of Charlemagne and the Holy Roman Empire.

For a long time the ruling class in the Philippines was recruited from Ateneo, La Salle and the University of the Philippines. Aside from the Magnificent Loners, Lorenzo Tañada, Jose Diokno, Alejandro Lichauco and Renato Constantino, this class has become insensitive to the crying needs of the nation, antagonistic to national interest when it conflicts with imperialist demands of the USA, and committed to keeping the Philippines a nation of poor dirt farmers and ersatz Americans.

Ranged against this is a new force headed by emerging leaders Rene Saguisag, Raul Roco, and others, from San Beda, committed to nationalism, social justice and human rights.

August 7, 1986

Part 18.   So Many Songs Unsung, Songs To Recapture Memories Of Today

There was a time during the Golden Years 1976-78 when Filipino songs celebrated the dreams, the longings, the smiles and tears in the very depths of the Filipino soul. "Sapagkat Kami ay Tao Lamang" was the campaign song of Doy, sung off-key by his wife Celia. "Kapalaran" was sung interminably over the air waves by Rico J. Puno; "Saranggola ni Pepe" by Celeste Legaspi; Ngayon at Kailan Man" by Basil Valdez; "Magellan" by Yoyoy Villame; "Kapantay ay Langit" by Pilita Corrales; and my favorite "Saan Ka Naroon". "Anak" by Freddie Aguilar became an international hit, and Imelda's favorite "Dahil Sa Iyo" did more to enhance the world image of the Filipino than any other until the February Revolution.

Today, we are being inundated by American rock and punk, discordant and deafening, drowning out once more the voices of Filipino music. Only one percent of the record releases are Filipino compositions sung by Filipino artists, thanks to the so-called Philippine Association of Recorders, Inc. (PARI) which should be renamed Association of American Licensees. Who are they?

Danilo Olivares (brother-in-law of Ninez), full-time president; Orly Ilacad, president of Octo Arts, licensees of RCA, CBS, Motown and Arista; Buddy de Vera of Alpha Records, licencees of MCA and A&M; Ramon Chuaing of WEA Records, licensees of Warner, Electra and Atlantic; James Dy of Dyna Records, licensees of EMI, Capitol, Polydor and Polygram; Vic del Rosario of Vicor Records which is now owned by CCP Cultural Center of the Philippines) and making only local records having lost RCA as of June 30.

According to Jose Mari Gonzales of Cinema Audio, there was a time that the PARI represented all the sectors of the recording industry -- not only the recording studios, but also the record producers, the singers, the musicians, the technicians, the duplicators, etc. whose interest was to promote Filipino music. One day, some asshole from the Marcos administration came into the picture, changed the by-laws of the PARI, and only the recording industries remained.

A mere four Filipino songs were played every hour on radio broadcasts, with the announcer with a false American accent braying, "This is a tribute to the Filipino artist" before every Filipino song, as if it were an obituary, a death notice for the Filipino Art. But even this is no longer being enforced since the Revolution.

The companies pay from $100,000 to $150,000 per year for exclusive license to make and sell foreign labels. This is paid strictly in cash to a visiting representative of the foreign company, without passing through the Central Bank or paying taxes to the BIR.

The company receives a series of demonstration tapes, badly recorded to discourage pirating, from which the licensee selects the records he wants, and he usually gets almost all offered. The company pays $2,000 production materials per album, also in cash, for which it receives a stamper (a metal mold for pressing phonograph records), or a master tape (open reel tape recorded at 15 inches per second, for copying into cassettes). These valuable materials are usually brought in at minimal reported cost and hardly is charged tariff duty.

Each record release from foreign sources have a initial direct cost of only $2,000 or P40,000 -- a very small portion of its actual cost. To produce an album locally with Filipino artists and compositions, will cost from P100,000 to P200,000. Do you wonder then that the PARI companies would rather produce and promote foreign records than our own?

Also, a Coca Cola Commercial made abroad a year ago, as well as an MTV promotional, are sold here at $30.00 while Philippine made TV Commercials and MTVs would cost at least P100,000 to produce. So why would advertisers use local talents?

In such countries as Australia and Singapore, every effort is made to preserve the national culture from unfair foreign competition and contamination. Heavy taxes are imposed on foreign records in Australia, so that foreign records sell for $12.00 while local records are sold for $9.00 per LP album. Singapore insists that most TV commercials shown be made in Singapore.

The television stations make a special effort to enhance the Filipino's image of himself, with such absolutely beautiful renditions of "Magka-isa", "Handog ng Pilipino sa Mundo", "Hindi Ako Papayag". There are also "Power of the People", and "Handang Umibig" by Kring-kring. But these are patriotic songs that arose out of the February Revolution. Where are the commercial songs, the "Kapalaran", the "Dahil Sa Iyo" of today?

Only 18% of Filipino families watch television, while 95% of our families have at least one radio and 77% have 2 radios. Here in the airwaves of AM and FM radio should we find the sounds and spirit of contemporary Philippines, but we do not.

So many songs still unsung! Where are the songs we dance to, our love songs, our theme songs, our screams of joy, our cries of pain, the songs we sing in the future to recapture the memories of today??

What then must we do to preserve the Filipino soul?

1. We must impose a sales tax on foreign records at least 30% higher than those imposed on locally made records.

2. We must lead up to the point that all radio stations are required as a franchise condition to play one Filipino record for every foreign record played.

3. We must reduce the taxes on equipment and materials for the recording industry, at least to the levels of those in the computer industry.

4. We must force TV advertisers to use for the most part locally made TV commercials, and more time for locally produced shows.

5. We must see to it that our artists and composers are paid "mechanical and performance royalties" such as those collected by ASCAP and BMI around the world.

August 9, 1986

Part 19. Import Lib Was Condition For IMF Support Of Martial Law

When President Ferdinand Edralin Marcos decided to declare Martial Law, he asked the permission of two foreign entities without whom he could not succeed -- Uncle Sam and the IMF/World Bank.

Uncle Sam answered: "Ferdie, I thought you'd never ask. You should have done it long ago, join Uncle Sam's buggers in making the world safe for democracy and profitable for multinational corporations. Welcome to the company of Rafael Trujillo of the Dominican Republic, Papa Doc and Baby Doc Duvalier of Haiti, Anastacio Somosa of Nicaragua, Augusto Pinochet of Chile, the militarists Videla and Galtieri of Argentina, Fulgencio Batista of Cuba, the Shah of Iran, the Chiangs of China and Taiwan, Syngman Rhee and Park Chung Hee of

South Korea, Ngo Diem of South Vietnam, Lon Nol of Kampuchea -- and all the rest of the dictators who kick the teeth of their own people, in the interest of Uncle Sam."

The IMF/World Bank answered, "Sure Ferdie, but on one condition. In 1961, we forced President Macapagal to open up your economy, float the dollar rate and devaluate. But he double-crossed us. He appointed Henares as NEC Chairman to raise tariff duties and protect your industries. As a result, your industries survived, and the value of the peso floated against the dollar never deviated from P3.90 to $1.00. We will give your martial law our blessing and support if you tear down all the last vestiges of economic protectionism in your country."

Marcos declared Martial Law on September 22, 1972. Three months later, on January 1, 1973, NEDA chief Gerardo Sicat, specially recruited upon IMF recommendation from the U.P. School of Economics, declared that Trade and Import Liberalization shall henceforth be the policy of the martial law government.

Today, 13 years later, NEDA chief Solita "Winnie" Monsod, also recruited with IMF approval from the U.P. School of Economics, declared that the last phase of the Import Liberalization is about to be accomplished.

And in between the dollar rate plunged from P7.00 to P20.50 per dollar, our industries and entire economy collapsed, while countries around us successfully weathered the economic recession.

The University of the Philippines is known to be the bastion of Philippine Nationalism, except for the U.P. School of Economics whose buildings, library, and "consultancy" appendages are subsidized by the Japanese Government, the Ford Foundation, the Rockefeller Foundation and other instruments of economic imperialism. On a raging sea of nationalism, the School of Economics has launched a Ship of Fools headed by such as NEDA Minister Gerardo Sicat, now gone to his reward as a minor World Bank Official highly paid with tax-free non-devaluable dollars; and his worthy successor NEDA Minister Winnie Monsod.

During the Martial Law, the IMF and its surrogates Finance Minister Cesar Virata and NEDA minister Vicente Valdepeñas, both rewarded as highly paid "consultants" of

American banks and corporations, succeeded in "rationalizing" tariff rates over a 5-year period down to an average of 28%, with a top rate of 50%. In contrast, at a comparative period of development in the 1840s, without comparable foreign competition, American producers were protected by the Morill Tariff equal to a weighted average of more than 50% of the value of imports.

World Bank experts came with their Structural Adjustment Loans, prescribing drastic devaluation, high interest rates, scarce money supply, import liberalization, and concentration on "export oriented, agricultural based, small scale, labor intensive, rurally dispersed" economic activities, like shell craft and hat weaving.

Import Liberalization was the official policy of the Marcos Martial Law government. From 1981 to 1985, Tariff rates were "rationalized", with Winnie and her U.P. gang demanding a non-protective uniform tariff rate on all imported goods whether it is a necessity or a luxury, whether manufactured locally or not. In 1981, 263 items were liberalized; in March 1982, 610 items were liberalized; because of the serious Balance of Payments in 1983, Marcos had at least the decency to suspend the Import Liberalization.

After the Revolution, Winnie took over and even though the economic situation has worsened, the IMF demanded that the new Cory government comply with Marcos' commitment to IMF for its support of martial law. A few months ago, 919 items were liberalized; and today NEDA minister Winnie Monsod, like NEDA minister Gerry Sicat before her, is demanding liberalization of the last 313 items.

Throughout the martial law, the IMF excremental conditionalities prevailed. Up to the time Ninoy Aquino was assassinated, the banned items and non-essential items imported totaled $12.6 billion, while the accumulated trade deficits during the same period was $12.9 billion. The external debt that was $950 million or less than a billion before martial law, was about $13.5 billion by the time Ninoy died, so that the increase in debt amounted to $12.5 billion.

To put it another way, we spent $12.5 billion to import things we did not need, so that we accumulated a deficit of $12.9 which we financed by borrowing $12.5 billion from international loan sharks. Now is that not stupid?

Not only that, when we took a closer look at our external debt, it was not only $13.5 billion, it was a staggering $26 billion, most of it in short term debt! Because of the unholy pact between Marcos, the Americans and the IMF, we were bankrupt long before Ninoy died, but our technocrats were "window dressing" our bankruptcy with short term debts!
August 12, 1986

Part 20. Why Are Our Best Heroes Also Our Worst Villains?

In the history of nations and in the hallowed pages of literature, the most admired and emulated of all heroes are daring quick-witted devil-may-care charlatans: Robin Hood, Sir Francis Drake, Captain Blood, Jean Lafitte, Jesse James, Bluebeard, Richard the Lion Heart, Clive of India, Laurence of Arabia -- pirates all, with the ability to move the world.

In the free-wheeling free-booting world of free enterprise, the greatest heroes are the robber barons, the empire builders, who bare-knuckled their way from the slums to the penthouses of the corporate world -- pirates too, with the ability to create wealth where none existed. In the eyes of social reformers and bleeding hearts, they are the cruel exploiters of the masses, the despoilers of the environment, who would sacrifice public interest for private greed.

In the United States, the land of the free enterprise and the home of the brave monopolists, the heroes most admired are those who demolish their competitors by fair means or foul, and create jobs and wealth. There is John D. Rockefeller, who set up the first billion dollar company over the bones of his competitors, the Standard Oil, which the anti-trust laws broke up into 32 companies, of which 7 are still among the biggest in the world. There is Henry Ford, the mechanical genius who hated labor unions, and who put America on wheels, selling cars "of any color, as long as it is black."

There is Andrew Carnegie who created the U.S. Steel monopoly; Henry DuPont who made the explosives that cleared the wilderness; Winchester who made the guns that made the Indian and the buffalo almost extinct; Sam Goldwyn (his name was originally Goldfish with a partner called Selwyn; he changed his name to Goldwyn, leaving his partner the big joke of

Hollywood, laughingly called Selfish or Sell-fish), Harry Cohn and the rest of the mob who created the motion picture industry. Howard Hughes, Stephen Jobs, Henry Kaiser, Thomas Watson... they are no angels, but they are the true heroes of our capitalist society. They are the entrepreneurs, the risk takers with initiative, imagination and talent for organization, who put men, money, machines and materials together in productive and profitable relationship.

In the Philippines, there is Teodoro Toribio, the shoe magnate who moved heaven and Quezon to give him exclusive rights to supply the army with footwear. There is Vicente Madrigal who found himself with a shipment of coal at the outset of World War I, soaked it with water to double its weight and made a killing. There is Gonzalo Puyat, the furniture and bowling alley king, who somehow cornered the supply of narra; then spawned a second and third generation of lusty no-holds-barred entrepreneurs. There is Don Andres Soriano, the beer magnate who destroyed the Japanese competition at the Balintawak Beer, and the poor Halili Beer in a manner that would make your hair curl.

In the post war years, we see Jose P. Marcelo who pioneered in rubber and steel nail monopoly; Harry Stonehill who smuggled tobacco seeds from the United States and created our Virginia tobacco industry; Philip Ysmael and his Admiral refrigerators; Lucio Tan and his Fortune Tobacco; John Gokongwei and his food conglomerate; Jose Y. Campos and his drug monopoly; P.L. Lim and his textiles; Ricardo Silverio and his Delta Motors, Rodolfo Cuenca and his CDCP, and the biggest of them all, the legendary PACMAN, Eduardo Cojuangco Jr. -- they are not lovable characters, they are considered greedy, selfish and vicious, they are the despicable cronies of Presidents. But in our dog-eat-dog devil-take-the-hindmost survival-of-the-fittest kind of a free enterprise jungle, these characters are the heroes and creators of wealth.

As part of a delegation into Mainland China, I encountered a Chinese intellectual who characterized the Capitalist Entrepreneur as a Competitive Man, comprising only 2% of the population, who has a compulsive obsessive drive to prove himself better than other men, even if he has to take the food out of mouths of the other 98% to prove it.

Money is no longer of any importance to him, since he has more than enough to keep himself alive, to provide for all his basic needs. Yet he will spend all his time, even to the extent of neglecting his family, to the determined pursuit of wealth that he does not need, of more wealth than he can ever spend in twenty lifetimes, while others live a precarious existence from hand to mouth.

For Money has become a means of keeping score in the Great Game of Life, and the amount of money he has is the measure of his worth as a man, as compared to other men.

"What will happen to entrepreneurs like me if the Communists take over?" I asked, and he answered, "You are as dangerous as a lion in the streets. If we cannot re-educate you to be a Socialist Man, we will have to put you where the lion should be -- in a cage."

August 17,1986

Part 21.　Bankers, Managers And Speculators Are Peripheral But Essential

In our capitalist world, the real creators of wealth are the Entrepreneurs, the initiators, the organizers, the risk-takers, the producers of goods and services for the marketplace.

In the boardrooms of the capitalist jungle, there are other characters, but they do not create wealth. Schumpeter calls them the entrepreneurs' "cluster of followers". They sometimes help, they sometimes conflict with the entrepreneurs, and usually, they wind up with all the wealth. Who are they?

They are the corporate raiders like Uncle Dan Drew, Jay Gould and James Fisk in the United States; in the Philippines, they are the stock speculators, the financial manipulators, the power brokers -- ask Irving Ackermann or Luis Ongpin Sr. and Jr., they know the ones. When Imelda, Kokoy and Vincent Recto forced the price of Oriental shares up, unloaded their shares while the public was left with high priced stock no one would buy -- when Kokoy and Rolly Gapud took over control of Oriental and other companies, by issuing watered stock and borrowing money from government banks with inadequate collaterals -- they were engaging in corporate raids.

These also include the ones who corner the market for sugar, rice and other commodities like Roberto Benedicto, Tony

Chan, Antonio Roxas Chua. The worst of these are those who use political power to take over the wealth others create, like Herminio Disini with his overprice and commissions; Kokoy Romualdez and his corporate takeovers; and the greatest plundering pirate of them all, Ferdinand Edralin Marcos.

Notice I make a distinction between Carding Silverio, Rudy Cuenca, Lucio Tan, Jose Yao Campos and Danding Cojuangco, the creators of wealth -- and Bobby Benedicto, Count Herminio Disini, Kokoy Romualdez and Ferdie Marcos, who are the parasites, bloodsuckers, and barnacles of the economy.

But stock market speculators and their ilk have a peripheral but a very valid role to play. Because they put their money in and out of the stock market, to the extent that they leave some in, they contribute to the pool of capital available to the Entrepreneur.

More important than that, stock speculators provide liquidity for capital already sunk into the enterprise. A ready market for shares of stocks provided for by speculators who gamble on the future value of such securities, is invaluable to the entrepreneur who can count on the "liquidity" or "stability" of his investment.

There are the financial intermediaries, the fat cat bankers, also known in the business world as "loan sharks in grey suits", who skim their interests and financial charges right off the top and use the money of others to make money for themselves. Like J. Pierpont Morgan, the Mellons and the Rothchilds. In the Philippines, there are Dee K. Chung, Vic Puyat, Ralph Nubla and the quintessential banker of them all, Jobo Fernandez of Far East Bank & Trust.

While the whole economy is in great recession, Far East Bank had one of its most profitable years. By creating jobs and wealth? Ha ha, by the appreciation of their dollar accounts after a series of devaluations painful to the rest of us; by the interest earned on Jobo Bills; by "arbitrage" or trading on the difference of dollar exchange rates in different parts of the world. Did Far East Bank make a single marketable nail, or relieved the misery of one single unemployed? Ha ha ha.

But financial intermediaries also have their uses. Banks mobilize the savings of the nation, and channel them into useful investments.

Then there are the so-called Professional Managers. They do not risk anything nor do they create wealth; they are the hired help, the *bantay*, the *pagkatiwalaan*, the guards of the sultan's harem. They have to be honest and upright, have to change underwear often, wear clean shirts and brush their teeth thrice a day, otherwise they don't get hired. The big boys of the Opus Dei and the Jesuit Mafia belong to this category. So do the Filipino managers of multinational corporations. Jaime Ongpin is the classic example of this breed, and he thinks he is God's gift to the Filipino people.

Sufficiently restrained by anti-trust laws and pertinent government regulations, the pirates of our capitalist jungle can be instruments of economic progress, engines for the development and growth of our economy. Yet it is a sad commentary on the state of mind of our people that they consider as villains and devils, such creators of wealth and jobs, as Danding Cojuangco, Harry Stonehill and Rudy Cuenca.... and worship such peripheral actors on the economic stage as Jobo Fernandez, Jaime Ongpin, and stockbroker Irving Ackermann.

It is sobering to realize that Eugenio P. Esguerra of 894 Quezon Boulevard, a humble shoe maker, creates more wealth for this country in a single day than multimillionaires Jobo, Jimmy and Irving can ever create in their combined lifetimes.

August 18, 1986

Part 22.   Angara Assaults PGH, The PGH In Critical Condition

My parents were born in their own houses. Mine was the first generation that was born in a modern hospital. It was in the Obstetrics Ward 18 of the Philippine General Hospital, where most citizens of my generation were born. The PGH was the first, the biggest and most modern hospital of its day, its crowded corridors evoking memories of Quezon, Osmeña, Roxas being probed, poked and examined by the great doctors of the time; of President Laurel, felled by an assassin's bullet during the war; of Congressman Felix Amante with multiple machine gun wounds, bleeding like a sieve. The PGH bears the mark of our history as a nation.

During the "liberation" of Manila, while all around were scenes of bloodshed and devastation, it was the sanctuary of thousands of the wounded and the dying. Even now when people face emergencies where they do not have the money needed for deposits, it is only to the PGH where they are brought. *"Dalhin nyo na ako sa PGH!"* is often the anguished cry of the impoverished patient.

The PGH itself is now in a critical condition, its status as an autonomous unit dedicated to the health and welfare of the Filipino, is now changed to being an appendage to an educational institution whose primary purpose is to train medical workers.

John H. Knowles, MD, in his book "The Teaching Hospital" makes a distinction between the goals of a medical school and that of a modern hospital. "The goals of a medical school," he wrote, "is the teaching of medical students... for tomorrow's health wants and needs. The goals of a teaching hospital is first and foremos... the care of the sick and service to the community today." The PGH is being subjected to the demands of Tomorrow, at the expense of the crying needs of Today.

During the Martial Law, President Marcos, by Executive Order 519, established the Health Science Center, in which PGH became one of 13 units, with a total budget of P125 million, of which P100 million was supposed to be allocated to PGH. Marcos' appointee UP President Edong Angara then issued his own Executive Order 10 and 11, by which he authorized himself to transfer funds from the PGH budget to the University proper, redefining the role of PGH to provide medical service to the community strictly secondary to, and as a consequence of its teaching, training and research activities; and to provide medical services to the faculty, students and employees of the University.

What villainy is this? This People's Hospital converted into a training school? a medical clinic for a lone institution?

What villainy is this? The PGH which was created by law, Revised Administrative Code, Chapter 29, and conferred the status of an independent Bureau, to serve the needs of all the people, is being illegally dismembered by executive fiat of the

U.P. president, its facilities and offices, powers and responsibilities, being transferred and distributed to other offices of the University, to satisfy the lust for power of President Ed Angara, Dr. Conrado Lorenzo, Dr. Clemente Gatmaitan Jr., Dr. Yolando Sulit, Dr. Felipe Estrella, Dr. George Eufemio, Dr. Richard Tiongco, and all the faculty members of the U.P. College of Medicine who look upon the poor patients of PGH as "clinical teaching material" or guinea pigs for doctors under training. These doctors who swore the Hippocratic hypocritical oath should know better than to strip the PGH of its original noble purpose.

What villainy is this? The U.P. Law Center in a memorandum on the effect of Marcos Executive Order 519, on the Bureau Status of the PGH, the powers of its director as well as its budget, opined that the PGH retains its legal status as an independent bureau, created by law; and consequently, neither the Board of Regents or the U.P. President can change its power and functions which are fixed in the administrative code. In other words, Attorney Edgardo Angara, head of the most prestigious law firm of the country, ACCRA, nemesis of PECABAR, has acted ILLEGALLY in emasculating the PGH's ability to respond to the people's needs. And this according to his own prestigious legal think-thank, the U.P. Law Center!

What villainy is this? The PGH historically and presently is still the foremost medical center of its kind, serving over 300,000 patients a year, more than any other hospital, without any motive for profit or gain, for three quarters of a century, the first really modern hospital in the Philippines, a living institution that has been the oasis of the poor and the neglected among us, the friendless, the cheated and the beaten.

Mrs. President Corazon Aquino should resolve this problem by revoking the Marcos Executive Order 519, revert the PGH back to the Office of the President as it was before, and reconfirm its autonomy and mandate as a People's Hospital. The people-oriented Cory administration must realize that the PGH is an immediate and direct interface between the caring concern of highest executive of the land and urgencies of life and death among the lowest of the low.

Our history as a nation, our consciousness as a people, our humanity as the children of God, are reflected in the dedication of its doctors, nurses and paramedics, and in the faces of those cured, comforted and cared for within its hallowed walls.

May it long endure, despite Ed Angara and his cohorts!

Part 23. Angara And Maceda Are Empire Builders

Radyo ng Bayan keeps blasting away at UP president Angara, "*Ibalik ang PGH sa mamamayan!* Give PGH back to the people!" supported by cause-oriented demonstrators. Practically 80% of the cabinet members were born in the PGH Ward 18; so was Cory and Ninoy. There is a groundswell of support for PGH against the unabashed empire building of Edong Angara.

We received a howl of protest from Sally Perez, our comrade in Cory's Crusade, cousin of Evelio Javier, secretary to U.P. president Edong Angara, "&%#'$!! Stop picking on my boss!" Edong is lucky to have such partisans who will defend him, right or wrong, without even knowing the issues involved. In the adversarial atmosphere of Philippine society, this is sad and dangerous.

We received a nice letter from Dr. Conrado "Clipper" Lorenzo, gently reminding us that the PGH hospital had formal links with the UP as early as 1914, was transferred from the Office of the President to the UP in 1947, and incorporated into the UP Health Science Center by Marcos in 1967.

Clipper and his loving wife also intimated that there are people who are just gunning for them -- two lady doctors, one of whom I never met, the other a cousin whom I do not see when I am in a state of health because she tends to browbeat me like Winnie Monsod does. No, no one put me up to this -- I   picked it up from some folders submitted to the cabinet.

No one quarrels with Clipper about the desirability of having PGH affiliated with UP Medicine. But up to 1983, PGH by the Administrative Code, always had the status of a separate bureau with its own separate budget, and operated primarily as a People's Hospital rather than a medical clinic for UP.

With his Executive Order No. 10 and 11, President Angara and the Board of Regents illegally arrogated unto themselves the power to denigrate the status of the PGH as a PEOPLE'S HOSPITAL, subordinate to its primary role as a teaching facility and a medical clinic for UP staff and employees;

and worse than that, the power to TRANSFER budgetary funds out of PGH for other purposes.

To have the People's Hospital PGH exist under the control and sufferance of the lawyers and politicians of the Board of Regents, that's really dung! "Power grabbing and Empire building" is the sickness that Angara is afflicted with, and not even a doctor like Clipper can cure him of it.

"Power grabbing and Empire building" is a contagious incurable disease that has contaminated every one in this government. Cabinet members fall over each other getting choice board seats in government and sequestered corporations.

Tourism Minister Tony Gonzales is also chairman of PAL; Dante Santos is PAL President and GSIS Chairman; Sonny Belmonte is GSIS Manager and President of Manila Hotel (and reportedly wants to replace Vic Sison as General Manager of Manila Hotel too, because Manila Hotel is a more comfortable place to work in than GSIS. Our Palace sources say the PAL/GSIS/MH is an empire exclusive to this Troika of emperors.

Jimmy Ongpin of course has the biggest empire, comprising the Monetary Board, PNB/DPB complex with tentacles to Filipino businessmen and American corporations. Winnie Monsod, according to sources, earns P35,000 a month in various capacities, and returns half the amount, but not the positions.

But the most active of all empire builders is Resources Minister Ernesto Maceda, but he is such a charming rogue, it is almost a pleasure watching him do his stuff.

Ernie started in the early days when he made a nuisance of himself sidling up to Cory every time a photographer aims his camera, driving Teddyboy Locsin bananas cutting the face of Ernie out of every picture for release to the press. To get rid of him, the boys made Cory sign the papers he brought with him, and the nation woke up one morning to find Ernie Maceda taking over most of the defunct Energy Ministry.

One day Malacañang called up PNB President "Ting" Jaime, saying there were papers for Cory's signature, appointing Ernie Maceda to the PNB Board. Ting Jaime almost choked on his Adam's apple, and managed to blurt out, "*Pare,* please change the letters PNB to DBP, and do not tell Jess Estanislao!"

DBP Chairman Jess Estanislao found himself one bright morning with Ernie Maceda in his Board. In panic, Jess and his boss Jimmy Ongpin went to Malacañang to protest; too late, Cory signed the papers. And while Jess and Jimmy were in Malacañang, Ernie Maceda got himself elected as Chairman of the Board of Associated Banking, an affiliate of DBP. What an operator!

Realizing that only God can pry Ernie loose from their territory, Jess Estanislao and Jimmy Ongpin are marshalling the resources of the Opus Dei and the Jesuit Mafia, to get Ernie transferred to PAL and Manila Hotel, dangling the prospects of first class travel and hotel facilities to Ernie Maceda. But the Troika of Tony/Dante/Sonny have sworn that bananas will grow in the North Pole before Maceda lands in the PAL board.

August 19, 1986

Part 24. Let's Export Our Soldiers

Let's face it. Our greatest problem is our military. We have too many of them -- 250,000 instead of the 50,000 we should have, as we did before Martial Law. These guys take up a third of our budget, and many of them have nothing better to do than to plot coups, rob banks, carnap our cars, shoot at each other, bully bar girls and customers, machine gun families wholesale, or hire themselves out as assassins.

To fire them outright is to invite civil war. To retrain them for other jobs is useless; there are no jobs to give. Their very existence is a constant temptation for any strong man to use them to gain or maintain power, as is the case in every banana republic from Indonesia and Thailand in Asia, to Chile and Argentina in Latin America, to Ethiopia and Uganda in Africa. We must get rid of them fast.

Why don't we just export our soldiers to the United States for use as a "volunteer army" for Reagan's military adventures in El Salvador, Nicaragua, and the Middle East? If the British have their Ghurkas, the French their Foreign Legion, the Russians their Cubans and Vietnamese, why can't the Americans have their little brown brothers as cannon fodder and surrogate army?

The Filipino soldier is the best in the world as long as he fights for good old Uncle Sam. He fought well during World War II when he sustained the greenhorn American troops through the ordeal of Bataan and Corregidor, then kept America's enemies at bay while all the rest of Asia took the opportunity to shake off their colonial masters. He did so in Korea and in Vietnam, fighting America's war to keep the world safe for democracy and multinational corporations.

Wouldn't we rather have Filipino soldiers fight Nicaraguans, Salvadoreans, Grenadans and Lebanese abroad, than have them commit mischief and mayhem on our own people? Wouldn't we rather have them fight for democracy abroad than sustain a dictatorship in their own country? Invite the "Movement for Philippine Statehood" to join them as well as Jimmy Ongpin, Christian Monsod and Blas Ople, and we hit two birds with one stone.

Ask Uncle Sam to pay us in dollars for our soldiers, at $1,000 per month per soldier for 200,000 soldiers, and we earn $2.4 billion a year, enough to cover our trade deficit as well as save budgetary expense and balance our budget. That's three birds with the same stone.

Come to think of it, why not export our Bangsa Moro Army to the Arabs for use in fighting the Israelis? The Arabs are such lousy soldiers, with 60 million population they could not beat Israel with only 6 million population. I am sure that the Moros who have never been conquered by the Spaniards, Americans or Christian Filipinos, can do better than the Arabs, and with petro dollars in their pockets, can beat the hell out of the Jews in Palestine. That's four birds with the same stone.

The biggest problem of US President Ronald Reagan is how to get the US Congress to authorize the sending of American troops to foreign lands to counter leftist revolts supported by the Soviet Union. The US Congress simply refuses to cooperate, afflicted as it is with the Vietnam syndrome, and has bound President Reagan to withdraw his troops within 60 days unless he is specifically authorized by Congress to keep them there.

That is the reason Reagan cannot mount a war against Nicaragua (3 million population, less than half of Metro Manila), and can do nothing better than to invade an itsy bitsy country like Grenada (88,000 population, less than Binondo). But suppose Reagan had at his disposal a volunteer army of Filipinos specifically charged by the Philippine government to keep the world safe for Americans?

There are many advantages in this arrangement for Mr. Reagan. First, he will have an army of Filipinos more loyal to America than Americans themselves. Second, he will have such an army, already combat trained, at less than one tenth of the cost of training and maintaining American soldiers. Third, he can go to war without risking precious American lives. Fourth, he will have an army much better than his own, which is full of sex-starved females, lesbians and homosexuals insisting on their constitutional right to serve alongside red-blooded American soldiers.

What a delicious idea! And one worth thinking about, considering that in this country many Filipinos are still afflicted with colonial double allegiance, an anomaly that must be resolved if we are to proceed with our nation building. How much more wonderful if it can be resolved while at the same time earning precious foreign exchange (THIRTEEN TIMES more than we earn from the bases), relieving our unemployment problem, giving reality to the aspirations of "American Statehood" supporters and other Americanophiles, purging our society of a potential threat to our democratic way of life, and getting rid of our military without getting shot.

August 25, 1986

Part 25. Filipino Soldiers Love America

One curious characteristic of Philippine soldiery is its special relations with the US Armed Forces. For a long time since its inception, it has been commanded by American officers. Led by Americans, Filipinos betrayed and captured General Emilio Aguinaldo and put an end to our Philippine Revolution. Then they "pacified" various *insurrectos*, *tulisanes*, *colorums*, and other rebels, including the intractable Muslims in Mindanao, all for the Old Glory.

During the World War II, while the Indonesians, Malays, Burmese, Vietnamese, and other Asians were letting their colonial masters fight their own battles while preparing for their own War of Independence, Filipino soldiers chose to cast their lot with the Americans. While green horn Americans were feasting on apples and ham in Corregidor, Filipinos were dying in Bataan.

Were the Filipinos really fighting for their country? How come most Filipino heroes of that war, as well as many veterans, chose to be American citizens rather than be citizens of a free republic? That what's-his-name who was the first Filipino to win a Congressional Medal of Honor became an American citizen, preferring to be a American gas station attendant than an honored Filipino soldier. So did the great Norman Reyes who broadcast the famous "Bataan has fallen!" So did our Filipino ace, Jesus Villamor, for whom our Villamor Air Base is named. So did architect Carlos Arguelles, accountant Washington Sycip; businessmen Andres Soriano, Sebastian Ugarte, Adolfo Roensch; soldier Napoleon Valeriano, engineer Luis "Tito" Luzurriaga. They all became American citizens.

For this act of Filipino loyalty to Mother America, Manila suffered the greatest destruction and devastation during World War II, comparable to that of Warsaw and Leningrad. We were after all American nationals fighting under American flag, not yet citizens of a free republic. Americans did not fight for us, dammit, we fought for them!

We were awarded by the United States "war damage" payments at less than five cents on the dollar, with a plaque on every rebuilt building reminding us of the "generosity of the American people". We were given war surplus equipment, worth less than one percent of its value new, but kept on the books at its original war-inflated value ($3 billion) by the Americans just to show the world the extent of our beggary. And our loyal soldiers who served under the US Army were paid in pesos, a fraction of what was paid in dollars to Polish, Chinese, Czechs and all other volunteers for the same US Army.

After Independence, the Philippine Army was equipped with outmoded US military equipment and about three days supply of ammunition for a full scale war, and practically run by American advisers in the JUSMAG (Joint U.S. Military Advisory Group). High Filipino officers were given privileges in the PX, officer's clubs, and Bingo games. Such Filipino officers cultivated an atrocious American accent, and strutted around as if they were part of the American Army of Occupation. It is demeaning for us Filipinos to see Filipino generals saluting and kowtowing to illiterate American mess sergeants.

Filipino soldiers were brainwashed to believe that their primary duty is not to the Philippine government or even to the Filipino people, but to the higher duty of hunting and killing Communists. "Communists" are defined as anyone who does not like Americans, do not agree with American policies, or resent the monopolies of American multinational corporations.

And under orders from Americans, the Philippine military went to war against the enemies of Americans among Filipinos. Philippine military intelligence compiled for the CIA, secret dossiers of Filipino Nationalists like Claro M. Recto, Leon Ma. Guerrero, Salvador Araneta and Renato Constantino (even Blas Ople, their supporter today), and sent many of them (like Amado Hernandez) to jail as subversives. Many Filipinos served as spies and hit-men for the American CIA.

Up to now, lack of loyalty to Mother America is still considered foul treason by Filipino military agents. Up to now, any attempt of Cory Aquino to reconcile with Communist rebels, asking them to abandon violence and peacefully compete with other ideologies in the market place of ideas, as they do in Europe, is looked upon by the military as just cause for a military coup d'etat.

What we are really leading up to is this. If we are to offer our surplus army to the United States for cash, for use in their military adventures in El Salvador, Nicaragua, Lebanon, even in Cambodia, or even New Zealand if it persists in opposing American nuclear warships in its area -- let us be sure that certain conditions are met.

We must insist that those who serve in such an Army, which should include "Statehood" proponents and green card holders, should in time, say ten years, be given the privilege of being inducted as American citizens.

Most important of all, we must insist that none of this volunteer army be stationed in the Philippines to defend American interests. We do not need a Second War of Liberation.

August 30, 1986

Part 26. Doroy Valenzona Writes Again!

Hey, I must be slipping. I wrote as Maurice Arcadia, and everyone assumes I wrote in the style of Maurice Arcache, the Arab Shriek who is a society columnist. Then I write twice as Teodoro Valenzona, and nobody even thinks I am writing in the style of Teodoro Valencia. I looked for an explanation; though many know Doroy as a Park attendant and controversial friend of you-know-who, few have the habit of reading his stuff in Daily Express.

Be informed, youngsters, that Doroy Valencia is a venerable institution in the world of Philippine Journalism. He was the most influential and the highest paid columnist, and probably still is, except for the Immensity that is Luis Beltran. So doff your hats, kids, whenever you see this smirk with the high-pitched voice that Willie Nepomoceno mimics so well. He is the greatest, he is part of our history.

Well Doroy Valenzona writes again.

Commenting on my survey of newspaper circulation, Baldomero Baltik of Manila Times commented on the impossibility of any newspaper having an odd number of pages, 15 or 19 or 39 as I cited, since every leaf has to printed on both sides. "Accuracy, Larry, accuracy!" he gently chided.

True, true, Baltik old boy (who is one of my favorite columnists), if you are talking of one issue. But if you describe a series of issues over a period of time (July 8 to 22), then you cite the AVERAGE number of pages (to calculate the circulation from the weight of the paper used).

If half the issues had 20 pages, and the other half had 18 pages, then the AVERAGE would be 19 pages, an odd number. Take it from a guy who is better in Mathematics than Bosworth, Bernie or Blas Ople. Logik, Baltik, Logik!!

The Cory government made an election promise of Privatization. She may be surprised to know that the whole banking system is practically nationalized.

Seventeen government Banks dominate the field: Philippine National Bank, Land Bank, Associated Bank (DBP), ComBank (GSIS), Pilipinas Bank (PNB), InterBank (NDC), Union Bank (SSS); Philippine Veterans Bank, Pacific Bank, Producers Bank, all under Central Bank receivership; the sequestered

CocoBank, Republic Planters Bank, Traders Royal Bank, PCIBank (with IBAA), Security Bank (sold), Allied Bank (?).

The only Filipino private banks left are thirteen: China Bank, Bank of the Philippine Islands (BPI), Solid Bank, Equitable Bank, Far East Bank, Metro Bank, Manila Bank, PBCom, PhilTrust, PhilBanking, Prudential Bank, Rizal Commercial RCBC), CityTrust.

Foreign Branch Banks are only four: CitiBank, Bank of America, Hong Kong Bank, Chartered Bank. There are over 20 Offshore Banking Units (OBUs), including First National Bank of Chicago.

There are 29 companies actively engaged in the assembly of semiconductors. Of these 17 are multinationals, among whom are the familiar Data General, Intel, Motorola, National Semiconductors, Philipps, Sprague, Telefunken, Zilog, Fairchild, Timex and Texas Instruments. All are operating, although many are thinking of moving out to Malaysia, where many firms are operating at 60%.

Twelve are local companies, six of which have already stopped operations, mostly because of labor problems: Filipinas Micro-Circuits, Integrated Circuits, Semiconductors Devices, Silicon Technology, Dynetics of Vicente Chuidian and Tony Garcia, and Stanford Microsystems of Cristino Concepcion.

Pricon Microelectronics has received a strike notice. And so has Dyna-Sem, run by the creditors of Dynetics, which took over the assets and labor force of Dynetics. The laborers are striking because they did not get their severance pay from Dynetics. What Dyna-Sem has to do with Dynatics is beyond me.

There are only four Filipino firms operating: Asionics, Complex Electronics, Labtech and Integrated Microelectronics IMI). Labtech of Julius Labrador just settled a disastrous month long strike, which made it fail to keep schedules for the first time in 9 years, forcing Sony almost to stop production. It is now operating at 140% of capacity to catch up on its commitments for the next two years. But with its labor costs and prices gone so sky high, there is great probability that Labtech will fail to get orders in the future. The IMI owned by Ayala and the Carloses of Resins, Inc. has not yet been unionized, and is operating at 60% of capacity.

ATTENTION Minister Bobbit Sanchez. Do something, strikes are fatal to these industries operating on tight schedules. The turn-around time (interval between receiving the materials and shipping the finished products) is only a week. Filipino companies get orders only when firms in the USA are operating at full capacity.   If they fail to deliver on time, they are out of business.

All these companies, including the multinationals, want is a guarantee that they meet schedules. They want Compulsory Arbitration to settle labor grievances without strikes. That is not too much to ask, is it, Bobbit?

September 3, 1986

Part 27. Betamax Raids Are Really Dung!

Betamax raids are really dung! So are raids on cassette stores and on stores for trade mark violations, designed to protect the interests of American companies at the expense of small Filipino businessmen and consumers.

Don't get me wrong. We must protect Filipino movie makers, Filipino song writers and singers, Filipino trademark owners -- these we should do with all our resources.

But why should we spend P9 million of our people's money to protect the interest of the 20th Century Fox and the Motion Picture Association of America (MPAA) against the interest of our own people: 3,000 registered video establishments employing 20,000 people, plus 50% more unregistered, and above all, the more than 1 million families who own a Betamax?

For that matter, why do we spend P million to protect the patents of American drug companies, so that they can sell us medicines at up to 20 times the price they charge in other countries? Why should we protect foreign interests at the expense of the health and well-being of its own citizens?

Why do we borrow dollars from abroad to print textbooks on which we pay royalties, limiting our access to knowledge and paying through the nose for the privilege? Why can we not be like Taiwan who refused to be a signatory to the Copyright Convention, so that her citizens can buy books at one tenth what it costs in the United States?

Universal Access to Knowledge is the principle that governs our way of life. This principle is reflected in Freedom of Speech and of the Press, Freedom of Assembly, Academic Freedom, Universal Suffrage, Universal Education, Wilson's Open Covenants Openly Arrived at.

Knowledge is public domain and the use of it is limited only in Patent and Copyright laws, for one good reason -- the State assumes the obligation to encourage the creativity and inventiveness of its citizens.

The Philippines has an obligation to reward the creativity of Filipino citizens. It has NO OBLIGATION to reward the creativity of American citizens.

If the Philippines is signatory to the Patent and Copyright Conventions, and protects the patents of Americans, it is only for ONE VALID REASON -- Reciprocity. We will protect American patents, if Americans will protect ours!

But suppose we do not have patents or copyrights for Americans protect, suppose 94% of all patents here belong to American companies, suppose there is no real reciprocity -- why the hell do we protect American patents and copyrights?!!!

Japan (the prewar Copycat), Italy (the postwar industrial pirate), and the Soviet Union did not join the Patent Convention till they were on the same technological level as the industrial countries; China, Cuba, and others refuse to join because they derive no reciprocal benefits; Taiwan is out of the Copyright Convention, and so were we until Marcos sold us out to the Americans; and more than 60 untries refused to grant product patents on drugs; Brazil and Soth Korea recognize no drug patents at all.

The greatest and most abusive cronies of Marcos are the Americans. There are at least 14 presidential decrees promulgated by Marcos to favor them, but Ongpin is there to see to it they all are in force. Pollution standards are relaxed to allow PMC, PRC and Colgate to pollute our environment with non-biodegradable detergents; Goodyear, Goodrich and Firestone are given monopoly of rubber tires without being forced to plant a single rubber tree; Kawasaki is invited here to inflict mercury poisoning on our people; retail trade is redefined to favor Americans; constitutional prohibitions are subverted to   allow Americans to own land and exploit natural resources, even to plant rice and corn; at one time family corporations paid more in income tax (45%) than foreign subsidiaries (35%).

The most recent imposition is the Marcos decree for the "Protection of Intellectual Property". According to this and other laws, if a Filipino song is broadcast before copyright is applied for, the Filipino song can no longer be copyrighted. On the other hand, the Superman logo may have been used here for 30 years without copyright, but still it is copyrightable upon the option of DC Comics, Inc., of America.

Another is Marcos PD 1987 creating the Videogram Regulatory Board, and taxing the video business to death -- a law even the United States does not have because it infringes on the First Amendment and is unenforceable. Walt Disney Inc. sued Sony seeking to stop the manufacture of video recorders, and lost. Scientific advances have made it impossible to prevent recordings of songs and movies off the air waves. And in the U.S., there are no damn raids on video rent companies.

What the Americans cannot do in their own country, they force us to do in the Philippines. A month ago, an American named Frank Knight, strutting like he owned the country, led lawyers of the Siguion Reyna Law Offices and government agents to raid the Video Sonix at Forbes, without even certificates of copyrights from the National Library, confiscated scores of tapes, video machines used for viewing and rewinders. Just like Storm Troopers.

President Cory should repeal PD 1987.
September 11, 1986

Part 28. Rise, Betamax Users And Sick People!

Betamax users and video rental outlets are victims of the PD 1987 and the Marcos decree on Intellectual Property, imposed upon President Marcos by the American Embassy and the American Chamber of Commerce.

In the United States itself there is no such law to regulate and tax the rental of videotapes. It is considered unconstitutional and unenforceable. But what Americans cannot do to their own people, they will do to Filipinos, because we are considered a stupid, colonial, self-sacrificial race.   Because we allow an imperial American like Frank Knight, companied by government agents, to strut around like a storm trooper, raiding Filipino businesses and confiscating videotapes, video players and even rewinders, for Christ's sake.

When Marcos became a signatory to the Geneva and Paris Convention on Copyrights and Patents, he gave American drug companies complete monopoly of our domestic market, not only against the authorized use of drug processes, but also against the sale of competitive drugs. We give the Americans completely monopoly even if they do not make a single aspirin in this   country.

Out of 16 drug manufacturers, 13 are multinationals with 57% of the market; and out of the 12 major drug importers, 10 are multinationals with 60% of the market. The U.P. Law Center studies show how American drug companies abuse the Filipino people: Ampicillin sells 4.10 times higher here than in Malaysia; Tetracyline, 7.24 times; Chloramphenicol, 3.84 times; Erythromycin, 5.44 times. Librium sells here 8.67 times more than in Great Britain, and Valium an incredible 14.29 times.

If there is any serious sickness in the family, Filipinos are driven to bankruptcy buying American drugs, while characters like Lewis Burridge of Sterling Drugs receive more than P2,000,000 a month in salary, allowances, bonuses and perquisites, a lot more than he earned when he worked Stateside and lived in a one room cold water flat in the seamy seedy side of New York.

Rise, Betamax users and sick people of the Philippines, you have nothing to lose but your colonial mentality. You will gain self-respect, a sense of self-worth, and the scorn of those who make their living, like barnacles and leeches, serving the interest of their colonial masters.

First, organize yourselves. Join up with NEPA and the cause-oriented groups. Marshall your people's power to exert pressure on the government.

Second, go to the Constitutional Commission. Insist that one provision be inserted in the new constitution: THE PHILIPPINES SHALL BE A SIGNATORY TO THE PATENT OR COPYRIGHT CONVENTIONS ONLY UNDER CONDITIONS OF FULL RECIPROCITY OF BENEFITS.

Go to ConCommissioners Christian Monsod, Bernardo Villegas, Jose Bengson Jr., and Ricardo Romulo, the "patriotic" Four Horsemen of the Apocalypse. See how patriotic they really are. You will probably get a lecture about sanctity of private Intellectual Property recognized by most countries except the devil communists. Also a lecture on the dangers of courting American displeasure and vengeance.

Do not let them disappoint you. The Four Horsemen are there to protect American interests, not yours. Remind these little brown brothers that Private Property is not Sacrosanct; that Private Property is considered Public Stewardship of a precious resource, held in trust for public benefit; that Private Property is morally justified only if it serves Public Interest. Remind them that "Knowledge is public domain", that the great works of Shakespeare, of Leonardo da Vinci, of Sir Isaac Newton, of Aristotle are not the property of any individual or any nation, but of all mankind; that Frank Knight does not represent mankind, but the greedy pushy characters of Wall Street whose interest conflict with ours.

Go to ConCommissioners Jose Suarez, Willie Villacorta, Minda Luz Quesada, Julie Amargo, Rene Sarmiento, Ponciano Bennagen, Jimmy Tadeo, and the wonderful Lino Brocka if he ever comes back. They will listen to you, because they are nationalists, they love their country more than they love America. And they love you more than they like Frank Knight.

Don't bother to see Blas Ople.

Third, send a delegation to Joker Arroyo, Executive Secretary of President Cory, with a petition for the repeal of the Marcos PD 1985, specially the onerous provisions that tax the video businesses 30% of gross. Come to terms with Filipino movie makers, Filipino singers and song writers, to police the industry and pay them royalties for their intellectual property; and let the Bureau of Commerce in the Ministry of Trade take care of "unfair trade practices".

Above all support Filipinos against greedy arrogant foreigners. We must stick together or hang separately.

September 16, 1986

Part 29. Teddyman, Chicken Shit And Shakespeare

I know it is irritating, but our program "ConCom and You" has been pre-empted to make way for something important, and has been moved from Sunday to Monday, tonight at 10:00 PM,

Channel 4 as usual, this time on the subject of Human Rights... Education, Science, Culture, Technology and Sports.

We are broadcasting it live, and our guests are the eloquent Minda Luz (her parents forgot the Visayas) Quesada; Florenz Regalado; Wilfredo Villacorta; and my favorite Jesuit Father Joaquin Bernas -- all Commissioners, and NSTA Director General Antonio Arizabal.

For eight bucks you can buy the latest issue of Philippines Free Press where Alejandro Roces was criticized and ably defended for his lapses in English in the wordings he composed for the Ninoy Marker on the tarmac; and myself for the two articles I wrote on Christine and the Cockpit, which Teddyman Locsin Sr. intimated is full of chicken excrement:

"The cockfight is one of the lowest forms of human activity. It's not only bloodthirsty, it is cowardly. If you want to see blood shed, why not shed your own or your opponent's in combat? Why let the chickens do the job for you? That's being chicken. The most publicized raiser of fighting cocks in this country whom we knew was a certified coward.

"In the United States and other civilized countries, cockfighting is banned. A crime. Cruelty to animals, you know. Animals hurt. They're animals, not plants. Aficionados in such states as Texas indulge their lust for chicken blood in secret, always in danger of raid by law-enforcement agents.

"Ah, but what about Washington, Lincoln and others of some fame who had fighting cocks and enjoyed the game? Well, Washington was the Father of his country all right, and no coward, but he wore some crude contrivance to replace his lost natural chewing apparatus, and he must have wanted to make somebody else share his pain, even if it is only a cock. As for Lincoln, the noblest American of all, his wife went nuts and perhaps he saw in the cockfight a replica, bloody but purging, of the contest between sanity and his wife's state. This is a lowdown analysis of their addiction to the cockfight, but the dead, especially the noble ones, will understand and forgive the living. To know all, and if the dead don't know, who does? -- is to forgive all. So okay, Wash and Abe?"

Teddyman rants on about His Immensity Luis Beltran, Minister Ramon Mitra, and myself for being aficionados of cockfighting, but, friends, if you want to have a laugh at our expense, you should spend your own 8 bucks. And I have news for Teddyman, I have been to a cockpit only once in my life.

Anding Roces is offended. After all, Teddyman has questioned his area of expertise, the English Language -- which parenthetically speaking, is not mine. I am an engineer and my first love is not English, but Mathematics.

Teddyman questions Anding's English in the passage: "The sun can bleach, the wind cannot blow, the rain cannot wash that sanctity away. From ground like this springs that which forever makes the Filipino great."

Teddyman carps: "As for the sun's inability to 'bleach', what do we have here –- laundry? To bleach is to whiten or make colorless, and the tarmac is surely white or colorless enough. An unnecessary effort on the part of the sun.

"... 'the wind cannot blow' -- but the wind is usually blowing at the airport. Ah but there is an 'away' six words further down the line. So, okay, 'blow... away' it is. But have you ever seen a slab of concrete being blown away, flying -- like the daring young man on the flying trapeze?...

"As for that part about not 'washing that sanctity away' –- what's it, a stain? There's that laundry business again!

"The whole thing is like something out of a high school oratorical contest which is characterized as high flown language – 'full of sound and fury,' to quote the Bard, 'signifying nothing,' or something trite, which is forgivable   in the very young but not to the grown-up. 'A tale told by an idiot.'"

A Professor of Harvard, David Brown, Ph.D. English, wrote in to twit Teddyman: "Your reading of 'bleach' shows that you have no sensitivity to metaphorical uses of language. The three parallel and climatic clauses in the third sentence of the marker use 'sanctity' as a tangible symbol.

"The next time you try literary analysis, I suggest you consult a professional. Or at least consult a native speaker of English. By the way, I am a Shakespearian Scholar, and I am offended by your misquoting of Shakespeare. The lines you referred to about sound and fury are meant to be read as poetry, not literally... You will discover that the 'idiot' referred to there is far from being an idiot. If there were any idiotic words on (that) page, they were yours."

September 29, 1986

Part 30. The Storm Troopers Of Rico Domingo

Dear Cory, remember the news blackout in the period between the assassination of Ninoy and his burial 11 days later? remember how during the political campaign the Marcos administration effectively blacked us out of the television stations and the movie houses? remember how the whole world through foreign cameramen, knew more what was happening in the Philippines than we ourselves?

It was the Betamax that proved to be our medium of mass communication. I remember when the MABINI lawyers -- Joker Arroyo, Rene Saguisag, Bobbit Sanchez, and others -- sneaked into my house in the dead of night with a U-Matic Tape of a Ninoy speech for re-recording to Betamax. Foreign news about our street demonstrations, the Ninoy assassination, hidden wealth, and Cory campaign materials were duplicated, triplicated a thousand times throughout the whole country till almost everyone was familiar with our call for freedom. Betamax helped bring about the February revolution, Cory.

In the heat of the campaign, on October 5, 1985, President Marcos issued P.D. 1987 to control and kill the video industry, by imposing an excessively heavy tax of 30% of gross receipts, and creating a Videogram Regulatory Board with police powers to conduct raids and confiscate equipment. Marcos did this for many reasons: (1) to prevent and to punish the Betamax industry from/for propagating Cory Campaign materials; (2) to prepare the way for son-in-law Greggy Araneta to monopolize the Video Industry; (3) to give the Americans non-reciprocal advantages at the expense of his own people.

In July, only a few months before the decree was signed, Greedy Araneta Marcos bought out 50% of the TECHNICA VIDEO INC., one of the largest duplicators in the business, with the other 50% owned by Nanding Yotoko, Manny Mendoza, etc. The idea of Greedy was to utilize the Videogram Regulatory Board (VRB)to kill all the competition, so that he can have a Monopoly.

The funny thing is that TECHNICA VIDEO has not given up the idea of a monopoly. With the VRB reducing the authorized reproducers from 5,000 to only 13, the three biggest ones -- FOX VIDEO (Fred Ongyangco), GALACTIC VIDEO (Eric Apolonio), and TECHNICA VIDEO (Greedy Araneta) are merging into one huge monopolistic corporation, the FGT VIDEO INC.

The first chairman of the VRB was Justice Juan Sison, at the same time chairman of the board of Censors. After the Revolution, Cirio Santiago the Movie Czar appointed a Rico Domingo to head the VRB.

Who is Rico Domingo? He is a lawyer in the Siguion Reyna Law Offices, who is the legal counsel for the 20th Century Fox, and the Motion Picture Association of America. Rico Domingo was the one who, without a fair public hearing, railroaded the Marcos P.D. 1987 into effect, assessed the video operators illegally, and harassed them with raids.

This Rico Domingo has given way to OIC Eduardo Sazon, formerly of Solar Film Distributors, with VRB board composed of film people -- Espiritu Laxa of Tagalog Ilang Ilang, Bobby Yang of Odeon Theater, Alex Tiu and William Ching of IMPIDAP, Ramon Revilla, actor and producer.

This Rico Domingo, no longer with VRB, with his bodyguard Mike leads the raids into the video establishments. According to reports, he led a contingent of 15 men armed with armalites, with several bodyguards and civilian "volunteers" to the house of George Rodriguez, owner of Group A Video.

Raiding the place after office hours at 5 PM so that one cannot call a judge or lawyer, this Rico Domingo terrorized the wife Fe who was alone, shouting, "You have 3 minutes to open up, or we will break your door down!" and shouting "*Magnanakaw!*". Mike pointed a gun at a maid, and said to Joey Chan, who came over to help: "*Bilang nang araw ninyo!*" Then Rico Domingo the Storm Trooper pushed Joey to provoke a fight. He would contemptuously point a finger to Steve Salonga who also came around to help: "*Saan ka ba nag graduate?*"

And later, realizing the scandal he was causing, he got out of the house and hid inside a Metrocom car.

Among the things the storm troopers of Rico Domingo confiscated in the house of George Rodriguez were 47 video machines, 6 video amps, 3 video switches, more than 1,000 tapes, 5 rewinders, 5 head cleaners, a Sony computer, an Olympus typewriter, and a Signature watch missing from a drawer.

When a Filipino becomes a lackey of the Americans, he acquires the attitude and manners of a California fruit picker. He is afflicted by the KAKA (Kiss Ass, Kick Ass) syndrome, i.e., he kisses the ass of every American within reach, and kicks the ass of every Filipino he meets.

Tomorrow October 2, the 21st anniversary of the death of Claro M. Recto, there will be an 8 AM Mass at the Lady Of Sorrows Church (where Ninoy and Cory Aquino got married; also my wife Cecilia and myself), F.B. Harrison, Pasay, followed by the Unveiling and Blessing of a Historical Marker in the old Recto residence in 1750 Leveriza, Pasay.

October 1, 1986

Part 31. The Movie Boys Fight Back

The following letter was signed by Manuel M. Nuqui, President of the Philippine Motion Picture Producers Association (PMPPA); Sixto A. Dy, president of the Integrated Movie Producers Importers Distributors Association of the Philippines (IMPIDAP); my friend, Marcos B. Roces, president of Greater Manila Theaters Association (GMTA); Ng Meng Tam, vice president of Metro Manila Theaters Association (MMTA; my old schoolmate, Lamberto V. Avellana, Deputy Director General of the Film Academy of the Philippines (FAP); and a son of a classmate, Primitivo Garcia III, president of Kapisanan ng maga Sinehan ng Pilipinas (KSP):

Dear Mr. Henares, at the outset, we cannot resist expressing our admiration for your keen spirit of nationalism for which many of our countrymen regard you with respect and high esteem. It is for this reason that we note with a tinge of sadness and a sense of loss that such revered spirit of nationalism is being demonstrated in defense of the video or Betamax tape industry without your knowing it, we are sure, that the industry you are defending and promoting is, with the exception of a handful and some members of the Philippine Video Association and Philippine Association of Video Reproducers, composed of countless unscrupulous businessmen who reproduce, sell, rent, and exhibit our films in video cassettes without a single centavo, thereby enriching themselves at our expense. This is plain and simple robbery which must be condemned instead of supporting and abetting it. Giving such lewdness a haven in a civilized and law-abiding society like ours is, to put it mildly, not in keeping with your brand of nationalism.

Making matters worse, the videotapes pirates, aided by their well-funded nationwide distribution network that operates with fantastic speed and clock-work precision, flood the market from Aparri to Jolo with Beta tapes illegally reproduced from our films even before such films are shown in the movie houses, thus reducing our income potentials by fifty percent and correspondingly decreasing amusement taxes to the prejudice of the government.

Indeed, the horrendous callousness with which the video pirates steal our film rights -- dwarfing all forms of theft known to Filipinos due to its national scope and syndicated viciousness -- cuts deep into our financial resources to the point of near exhaustion. To the consternation of the local film owners, the entire motion picture industry looked virtually helpless and hopeless several years ago. And then by some happy twist of fate, the government has seen it fit and necessary to issue P.D. 1987 creating the Videogram Regulatory Board which offers a flicker of hope to the beleaguered film industry amidst the pall of darkness cast upon it by the video bootleggers. But this one remaining flicker of hope for the survival of the film industry might be blown out by the repeal of P.D. 1987 which you so fiercely advocate.

Killing the video industry as unjustifiably feared by some quarters is farthest from our minds. All we want is to see it legitimized by the Videogram Regulatory Board by requiring it to pay just royalties to the film owners, pay taxes to the government, and submit video tapes for proper classification according to audience suitability in order to safeguard the moral values of our people, especially the youth. Is this asking too much from the video industry which after all lives on our film industry?

In the interests of fair play, we hope you will devote some space in your column to ventilate our side of the issue as expressed above so that your readers will be properly enlightened regarding our espousal of P.D. 1987 and our position against the illicit video industry.

After putting things mentioned above in their right perspective, it is hoped that you will find the film industry, a seven-decades old institution, which employs thousands of Filipinos and pays about P450 million taxes annually to the government, more deserving of your support than the video industry which takes the road paved with non-adherence to the rule of law, dishonesty of purpose, and unwillingness to pay royalties for film rights.

October 2, 1986

Part 32. The CIA In Namfrel Again?

A news dispatch datelined Washington September 20 featured a joint announcement by Allen Weinstein, president of Center for Democracy, and Edgardo Angara, vice chairman of the Namfrel, to the effect that a group of American companies have accepted an invitation from Comelec chairman Ramon Felipe and the Namfrel chairman Christian Monsod to provide technical advice and support in the revamping of the electoral process. Augusto C. Lagman, Namfrel's chief technical adviser, briefed a group of four companies involved in this mission: Lotus Development Corporation (computer software); Digital Equipment Corporation (computer mainframes); the Polaroid Corporation (instant photos); and Coopers & Lybrand. And Senator John F. Kerry was on hand to assure President Aquino of his support of US funding of Philippine electoral reform.

Well and good, except that Chairman Ramon Felipe of the Comelec, categorically DENIED at the Philippine Columbian Club, that he ever issued an invitation to any U.S. group.

Well and good, except for two characters involved: Christian Monsod, one of the Four Horsemen of the Apocalypse in the ConCom, who rammed through provisions favoring his Mother America and is interested to make sure these provisions are approved by plebiscite; and Augusto C. Lagman who is in the computer business, and in a situation where he may be accused of making business connections for personal gain.

This Lagman was twice shown a device invented by a Filipino, Miguel L. Lorza Jr., called "Operation Abacus" and never called it to the attention of the Comelec or the Namfrel. Instead he flew off to the United States to gain an audience with American companies. This "Operation Abacus" was shown to the Comelec en banc who opined that at least it deserved to be tested on a pilot basis.

I have seen the device and it really works. Me, I am not particularly enthusiastic about electronic devices, because its workings are not readily understood and is prone to accusations of being rigged. But certainly if Namfrel intends to ram an electronic system down our throats, they better give more than due consideration to one invented by a Filipino.

Considering that (1) Namfrel Chairman Christian Monsod is an indefatigable champion of the American cause, (2) Namfrel has a previous history of CIA involvement in the 1950s, (3) electronic electoral equipment may be supplied as "American Aid", (4) the question of the US bases, the nuclear-free zone and foreign investment may be submitted separately to the electorate -- it may not amiss to suspect that a CIA operation is afoot to subvert the people's will.

How easy it would be to make a few changes in the computer program to give undue advantage to the Americans. I am not being funny. The CIA has done worse -- promoting civil war, assassinating leaders, even subverting religions -- for much less than they expect to get in the Philippines.

First, it's important that Christian Monsod be made to resign from the Namfrel. He is not non-partisan; he is a passionate partisan of surrendering the bases and the Philippine economy to the Americans.

Second, we should not accept American aid and advice on our electoral process. To do so is to give the CIA a chance to subvert the people's will.

Third, we should consider seriously the "Operation Abacus" of Mike Lorza, which cranks in nicely into the PC micro computers already bought by the Commelec. He offers 90,000 "ballot tabulators" at $55 each or a total of $5 million, a fraction of what it would cost to set up an American system.

Who is Mike Lorza? He is a 32 year old Assistant Vice President of Ayala Corporation, the youngest ever. In Kuang Chi (Xavier School), he garnered medals and honors in Mathematics, History, Languages, Literature and Composition; and won gold and silver medals in all elocution contests in English, Pilipino and Mandarin. He participated in an interscholastic elocution contest in Mandarin together with 33 Chinese orators, and won 2nd Prize!

As a student in Milwaukee School of Engineering, he headed a team that won an interscholastic competition among 18 universities, in the design, assembly and performance of an all terrain buggy, which won again for 2 consecutive years. Mike worked with General Motors and Wormald International of Australia, managing projects all over the world.

Mike is a natural born Filipino genius, with an IQ much higher than those whose only purpose in life is to serve Americans. It's a same to waste his talents.

October 4, 1986

Part 33. Balance, And The Business Cycle

Every one of us dreams about being the richest person on earth, with a fleet of Rolls Royce and Lear Jets at our command, with a beautiful mansion in every important city in the world, with a mountain of gold to rival Fort Knox.

There is NO LIMIT to what we want to have, but there IS A LIMIT to what is available, a limit to the resources of this earth. There are not enough Rolls Royce, Lear Jets, mansions or gold for everybody. And this is what Economics is all about.

Economics is the science and art of allocating SCARCE resources for UNLIMITED needs and wants. It is a science because in many ways the economic factors are often predictable and measurable. It is an art too because it involves people, and what people think and do are too often unpredictable.

Allocating scarce resources for unlimited needs and wants, involves BALANCE above all, balance between supply and demand, balance between too much money and too little, balance between too high and too low prices, balance, balance, balance. There are fancier words for it: EQUILIBRIUM, STABILITY.

To achieve GROWTH, we may unbalance the factors a little, by creating new demands or finding new sources of supply, but in the end, we must restore BALANCE. Restoring this balance is the hardest task of all. Like the pendulum of the Grandfather Clock; once it starts swinging, it takes time to get it to rest in an equilibrium position.

In the United States many years back, there was a great demand for food and other farm products, which people bought at very high prices. More and more farmers planted more and more crops to take advantage of the high prices. Just before harvest, it became obvious that there were more wheat and corn than what people are willing to buy. And the prices suddenly plummeted way below the cost of harvesting the crops.

There followed one of the most bizarre economic situations ever. Because the low prices could not cover the cost of harvesting, the farmers decided not to harvest, and left the crops unattended in the fields. Suddenly there were no wheat and corn in the market, prices went up skyrocketing, but there was nothing to buy. People were starving in the cities while the wheat was rotting in the fields.

The farmers were bankrupt, the banks took over the farms but could not generate enough cash to prevent bank runs. A series of bank failures, a shortage of money, a drop in demand, closing of factories and mass unemployment followed. Thus the Great Depression came upon the United States, and eventually the rest of the world. This was from 1929 to the 1930s. The above may be Simplification, but is essentially what happens when there are violent swings between oversupply and over-demand. The economic machinery simply breaks down.

Chronic imbalance resulting in a succession of "business cycles" is a characteristic typical of the CAPITALIST SYSTEM, or what the Americans fondly refer to as "Free Enterprise". Too many people are making separate decisions at the same time that supply and demand cannot quite remain in balance.

Start with high prices and a good market for textiles. And sooner or later competition starts to grow as new textile mills are set up and old ones start expanding their facilities. The result is overproduction and a dip in prices. A few textile mills will close, and the workers are laid off. And later the supply of textiles will diminish, and prices will be high again. The cycle has come to a full circle.

The swing of the pendulum between oversupply and over-demand, recession and prosperity, deflation and inflation, high prices and low prices, exact their toll in waste of resources. Factories close, companies face bankruptcy, workers are laid off. Fortunes are lost, and assets are idled.

The Capitalism as envisioned by Adam Smith in his book "The Wealth of Nations" presupposes that every man pursuing his own self-interest, will ultimately contribute to the interest of all. The Whip of Necessity, the Hidden Hand of market forces, Free Competition, are the standard jargon of such Smithsonian economists as Bernardo Villegas and the CRC.

Fortunately, there came a mathematician named Lord Maynard Keynes, who proposed a way to moderate the effects of the Business Cycle and promote desirable Growth, by manipulating Government policies. If there is oversupply and the prices drop, one may increase demand by putting more money in circulation. If there is an undersupply and the prices skyrocket, one may decrease demand by reducing the amount of money in circulation. And such can be achieved by increasing or decreasing taxes, reserve requirements, rediscounting rates, government spending, tariff duties -- what the Keynesian economist Alejandro Lichauco is talking about.

October 9, 1986

Part 34. Making Hicks Happy On Sexy Sunday

Architect J. Antonio "Toti" Mendoza called to ask what is on the agenda and I said I am writing on Ed Sazon, Alita Akester, on Cory, Enrile and the ConCom.

And Toti said Whoa, why not write something to ease the strain on the brain, like a few rewrites of the classic vintage Henares articles of the past years, something to make Sunday pleasant for Douglas Hicks? Good idea, we'll do a piece every Sunday.

Well, if Hicks really wants to see sexual depravity, he should buy *sampaguitas* or roses for his beloved. For according to biologist Mary Batten, plants are avid practitioners of *Menage a Trois* or three way sex, and shameless sex exhibitionists.

Flowers are really the sex organs of a plant, enlarged, colored and perfumed in order to attract. The roses you send to the beloved reek of sex in the most blatant way. A flowering plant is a creature in heat, and it bares its sex organs as brazenly as Marilyn Chambers. To cut flowers is to castrate.

For most organisms, it takes only two, male and female, in order to mate. But for plants, three is a necessity. Imagine trying to have sex without being able to move around. Imagine if the object of your affections is rooted one kilometer away, and she cannot move either. This is quite a problem, but one way plants

solve this dilemma is to enlist the services of a third creature --
bees, butterflies, wasps, monkeys, even rats -- in a kind of three-
way sex, or *menage a trois*. The idea is to get this third creature
to bring the plant's sperms (pollen) to the female part of the
blossoms.

How do plants do this? Plants are the greatest
manipulators of behavior. Most of them offer food for sex, just
like the executive who invites his officemate to an intimate
dinner. Plants offer nectar, a high carbohydrate food convertible
to honey, to bees and birds if they would participate in the mating
game.

Other plants arouse the sexual appetite. Certain orchids,
such as the Ophrys and the Cryptostylus arouse ale bees and
wasps by mimicking not only the feel and appearance of females
but also their sexual odor. Attracted by what he thinks is a
turned-on female, a male finds himself in the ridiculous position
of trying to mate with a flower.

I remember how shocked the world was when a man from
Denmark named Christian Jorgenson announced that he went
through a sex change operation to become a female Christine
Jorgenson. But sex change may be found among plants.
Avocados for instance are not as innocent as they seem. Every
24 hours they change sex openly, but no one except the
avocado knows the difference. Avocados are of two types. The
first type's flowers open as female in the morning, close in the
afternoon, then open as male in the next afternoon. The second
type does exactly the opposite. And the purpose is to prevent
incest and insure diversity by guaranteeing that a tree will be
fertilized by pollen from another tree rather than from its own
blossoms.

Talk about sex maniacs. The male lion was observed to
have mated 157 times in fifty-five hours, an average of once
every twenty-one minutes; female lions need repeated
copulation to stimulate the release of eggs in the ovary. Wolves
do it like dogs do, but during the entire half-hour the male and
female are locked together, the male ejaculates approximately
once every minute. Now you know why a tireless lover is called a
Lion, and a persistent Romeo is called a Wolf.

Sex for human beings is easy and not dangerous unless
you are caught messing around with somebody's wife, but sex is

no picnic for some creatures. The ordinary pussy cat female lets out a bloodcurling yowl when the male withdraws, and no wonder, since the male's penis is covered with hard barbs, directed backward like fish hooks.

Great loves are born to die, as evidenced by the tragic romances of Romeo and Juliet, Tristan and Isolde, Antony and Cleopatra, and the angler fish. The male angler fish, at an early age loses his teeth; so he attaches himself like a parasite to a female twenty times his size. There he feeds on the female until his mission is carried out. When the female's eggs are released, the male's sperm is synchronized to follow. Then his body degenerates till all that remains is a wart on the female's body. A heroic death for love.

And the praying mantis. If the male fails to jump on the female in just the right way, she bites off his head and eats it -- giving him a headache from which he never recovers. But his neuro-anatomy is such that losing his head only triggers a nervous reflex that has him going through a post-mortem sexual intercourse. He passes on his genes while he passes on. What a way to go! Decapitation as a cure for impotence!

Happy now, Hicks?
October 12, 1986

Part 35.   The Greatness Of Cory: Doing The Unexpected

I have a sneaky feeling Cory Aquino will turn out to be the best president we ever had. Women leaders have always the best. Elizabeth I, Queen Victoria, Margaret Thatcher; Siri Bandaranaike, Indira Gandhi, Golde Meir -- each brought a golden age to their countries in war and peace. Cory will do no less.

Cory Aquino came out of nowhere like Joan of Arc and delivered this nation of ours from 14 years of cruel bondage, without shedding a single drop of blood -- a feat that still astounds the world.

Cory Aquino is the most astute politician we ever had, holding together the most disparate and rambunctious coalition of malaperts every assembled in a cabinet -- not by the exercise of naked power, but by friendly persuasion. This outstanding quality is rooted in her being a woman. All her life a woman has to persuade a husband to curb his polygamous instincts; recalcitrant children from going out of control; greedy vendors from charging too much. And making peace with a mother-in-law requires more tact and persuasiveness that it needs to pursue peace with the communists.

Cory, like any woman, is a generalist, not a specialist. She does not, like Enrile, act within the narrow confines of being a lawyer and soldier; nor like Bert Romulo the accountant; nor like Alran Bengson the medical doctor; nor like Mitra the agriculturist; nor like Mita Pardo de Tavera the social worker; nor like Jimmy Ongpin the financier, nor like Winnie Monsod the economist. Cory's mind encompasses all these areas of specialization with an appreciation of what each contributes to the over-all objectives of her administration. Thus she marshals the efforts of all toward a common goal.

As a generalist, Cory is proving to be a good president; and infusing into all these mundane endeavors, a keen sense of humanity that can only come from a mother and a widow, she is well becoming a really great president.

Like the lioness caring for her cubs, Cory Aquino is ever conscious of being the mother of the nation and president of all the people, including the subversives. And this is what makes her unique among all our presidents. The usual scenario is for Filipino presidents is to go into an all-out war against fellow Filipinos whom Americans do not like. But Cory continues to confound Americans by resisting all pressures for a bloodbath, refusing to make war on her own people.

Troublesome cabinet officials from Bobbit Sanchez to Johnny Ponce Enrile think they are rocking the boat -- ha ha ha -- when they get to within ten feet of Cory, they are putty, they start eating out of her hand! Perhaps a few months from now, she may even have Marcos beating a path to her door.

You think she is weak? Listen, a man can only work 8 hours a day, 9AM to 5PM, and he comes home all pooped out. But the woman of the house has to face family crises, 24 hours a day, day in day out including Sundays -- which is what a president has to do when he takes the helm of the nation. A woman can stand the pain of childbirth, the hazards of the home without a nervous breakdown, and still manages to outlive her husband. Who is better equipped to lead the nation?

Great presidents become great by doing the Unexpected. There is something about the summit of power that frees a leader from the constraints and habits of a lifetime, and makes him do the opposite of what he is expected to do. By doing so, he embraces his enemies without losing his friends, and achieves National Unity, an imperative during times of crisis.

It took an aristocratic capitalist Franklin D. Roosevelt to turn the United States into a welfare state with the New Deal program. If Henry Wallace, his Socialist vice president, did it, he would have been shot as a communist.

It took a peacenik Jack Kennedy to stand up to Khrushchev in Cuba and Berlin; and another peacenik Lyndon Johnson to escalate the war in Vietnam. If Nixon did it, he would have been shot as a war-monger.

It took a war-hawk Richard Nixon, the professional anti-Communist, to achieve detente with the Soviet Union and Mainland China. Nobody else could have done it without polarizing the nation

If President Cory Aquino ever becomes our greatest president, it will because she will be the first to do the Unexpected. An aristocrat, a devout Catholic, and educated by Americans, she will bring about the national reconciliation andpeace that has so far eluded this nation. She may repudiate the bases agreement, pursue a real industrialization program, and usher in a real sense of nationalism, that may stand up to all the world and say "I am a Filipino!" never more in shame.

October 13, 1986

Part 36.   Teddyman And Brown; Akester And The Coast Guard

Teddyman Locsin wrote to complain that in our column entitled, "Teddyman, Chicken Shit and Shakespeare", his reply to Professor David Brown was maliciously omitted. Not true, Teddyman, our piece was a bit too long, and was cut by the paste-up man. Our apologies to a writer we hero-worshipped since 19-forgotten. He said with understandable pride that his son Teddyboy can write better with his ass that we could with our pointed head. He can insult us anytime, it is an honor to be insulted in good grammar and impeccable style. The last part including the omitted portion is printed below.

A Professor of Harvard, David Brown, Ph.D. English, wrote in to twit Teddyman: ".... The next time you try literary analysis, I suggest you consult a professional. Or at least consult a native speaker of English. By the way, I am a Shakespearian Scholar, and I am offended by your misquoting of Shakespeare. The lines you referred to about sound and fury are meant to be read as poetry, not literally... You will discover that the 'idiot' referred to there is far from being an idiot. If there were any idiotic words on (that) page, they were yours."

The answer of Teddyman to this arrogant asshole is a classic in put-downs -- Shakespearean scholars being a dime a dozen, adding tirelessly to the store of useless knowledge -- who write English like badly translated German, turgid, flat, stale and unprofitable -- who not being able to write well, must therefore teach -- who like many native Americans, probably cannot read or write correctly in English anyway. Come on, you guys, buy your own Free Press and read it as written by a master. It is worth 8 pesos.

While I am handing out apologies, might as well extend one to Mrs. Julia G. Ugarte who writes to say that contrary to what I wrote, her husband Sebastian Ugarte, for whom the Makati park was named, was never an American citizen, was a Filipino till the day he died in a plane crash on the way to East Borneo. Pete Picornell, a close associate of Sebastian, said as much, adding our common friend Tito Luzarriaga's Christian name is Eusebio, not Luis.

I apologize for the mistake. But I would like to explain that in an argument with Sebastian in which I was fulminating against Americans, he silenced me by saying he was an American citizen, and if I continued, I may get a football kick in my donkey. He was obviously pulling my leg, a typical La Sallite trick at the expense of an Atenean.

Agnes Enriquez, the data on Russia and Romania, has been ready; leave phone number at the Inquirer; you too, Joey Dino of PWU. Bernie Noriega,I am flattered being called a genius, the only brain food I partake of are books, books, books. To those who like and/or comment on my articles, including Sharon Adams, A.F. Vermeulen, Allan Batuhan, Jose Abello, Fructuoso Capco, Augusto Garcia, Benjie Antonio, and Ernesto Tobas, I can't answer, but please continue to write.

Maria Alita C. Akester, who operates a tourist ferry boat between Batangas pier and Puerto Galera, is being harassed by a Lt. Ancheta of the Sta. Clara Coast Guard, who held her boat full of tourists two days (August 18-19) in a row for two hours, then held it indefinitely with its load of tourists on   the third day (Aug. 20) while the district commander of the 5th Coast Guard District, a Captain Mariano, blissfully had his siesta undisturbed. On the fourth day and fifth day (Aug. 21-22), the Coast Guard refused clearance to the Akester ferry and transferred the tourists to a banca, a banca for Christ's sake!

These two abusive officers, Lt. Ancheta and Capt. Mariano claim that the Akester boat's "provisional license has expired," while refusing to explain why they give clearance to the unlicensed banca M/Y Galera Express owned by one Silverio Atienza, or Princesa AC VI owned by a shipping line whose license expired three months earlier.

The fact is that these two abusive officers received a radio dispatch from the Manila Coast Guard that "Violation of Marina rules and regulations cannot be a basis for holding the departure of any vessel." And a Supreme Court ruling (Case no. 63 SCRA 215, Saumala vs. Saulog Trans) held that "where public service commission failed to act on a petition to extend the term of a provisional permit, the latter cannot be deemed to have lapsed automatically."

These two abusive officers are committing injustice on a woman citizen, and hurting the tourist trade. General Ramos is usually quick to order a prompt investigation, believe me.

General, please call Maria Akester's lawyer, Mr.Sam Magdamit, tel. 85-1758 or 89-8365. And nail those two abusive officers to the wall.

October 15, 1986

Part 37. Pirates And Taxes Bury A Dying Industry

I was handed a position paper called "Primer on Film Piracy" from a group headed by my friend Johnny Litton, with a view to presenting the side of the movie importers, producers, distributors and theater owners in the Betamax Raids Controversy. According to the list, this group comprises: Good ole Johnny as member of the Motion Picture Association of America (MPAA); Manny Nuqui, president of the Philippine

Motion Picture Producers Association (PMPPA); Sixto Dy, President of Integrated Movie Producers, Importers, Distributors Association of the Philippines (IMPIDAP); Tama Ng, vice president of Metro Manila Theater Association (MMTA); Bobby Yang, vice president Greater Manila Theater Association; Remy Monteverde, director, Motion Pictures Association; and Eduardo Suazon, the OIC of the Videogram Regulatory Board (VRB).

The statistics that they offer is a horror story in itself. There is a sharp decline in theater attendance by at least 40 percent resulting in substantial losses estimated at P450 million annually in government revenues.

In the last four years, theater attendance have dropped by 65 percent, while admission prices increased only by 38 percent. About 55 percent of theater expenses go to energy bills alone, and such overhead cannot be covered by an ever contracting market.

According to this group, some 75,000 families and 500,000 workers depend on their livehood on the movie industry which has an accumulated investment of P3 billion.

American film companies pay to the government an estimated P20 to P30 million in taxes -- specific taxes, import duties, income taxes, etc., excluding amusement taxes. They spend about P6 to P7 million pesos to advertise their pictures in the newspapers annually. Their film exchanges directly and indirectly employ 500 persons. The major American companies have gone down 37% from the level of their 1981 profits.

No statistics are given for local movie producers other than that some of them in desperation have resorted to making "cheap bold films."

The group blames the entire sad state of affairs on "the proliferation and unregulated circulation of videograms, including among others, videotapes, discs, cassettes or any technical improvement or variation thereof," and more specifically "rampant film piracy".

There are 3,000 video outlets, of which 1,433 are registered with the VRB, with 61.5% or 913 outlets in Metro Manila while 38.4% are in the provinces, according to the position paper. But there seems to be a slight mathematical error here, for 91 divided by 1,433 is 63.7%, not 61.5 percent.

Video Houses are beginning to proliferate, competing directly with movie theaters by showing the same film, and charging only P2 to P3 as against the movie ticket of P8.00. CATV or Cable Television have found its way into homes in Quezon province and the Bicol region, showing first run movies being shown in Metro Manila. Clubs, hotels, motels and restaurants also show videotapes to attract customers.

There is no question that the movie industry as we know it, is dying. It is dying everywhere else in the world due to the competition of television, the escalation of production costs especially of expensive performers, and above all because of the advent of the video recorders. Nothing can save it, any more than vaudeville could be saved after the motion picture came into being -- or any more than the silent movie could survive the advent of sound -- or black-and-white can exist after color movies swept the industry. The movie industry as we know it, is a sunset industry, it will soon be dead as a doornail. Technology has made it obsolete.

The reason it is dying here faster than anywhere else is because the Technoquacks under pressure from the IMF imposed oppressive taxes on the industry, equivalent to 40% of the gross ticket sales. Where in hell do you find taxes equivalent to 40% of gross? In the 17th century, the Mogul Emperors did it in India, and in the 18th century, the Kings of France imposed it on their people; both the Mogul Empire and the French monarchy were swept into the dustbin of history.

The least we can do is to relieve the industry of these taxes. Regulating videograms is as useless as the Prohibition of alcoholic drinks in the States. There is no video regulation in the States because it is unenforceable, and subject to abuse and racketeering.

Tell me, reader, wouldn't you rather rent a tape than go to a movie house? -- with thousands of titles to select from, no parking problems, no one to kick your seat from behind, or talk loudly, or pick a fight with you, and trample you down when there is a fire; with only a button to press if you want to go to the bathroom or feed the baby or kiss the wife?

Part 38. Junie Kalaw And Another Sexy Sunday

Talk about seduction pads of playboy bachelors, like those of Junie Kalaw, Boy Daza and Arthur Sales. The male bower birds, lacking fancy feathers to attract mates, build elaborate "bowers" on the ground, a mating station where the male struts and sings to attract as many females as possible. After mating, the male like many a human bachelor, kicks out the female, and tidies up the bower for the next conquest. As usual, the ugliest male builds the most ornate bower.

In the Paris Louvre, there is a Greek statue of Hermaphrodite, a creature with breasts and two sets of organs, male and female, which people may find bizarre. But take the sea hare, a large marine snail with a penis just to the right of its mouth and a vagina in the center of its back. Mating combinations for this anatomical wonder vary from conventional male-female couplings to orgiastic splendor that would titillate even the most sated hard-core porn aficionados. Imagine a "daisy chain" of several participants, in which each snail simultaneously performs both male and female functions. That's really the way to have our cake and eat it too.

Transvestites are different from hermaphrodites and homosexuals. They are males who have a fetish of wearing women's clothes but do not necessarily go for males as homos do. Consider the transvestite scorpion fly. Courtship etiquette among these flies demands that the male hunt down a large tasty prey and present it to the female. He has to risk his life exposing himself to predators as he hunts, but he is sure to die a virgin if he has no gifts to give to those gold-diggers. Now some opportunistic males have found a way to do this without risking life and limb. Becoming transvestites and pretending to be a female, these devious fellows grab a courting male's nuptial gift, and fly off to offer it to a female of their own. It was discovered that these transvestites mate more often than males who do their own hunting. Crime really pays among the scorpion flies.

And Oral Sex, the usual fare of the porno film, is prevalent among the cichlids, a species of tropical fish found in waters full of predators. As a protective strategy, the female carries her eggs and hatches the young in her mouth till they could swim. The problem of the male is how to fertilize the eggs in the female's mouth. Fortunately, the male has orange dots on his tail that look exactly like the female's eggs. The crafty male drags his fin over the sand, tricking the female into thinking she dropped some of her precious cargo. As she instinctively tries to scoop it up, she gets a mouthful of sperm that fertilize the real eggs in her mouth. Oral sex is a necessity among these tropical fish.

Male bedbugs and fleas have penises that are too short to reach the female vaginas, so they simply stab the females in the back and ejaculate there. Sex is done by inoculation, and if the female survives, the sperm reaches the egg by one of the most amazing journeys known.

The Snake which the embodiment of Evil is actually a pathetic creature when it comes to sex. The male snake still plugged into the female, may suddenly experience a female resistance so violent that his penis breaks off. Fortunately he has an extra penis as a backup. A male with two penises is more interesting than Nick Joaquin's woman with two navels.

Then there is the tiny male fly called J. Nitida who guards the chastity of his mate with his very life. After copulation, the female eats the male, leaving his sex organs locked in place, to prevent others from entering. So you see, the chastity belt was not invented by medieval knights going off to the wars. As a matter of fact, some insects, rodents and snakes safeguard their sperms by sealing up the female sperm storage chamber with a copulatory plug, a gluey secretion from their own bodies.

Homosexual rape is common among Anthocorid bugs. The male rapist forces his own sperm into the storage organ of another male while the victim is mating. When the latter copulates again, he passes on his attacker's sperm and genes.

Why do I tell you all these? According to biologist Mary Batten, "In the human world, love and romance have long embellished sex, while fears and anxieties often overshadow it. By broadening our perspective on sex to include its biological roots in the rest of the living world, we may achieve true sexual liberation. We can take the guilt-ridden ghosts from the closet, sweep up the tangled web of Freudian fantasies, and simply have fun!"

Without being promiscuous, adulterous or irresponsible, it is possible for us humans to simply enjoy sex. Why not, we may be the only animals who can!

October 19, 1986

Part 39. The Big Picture and Ed Sazon's Bully Boys

Life is made up of small confusing details, they say, and to make sense out of it, one must look at the Big Picture, the Over-all Pattern, the Grand Design.

In the Videogram Controversy, one begins to detect the Big Picture. Above all like a thunderhead, is Frank Knight, the British agent of American Imperialism, the Regional Director of East Asia Film & Video Security Office, the watchdog of American film interests. In the Philippines, he is represented by his surrogates, Rebecca Benitez Cruz (liaison officer and representative of 20th Century Fox) and Rico Domingo (lawyer of the Siguion Reyna Law Office, counsel of the Videogram Board and of the Motion Picture Association of America).

Then there is Rico Domingo's surrogate and successor as head of the Videogram Regulatory Board, Ed Sazon -- and his "volunteer" bully boys who are harassing Filipino businessmen, in a manner forbidden in the United States itself.

As usual the imperialist strategy is to divide and conquer, to consolidate and control. The first thing Knight and his Unoly Trio -- Benitez Cruz, Rico Domingo and Ed Sazon -- did was to drive a wedge between the big boys and the small boys of the video business. They recognized the big businessmen of Philippine Video Association (PVA), and concentrated their raids on the larger group of small businessmen in the Videogram Dealers Association of the Philippines (VDAP).

Then they offered the reproducing rights to a select group of 13 companies organized as the Philippine Association of Videogram Reproducers (PAVR). The 5,000 video companies who use to do their reproducing too, are now relegated to the status of distribution outlets.

Of the 13, there is a pattern of consolidation and monopoly. The three largest, Fox Video (Fred Ongyangco), Galactic (Eric Apolonio), and Technica (Manny Mendoza, Greggy Araneta) have merged into the giant FGT Video. The original owner of Technica Video was Manuel Arcangel, who sold the firm for P3 million to Greggy Araneta. Greggy paid for it with a check for P1 million, and never got around to pay the balance.

Of the rest of the 13, Trigon (Ching Zapanta), Viva (Ricky del Rosario) and Fujiwara (Arthur Co) are merging into one company; Stripes (Roland Siquijor) and New Dimension (Marcos Ong) are also merging into one. And the rest continue to operate as smalltime independents: Trade Mark (Faustino Salud); Precision (Philip Lee); Hennelyn (Henry See); Video Sonix (Rene Ledesma); and Aguila (Eddie Aguila).

The strategy is to concentrate the monopoly in a few firms, and then, an American take-over of the entire monopoly, freezing out the poor Filipinos. This happened in the banking business, which was forced into monopolistic Unibanking, and then forced to accept foreign equity. This happened in advertising when American companies Walter Thompson and McCann Ericcson simply took over the entire industry, leaving the scraps to the Flips. Most probably this is what Frank Knight and his Unholy Trio have in mind.

And how do Ed Sazon and his bully boys fit into this? Well, Ed Sazon, the head of the Videogram Board and former film distributor (Solar Films), was overheard to have said that he will retire soon and set up a service agency to facilitate the copyrighting of foreign films. He said this to Nathan Zulueta (at the baptismal party for Nathan's daughter), as overheard by Angel Calaguio, son of former MMC Commissioner Calaguio.

Boy, these guys learn a lot from their American masters. The American film companies will finally get their monopoly going under Frank Knight the Enforcer, with his Unholy Trio doing the dirty work: Benitez Cruz and Rico Domingo representing the Americans and bullying small Filipino businessmen, and Ed Sazon with a nice copyright facilitation business to service the monopoly.

In the meantime, Ed Sazon, is busy with a whole cast of "volunteer" bully boys harassing poor Filipinos.

Complaints are pouring in about a Joel Reyes, a "volunteer" from the VRB, who raided Eyeball Video (Marie Reyes) without a search warrant, confiscated 35 tapes, and allegedly asked for P4,500 to settle the case. He was given P1,500. This same Joel Reyes raided Vilman's without a search warrant, and was allegedly given P1,500. This same Joel Reyes went all the way to Batangas and allegedly confiscated 200 tapes from a Mr. Maglunoc, accompanied by armed men. This same Joel Reyes allegedly sells the confiscated tapes at P100.00 per tape, saying that his aunt is going to the States and asked him to   sell her tapes.

There are more horror stories, but space is limited, and they will have to be published in forthcoming articles. Come on, friends, send in more complaints, if possible with sworn affidavits. Let's send Ed Sazon and his bully boys to jail!
October 22, 1986

Part 40. Raiders Of The Lost Arse

We hate to press this, but we have so many horror stories of abusive officials of the Videogram Regulatory Board (VRB) that it would be a shame not to use them. What these guys have to learn is that the PD 1987 of Marcos and the grandiose plans of Greedy Araneta, Frank Knight and his Unholy Trio have no place in our democratic and humanist society, where human liberty and human dignity are sacrosanct. Nor are threats against this newspaper and this writer have a place in a free society where all ideas must meet the challenge of other ideas in open, free and unlimited debate.

We reiterate this paper's policy of absolute fairness in airing all sides of the controversy, and invite the representatives of the theaters and the movies to sit in with us to exchange views, with a promise to print in full within the limited space available (90 lines of 64 characters each) any views opposing ours. The invitation has been extended many times before, but was never accepted.

What is so frustrating is that, according to Justice Federico Moreno, legal adviser of the Philippine Video Association, the Philippines is NOT even a signatory to the Copyright Convention, and therefore is not obligated to protect American copyrights. And rightly so, because we hardly have any copyrights for Americans to protect. As a matter of fact, Filipino films are being copied and sold in the United States among Filipino Americans, and no royalty payments are made, nor any asshole raids conducted. Raids are forbidden in most of the United States because it is unconstitutional and unenforceable.

The Marcos PD 1987 which creates the Videogram Regulatory Board to protect American film copyrights and destroy Filipino video rental shops with a 30% tax on gross receipts, is a self-imposed abomination on the Filipino people. We are being made to pay the cost in tears and poverty, without any obligation to do so, so that Frank Knight, the Unholy Trio and their American masters can be prosperous, cultured and free. We are indeed, as Claro M. Recto once said, "a sacrificial race with a mysterious urge to suicide."

The Video Regulatory Board (VRB), as far as we can glean, is made up of Ed Sazon, OIC (formerly of Solar Films); Atty. Esperidion Laxa, (Tagalog Ilang Ilang); Bobby Yang (Odeon Theater, etc.); Alex Tiu (film distributor, IMPIDAP), Ramon Revilla (movie producer); William Ching (IMPIDAP); Faustino Salud (Trademark Video, reproducer). Rico Domingo, counsel for the Motion Pictures Association of America is also, it is said, counsel for the VRB, and lawyer from the Siguion Reyna Law Offices.

The Philippine Video Association (PVA) is headed by Atty. Faustino Pong Salud (Trademark Video), president; Rene Ledesma (Sonix); Fred Ongyanco (Fox); Eddie Barretto (Junction); Eric Apolonio (Galactic); Eddie Aguila (Aguila); Philip Lee (Precision); Arthus Cotoying (Fujiwara); Henry See (Hennelyn); Laura Larisma (Equus); Fred Contreras (House of Stereo); Manny Mendoza (Technica).

The Videogram Dealers Association of the Philippines (VDAP) which comprise the smaller shops, are headed by Atty. Roque Peran (Angie's), chairman; George Rodriguez (Group A), president; Paul Chan (Video Take-out); Lydia Nabong (Video Channel); Mike Bangayan (Golden Bean); Jimmy Lim (Astro Vision); Samuel Chua (Martin Lauren); Jose Chan (Group A); Rolly Manalo, Mr. Javier (Citizen); Miss Becky (Video Circle).

The VRB authorized 13 "reproducers" to copy and distribute the video cassettes. Every cassette must be identified with a distinctive yellow sticker, which is procured from one source, PORI, and sold at 30 centavos each. The reproducers can buy as many stickers as they want for placement on authorized cassettes, but some of them have gone into rackets of their own, selling those stickers to video outlets for P1.00 instead of 30 centavos. Like the Prohibition Era in the States, the

Betamax raids spawns rackets and destroys the moral fiber of our people.

Take the five simultaneous raids on video shops in Virra Mall. In the Astro Vision of Jimmy Lim, 3 VRB inspectors with armed policemen, appeared after 5 PM, waving a warrant and a new list of forbidden titles separate from the VRB forbidden list. On the basis of this list, comprising all titles from 20th Century Fox, Walt Disney, Warners, Paramount and Columbia, which nobody knew of before, the VRB inspectors began to wreak havoc and confiscate tapes.

"Basta kokonin namin. Wala kayong magagawa!" they shouted at the top of their lungs. George Rodriguez and Joey Chan came to help their VDAP member, only to find that the warrant was valid "anytime, day and night". At this point der Fuhrer Rico Domingo showed up, shouting as usual, *"Huwag ninyo pakinggan yan, magnanakaw yan! Kunin na yan tapes"*, and turning to Joey, he screamed, *"Ikaw na naman! Bakit kayo makiki-alam?"* Then he shouted to the police, "Arrest this man for contempt of court!" but the policeman embarrassed answered, "Hindi namin magagawa yan."

In a rump hearing before the VRB at the Experimental Cinema, Ms. Benitez Cruz of the 20th Century Fox, accused Eva Gecusa of Image Century Video of trafficking in forbidden tapes, showing a receipt for the purchase of "Police Academy III" by a Mr. Otto from Eva's shop. Subsequently, Eva showed her own the duplicate of the receipt, without "Police Academy III" and proved that the receipt of Benitez Cruz was tampered, and the case was dismissed. Whereupon der Fuhrer Rico Domingo stood up, and shouted at the top of his lungs as usual, *"Basta magnanakaw kayo!"* Eva is suing Benitez Cruz for a million pesos in damages.

Then again, VRB volunteers swooped down on Lydia Nabong's Video Channel for alleged non-registration, with civilians carrying guns, and armed with a closure order signed by Ed Sazon. No written notice was sent to Lydia prior to the closure. They just showed up after office hours and sealed the place. Yet later it was found out that Lydia's Video Channel was duly registered since January.

Dear Reader, do not think you are immune from the abominations of these VRB Raiders of the Lost Arse. Every time you rent or buy a "forbidden" tape, every time you copy a program off the air and lend it to a friend, every time you get a videocassette in the mail from your friends abroad -- you risk being harassed by these assholes, and being called "Magnanakaw" by der Fuhrer Rico Domingo at the top of his voice. He'll never do it to an American, but he will do it to you, you filthy Flip.

April 1987

Part 41.   Manila Times, casualty of the War of the Roces

Anding Roces is right again.

On February 15, 1986, he predicted that the Marcos will be toppled within the month and collected bets from Guy Pauker of Rand Corporation, John Shaplin of New Yorker, Melinda Liu of Newsweek, and myself.

On August 26, he told me that another coup attempt will happen soon, and it did two days later.

Last May 1, 1987, when he resigned from Manila Times, he predicted that the venerable newspaper will not last six months. On October 1, exactly six months later, Manila Times stopped publication.

The Manila Times was born after World War II, replacing the pre-war Manila Tribune that was taken over by the Japanese during the Occupation.

The Times was set up by Ramon Roces and his brothers and sisters: Isabel "Bebeng" Roces, Nenita Roces Verzosa, Joaquin "Chino" Roces, and Benito "Bibilo" Prieto, husband of sister Chuca.

The paper was managed by Chino Roces and was so successful that it printed 250,000 copies daily -- TWICE the circulation of all rival newspapers combined (Chronicle of the Lopezes, Herald of Soriano, Bulletin of Menzi, and others, among which was Ramon Roces's Evening News).

It had a stranglehold on classified ads and the obituaries, and had among its columnists, Doroy Valencia, Alfredo Roces, Jose Guevara, Max Sullivan, and a fifth column by J.V. Cruz.

Believe it or not, I had a front page column there called "Ways and Means" about economics -- to which Jobo Fernandez, Sixto Roxas and Salvador Araneta contributed.

Ninoy Aquino was a star reporter, along with a business reporter named Satur Ocampo.

The great Manila Times died by Marcos fiat on September 21, 1972.

The Bulletin, a business daily with 15,000 circulation, took over the classified ads and obituaries, and eventually reached 250,000 circulation, more than five times the rest (Times Journal, Daily Express).

In January 1986, Ramon Roces resumed publication of the Manila Times, and failing to get Chino to join him, got his cousin Titong Roces as editor.

After the Snap Elections, the Times suffered its first crisis -- Marcos crony Geronimo Velasco was exposed as a stockholder with Benny Tan as his front man. Titong was appointed ambassador to Taiwan, and his brother Alejandro, ex Education secretary became editor-in-chief.

Velasco's equity was returned to him, then a second crisis hit the Times -- managing editor Vergel Santos walked out with the staff, leaving Anding Roces, Joe Quirino, Napoleon Rama and Hernando Abaya to put out the paper. By midnight of the first day of the strike, they were able to put a 16 paged edition with a mocking one-inch notice, "The Manila Times staff walked out last night."

Vergel Santos and his men joined the Manila Chronicle then being set up by Chino Roces, formerly of the Times. Thus started the War of the Roces that eventually involved the Star (Antonio, once the president and editor) and the Bulletin (Anding as president).

Manila Times was number four paper, with a peak circulation of 50,000. The two top papers, Bulletin and Inquirer had peaks of 300,000; the number three, Malaya, had a peak of 120,000.

Anding Roces brought in as columnists such respected writers as economist Alejandro Lichauco and National Artist Nick Joaquin to whom he offered a top rate of P1,000 per column article.

Surprised, Nick murmured, "I am honored." Anding answered with his usual no-no, "No, no, Nick, YOU honor us!"

But Don Ramon is not too honored by literate writers. First, he fired Lichauco for an article on Cory that offended him.

Anding took him back, and Ramon fired him again for an article on Cardinal Sin. Then, Ramon fired Nick Joaquin for an article on Chino Roces that offended him.

Don Ramon Roces is no Bea Zobel. He is the publisher and he has the right to fire anyone he does not like.

His cousin Alejandro Roces resigned on May 1st, saying "I am giving the Times six months before the end."

Six months to the day, October 1st, the Times stopped publication.

Ah, the inevitable post-mortem!

Don Ramon Roces is probably the most successful publisher in the Philippines. His Capitol Publishing has printed over 85 publications -- comics, telephone directories, vernacular magazines -- and never lost money except in Evening News which he sold to Chick Parsons for P1.00.

His first magazine Liwayway made millions, because of Severino Reyes, author of the classic stage musical Walang Sugat, who wrote for Liwayway a series called Kwento ni Lola Basiang -- Pilipino translations of Grimm's Fairy Tales.

A Times insider says that Don Ramon loved to be called "Abraham Lincoln" but ran his businesses like an emperor. He and his grandson Chito Davila just did not have the background to appreciate good English writing, according to the scuttlebutt, and therefore could not hold together a good staff as do his cousins Chino at the Manila Chronicle, and Anding at the Bulletin.

And so the Manila Times circulation dived to less than half, and a venerable institution died, the latest casualty in the War of the Roces.

Recently two other papers, Tribune and Observer died and is resurrecting as the Globe, to compete with the giants of the field: Manila Bulletin (100,000 to 200,000 since the strike); Philippine Daily Inquirer (175,000 by recent audit, up to 200,000); Star including the evening and business editions (60,000 to 80,000); Malaya (35,000 to 50,000); Manila Chronicle (20,000 to 30,000); Standard (5,000); Journal (5,000).

The two top papers occupy the center of the political spectrum, Bulletin from center to right-of-center, and Inquirer from center to left-of-center.

Star is positioned right-of-center to far right. Malaya occupied left-of-center to far left -- but has disturbingly shifted to the right.

Chronicle is becoming a business paper with its shipping news, filling the void left by Business Day.

Part 42. *Et Tu Bruja*, then fall San Miguel!

Apply a few thousand volts of static electricity on a woman, and two things happen to her. First, her hair rises straight up so she looks like the Bride of Frankenstein. And second, she develops a visceral dislike for Little Boy Blue del Rosario, exec vice-president of San Miguel.

I know of two such women. One was someone I saw in front of the PCGG offices screaming about how she was going to send to jail the boss of Boy Blue, because thousands of San Miguel employees besieged her office the previous day.

The other is a cousin of mine, who inherited five shares of San Miguel, and feels that Boy Blue owes her an explanation for every paper clip he uses.

Early morning, a few hours after I saw the first Bride of Frankenstein, my cousin woke me up, waving pages of a dozen newspapers, screaming, "Why is Andy III using corporate funds to buy UCPB shares of San Miguel? Why does Andy and Boy Blue buy the shares at higher than market? Who are they fooling??

"Why is Anscor International, a private Soriano firm, cornering most of the supply of materials and services sold to SMC? A blood-sucking operation?

"Tell Blue Boy that the PCGG will press for amendments requiring transactions over P50,000 to be approved by two-thirds of the board!

"Tell Boy Blue that the PCGG will elect a new board of 9 to 6 majority, kick Andy up to the chairmanship, and run this corporation with board of respected businessmen!"

I stumbled out of bed half dazed by the sight of a nightmare, murmuring what Julius Caesar might have said, had his assailant Brutus been the Bride of Frankenstein, "*Et Tu Bruja*, then fall Boy Blue!"

O *Haesslichkeit*, O *Schrecklichkeit*, Oh Bride of Frankenstein, hearken to thy humble servant, and read the decision of the SEC Case 3152, dated April 28, 1987, which precisely dealt with the same issues you bring out!

In the first place, O *Haesslichkeit*, must you keep repeating the falsehood that Andy is buying the sequestered shares with company assets? The SEC conclusion precisely says that such a statement "appears not so far supported by the evidence on record."

Andy is not buying any of the shares. The institutional buyers -- SSS, Bond of Australia, the SMC Retirement Fund, and the Soriano Group of companies -- are buying most of the shares for cash. A portion is taken back through an offset deal in which advances to the CIIF companies and the non-voting preferred UCPB shares and dividends are exchanged for the sequestered shares -- this is to undo Danding's ploy to keep control of San Miguel.

In the second place, O Schrecklichkeit, the high price of the San Miguel shares is dictated by the seller, not the buyer. The sellers are UCPB, CIIF, and your PCGG, so what are you cackling about?

Bond of Australia is willing to buy at P150 per share, as long as management is vested with the Soriano Group. Why not, the government which hold the shares, benefits.

The Filipino buyers are willing to buy at P111 per share while the market is P95. Shares that contribute to control is usually sold at a premium. You know what Danding Cojuangco paid for the shares owned by Ayala? He paid P27 while the market was P18 per share, a 50 percent premium, because he wanted control.

The Filipino institutional buyers, employees and stockholders are paying P111, instead of P95 per share, a premium of only 17 percent, because they do not want PCGG control.

Thirdly, the buying agency Ansor, not Anscor, is based not in Stanford, Connecticut, but in Hong Kong. It is owned, not by Soriano but by Atlas Consolidated, PICOP and San Miguel Corporation.

It is meant to be a watchdog of purchase operations, including getting alternative bids and watching out for shipments not according to specs.

Now, witness this, O *Haesslichkeit*, in 1986 Ansor supplied only $250,000 of the over $6,000,000 worth, a mere 4 percent of all the supplies and materials bought by San Miguel. Ansor does not charge a commission, only a small handling charge, and it has LOST during 1986. Do not give me that dung about bloodsucking and overprice.

Fourthly, PCGG insists on having transactions over P50,000 approved by two-thirds of the board. Holy Moses, what does the PCGG take San Miguel for, a sari-sari store? If this were to take effect, the board has to meet 24 hours a day to get any business done! I am sure Andy III and Boy Blue will consider any reasonable check and balance to the powers of management.

Lawyers compared the by-laws of UCPB, PLDT, Benguet and the San Miguel -- and there are NO differences in the powers of management. Let's face it. The PCGG is playing favorites, they are forcing changes in the SMC by-laws that they are not demanding from UCPB, PLDT and Benguet. They are better friends to the Cojuangcos, Yuchengcos, Ongpins and the Allens than they are to Andy III and Boy Blue.

Fifth, Oh Bride of Frankenstein, is the hypocrisy with which you load the board with your dummies. You put Ben Guingona and Mario Locsin in the PLDT board, and when they cooperated with management, you threatened to oust them in the next stockholder's meeting.

You put Abe Sarmiento and Monchong Garcia in the San Miguel Board, but you won't allow them to exercise any discretion. They cooperated with Andy III, so you are not nominating them this year. What you really want is power, O Schrecklichkeit, you and Mr. Diaz and the PCGG.

Who are your nominees? Teddyboy Locsin, Ramon Sy, Jose Cuisia, Augusto Barcelon, Jose Mari Delgado, Oscar Hilado, Salvador Carlos, Quirico Camus, Jose Palma, Mariano Que, Jose Feliciano, Dindo de los Angeles, Roberto Coyuito, Sonny Belmonte. We'll talk of them later.

Andy III, his group have about 39 percent of the vote, enough for six board seats. PCGG plus the GSIS constitute 52 percent, enough for eight seats. One is up for grabs.

February 1988

Part 43. The Editor, Philippine Daily Inquirer, Manila
Dear sir,
Correct me if I am wrong but the persons being always referred to in Henares' column, Make My Day, are:
Arroyo, Joker: The Big Joke
Bengzon, Alran: St. Alran, The Saint
Bengzon, Jose: Little Brown Jug-ears
Bernas, Joaquin: Doc, Rasputin
Buenaventura, Cesar: Our Man Squint, Convexity of his Face
Fernandez, Jobo: Pompous Ass
Jayme, Vicente: The Big Sleep
Locsin, Teddyboy: Teodorus Filius, Theopolous, The Finger
Macaraig, Catalino: Mac the Knife, Father of Twink
Mangahas, Majar: Mumbles
Monsod, Christian: Uncle Tom, Tom Hearns, Raging Bull
Monsod, Solita: Screaming Banshee, Wicked Witch of the West, Holy Cow
Nieva, Teresa: Sta. Teresa, Our Lady of Zeroes
Platt, Nicholas: Hoy Kulas, Jeeves the Butler
Reyes, Rainerio: Pile of Pomade
Romulo, Ricardo: Small Dick
Soriano, Noel: Walter Mitty, Goldfinger, Dopey
Villegas, Bernardo: Alopecic Gynander
Yours truly
ENRIQUE VELASCO, Guerrero Street, Makati
March 28, 1988

Part 44. The Praetorian Guards of Emperor Kulas
The greatest threat to our democracy is the existence of a bloated, politicized and pro-American military. What was once a disciplined professional patriotic force of only 50,000 before martial law, became a Marcos goon squad of 260,000 during the dark age, taking over civilian posts, draining our budgetary resources, running murder-for-hire, car-napping, bank-robbing syndicates, and killing, mutilating anyone on CIA's shit list.
This bloated, politicized, pro-American force became a Frankenstein monster, a constant temptation for any strong man to use to gain power, such as Honasan and the RAMboys tried

to do. This Frankenstein monster continues to plague us long after Marcos is gone -- just as it does in Latin America and Africa where nations keep plunging into a succession of military dictatorships.

Such forces, supported by the Americans, betrayed and murdered leaders like Ngo Dinh Diem and Salvador Allende, and kept in power such bloody butchers as Batista, Somoza, Duvalier, Trujillo, Pinochet, Shah of Iran, Noriega, Marcos -- all of America's Free World, ha ha.

The Americans boiled us in our own oil by building up this force with base rental money that might be of better use in economic development. Then they create what Sen. Maceda calls "factionalism" in an obvious attempt to divide, conquer and control it.

First, they had vigilantes organized to bolster the army's ability to skewer poor patriotic peasants opposed to American bases and monopolies.

Second, they encouraged the RAMboys under Honasan to attempt a coup and destabilize our democracy just to strengthen their bargaining posture on the bases.

Third, they encourage such war-lords as Col. Rudy Aguinaldo (aka Colonel Kurtz), and Col. Rolando Abadilla to enter politics as an armed anti-communist goon.

Fourth, they cooperate with the pro-Marcos rightist fascist faction under Col. Cabauatan and General Zumel.

Fifth, they probably asked Secretary Ramos to swell the ranks of an already bloated, politicized and pro-American army by calling up the civilian reserves.

Sixth, through the JUSMAG, they still call the shots in the Army headquarters, with superspy US Colonel Dennison Lane assuming the role of CIA Col. Edward Lansdale, Ugly American of the 1950s.

Seventh, Ambassador Alexander Melchor of Opus Dei and Annapolis, has written his friends in Malacañang, suggesting a "total structuring of the AFP by legislation or by bringing in an outside advisory group (with) the specific mention of General Lee Hsien Loong." His statement, "I have asked Bernie Villegas to try to make sure that as many of our people in government and industry can listen to (Dr. Fernando Soto, his representative)," is very disturbing, considering that the counterparts of Bernie and

CRC in Chile (Pablo Baraona and IGS), conspired with the CIA to murder Allende and install a repressive dictatorship under General Pinochet.

Eighth, in effect American dungheaps, encouraging the PMA-ROTC rivalry, are factionalizing our armed forces into nine independent, sometimes mutually antagonistic groups, all pro-American: vigilantes, Ramboys, warlords, Marcos fascists, civilian reserves, the main Army, PMA grads, ROTC regulars, and Opus Dei.

Add to these armed defenders of Mother America, the pro-American Big Business complex: Council of Trent, MBC, BBC, CRC, Social Weather Station, UP-Economics, AmCham and the Australians of Mabini and Angeles -- there you are, we are a Banana Republic!

How could we allow these hillbillies to use us for their nefarious ends?

Whether Marcos or Cory is the president, it seems that the real head of our government is the American Ambassador who dictates our foreign policy and subjects our economy to the excrementalities of the IMF.

Clutching tightly around him the robes of false authority, Emperor Kulas Platt, who looks like Jeeves left much too long under the sun, is surrounded by Filipino sycophants (Dick), opportunists (Doy), courtiers (Blas), jesters (Bernie), and Praetorian Guards from our Armed Forces.

These Praetorian Guards like those of the decadent Roman Empire, may evolve from being the servants of the master to being the makers of that master, will one day sell the imperial dignity to the highest bidder, and change emperors as the mood strikes them from day to day.

It happened in Rome and in all banana republics. It can happen here.

April 1988

Part 45. SEC director is a pit bull terrier

The Securities Exchange Commission (SEC) upon the lifting of the Supreme Court restraining order on its futures trading regulations, promptly ordered Futurelink Commodities to cease and desist trading, and close shop. Probably the work of a Marcos-appointed SEC director whose pit bull terrier tenacity on behalf of the ruling Hong Kong Mafia is nothing less than legendary.

The pit bull terrier, everybody knows, is considered a congenitally vicious dog, bred for dogfights in which it fights to the death. This dog once it bites, never lets go, and has been known to kill children; it is in widespread use by gangsters to guard their illegal drugs. Several bills have been introduced in the USA to forbid the breeding of these dogs. There should be a law against human pit bull terriers too.

The SEC's pit bull terrier serves the purpose of a cartel Hong Kong traders in the Manila International Futures Exchange (MIFE) by:

o limiting futures trading to the local exchange because parallel international trading minimizes large scale manipulation of local prices.

o throwing out a Singapore firm, Futurelink, which assumed a spoiler's role in the Hong Kong traders' market manipulations.

o acting very slowly on the complaints of investors against unscrupulous brokers and unlicensed investment consultants.

The Philippine National Bank to hedge against sugar price fluctuations goes to the Chicago Board of Trade, not to local futures exchange. Whose fault is it? The SEC has been issuing regulations against trading abroad when it is the only way to prevent manipulation of the local prices.

The SEC has not in any way convinced users and producers to hedge against price fluctuations in the commodity futures market (its sole economic justification), instead left the market to the mercy of predatory gamblers and speculators.

The coconut plantation owners and oil mills, the coffee and soybean growers, the sugar planters and sugar centrals, and the buyers and users of these commodities -- PNB, San Miguel, Robina, Coca Cola, Pepsi Cola, Nestlè-- would not touch the local commodity futures market with a ten-foot pole as long as the SEC and its pit bull terrier call the shots.

The way the SEC runs the market gives a cabal of brokers the opportunity to trade on their own account and manipulate prices. The restraining hand of foreign commodity futures prices was summarily eliminated by SEC fiat. The *tayo-tayo* attitude of SEC and the organized brokers, and the utter neglect of client complaints by the SEC, have destroyed the confidence of legitimate hedgers in the local market.

The failure of the SEC to warn the public about the innate risks in the futures market, to limit market speculation to those who can afford to throw away their money in Jai-Alai and casino gambling -- has allowed unscrupulous investment counselors and brokers to entice orphans and widows living on insurance money, and poor employees with their retirement pay, into something more risky than buying sweepstakes tickets.

It breaks one's heart to listen to single parent Carmen de Leon with her three fatherless children losing her lifetime savings of almost P300,000 which she earned in the trucking business, often sleeping under the truck, climbing mountains alone, and going through two disastrous highjacks.

It breaks one's heart to listen to Fely Almeron who borrowed and lost P105,000 -- now in the grip of loan sharks and bloodsuckers; to Rosita Kho, small time junk dealer, losing P167,000 in one throw, all the capital she needed for her business.

It breaks one's heart to listen to Mary Rose Rosario who inherited and lost P155,000, with the broker attaching her Betamax and wedding ring, while she is dying slowly from tuberculosis and cannot even buy milk for her children.

How much blood, sweat and tears of the poor huddled masses were spilled because the SEC did not see to it that they were warned of the inherent risks of this game?

Today there is weeping and gnashing of teeth, there is chaos and consternation, turmoil and confusion, because of this Marcos appointed official and one Marcos-appointed commissioner.

God in heaven, when will the balance sheet be balanced in favor of the poor and the hungry among us, the friendless, the cheated and the beaten?

By whom? How?
August 4, 1988

Part 46. Where is Capt. Gutierrez who murdered the Santos Family?

My maid Ateng Zaragoza woke up one night in a sweat from a nightmare where she was pursued by soldiers intent on cutting off her head. She dreamt she was hiding in a closet while outside the whole village resounded with screams of women and children being butchered like pigs. It was then that she woke up. Why is it that our armed forces, in the minds of the poor, are associated with rape and plunder?

On the other hand, the communist rebels are never feared because they have specific highly visible targets -- men in uniform, Americans, rich pro-American businessmen -- that do not included their more unfortunate countrymen. Most Filipinos do not agree with the communism, but they do not fear the communist rebels.

Their greatest objects of fear are the soldiers of the republic who are sworn to protect them, and who in many cases, protect them out of their meager possessions, their chickens, their daughters, their sisters, their wives, and especially their lives. Soldiers wage war on their own people, according to the poor, and get away with it with the connivance of their officers.

At dawn on Wednesday, April 6, 1988, 11 Scout Rangers of the 4th Company under the command of Capt. Melvin Gutierrez, surrounded the house of Reynaldo de los Santos in Barrio Mambagaton, municipality of Himamaylan, Negros Occidental.

They shot up the house until they thought everyone inside was dead. Then, having shot the family carabao, as well as a pig, they ransacked the house, taking money and clothes, as well as eleven fighting cocks, worth a considerable amount of money.

The sole survivor in the house was Joaquin, age 17, who, though seriously wounded, had witnessed the death of his mother, father and one brother and two sisters. Both Joaquin and his mother, Serena de los Santos, were brought to the Bacolod Provincial Hospital. Mrs. de los Santos died shortly after arrival at the hospital, while Joaquin is being treated for a shattered upper left arm. Joaquin Recounts that the Scout Rangers entered the house, thinking all were dead. Though he escaped injury in the massive initial strafing, the soldiers shot him after entering the house.

The married sister of Joaquin, Jennelyn, also witnessed the whole event from her small house a few yards away, as did other neighbors. The Rangers have admitted the attack, but claimed that the house was full of NPAs. A military report said that they fired on the house, because they were on combat patrol in the area, and were informed that armed NPAs were having a meeting in the house. They also claimed that three rebels were killed, and an undetermined number had escaped. However, the only bodies found at the site were those of Reynaldo and Serena de los Santos, and three of their children, Joenes, 14 years, Mary Joy, 6 years, and Reynaldo Jr., age 5.

Reynaldo was employed in the office of the Provincial Engineer. He was active in the parish Himamaylan, serving as Vice Chairman of the Justice and Peace Committee of the Basic Ecclesial Community. He served also as chairman of the socio-economic committee of the Presentation Committee Center of the parish, and was the Himamaylan representative of the Promotion of Church Peoples' Rights (PCPR). Both he and his wife, Serena, were active in a volunteer feeding program for malnourished children in Himamaylan. If one is poor and active in church affairs in Negros Occidental, he automatically assumed to be a Communist.

The funeral services were held in the parish church in Himamaylan on Monday afternoon, April 11.

On a TV program we posed the question to Defense Secretary Fidel Ramos: "We depend upon the army and police to protect us from those who would violate our human rights. But who would protect us from our protectors? Nobody!

"The army and the police do the investigation of the crime and catch the criminals, but what if the criminals are themselves? Who is going to investigate them, who is going to catch them?

"If insurgents and criminal elements violate human rights, they are common criminals to be pursued and punished by the army and the police. But if the army and police violate human rights, they are worse than criminals. They are betrayers of the public trust. We pay them, feed them, cloth them, arm them, if they turn against us, they are worse than criminals, they are traitors.

"They have sworn to uphold the majesty of the law but if they violate it themselves, they are guilty of violating our constitution, the public who trusted them, and the nation."

Secretary Ramos strongly condemned criminal elements

in the army and the police, saying that soldiers are subject to military discipline not imposed on civilians. Under the Articles of War, soldiers maybe summarily and without trial, reprimanded, demoted, deprived of their duties, or even summarily executed for their crimes.

But we see no evidence that the army is bent on disciplining their own soldiers. On the contrary, they have gone out of their way even to forcibly rescue their fellow soldiers from jail and justice.

Where is Capt. Melvel Gutierrez and his ten Scout Rangers who perpetrated the terrible Himamaylan massacre? Has he been investigated, accused, suspended, tried, for the crime committed over four months ago? No one in the Defense Department would tell us.

There's no greater proof of his perfidious crime than the pictures seen on these pages, and the testimonies of those who have seen and survived the tragedy of Himamaylan.

Yet as far as we know, the murderers with the connivance of their officers, have gone unpunished and free to make a travesty of justice and the law.

Damn.

September 4, 1988

Part 47. Fools: Bacani, Remy, Roger, Ray

Today April 1 is All Fool's Day, American equivalent of our Holy Innocents Day (December 28). Since we have a colonial mentality, expect a lot of Flips to go around borrowing money they do not intend to pay back, and playing tricks and practical jokes on the unwary.

An April Fool is called in France *un poisson d'avril* (fish of April), and in Scotland a *gowk* (cuckoo), a person befooled or tricked on this day.

In India similar tricks are played at the Holi Festival (March 31) when the weather is pleasant, so that All Fool's Day cannot refer to the uncertainty of the weather, nor yet to the mockery of our Redeemer, the two most popular explanations. A better explanation is that March 25 used to be New Year's Day, and April 1 was its octave, when festivities culminated and ended.

It may be a relic of the Roman *Cerealia*, held at the beginning of April. The tale is that Proserpina was sporting in the Elysian meadows, and had just filled her lap with daffodils, when Pluto (brother of Jupiter) carried her off to the lower world and made her his Queen.

Her mother Ceres (Mother Earth) heard the echo of her screams, and went in search of the voice. But her search was a fool's errand: it was "hunting the gowk,'" or looking for the "echo of the scream."

Of all the practical jokers, few come close to Ferdinand Waldo Demara Jr. of Massachusetts, now a Fundamentalist preacher, like Ronald Remy, Ray Orosa and Roger Arienda.

Known as the Great Impostor, Demara in the 1940s posed as a Trappist monk in a Kentucky monastery, a psychology professor at a Pennsylvania college, a biologist doing cancer research near Seattle, and a recreational officer in a Texas penitentiary.

His greatest feat was during the Korean War, when he served as a lieutenant-surgeon with the Canadian Navy. With the aid of medical books aboard ship, he pulled teeth, removed tonsils, amputated limbs, and successfully removed a bullet lodged near the heart of a wounded South Korean soldier. Eventually discovered, he was discharged and deported to the USA, where in 1956 he was caught impersonating a school teacher in Maine.

Asked why he impersonated so many people, Demara now a Fundamentalist preacher, replied, "Rascality, pure rascality." I always wondered about the Three Rs -- Ronald, Ray and Roger -- who look infected by the fourth R, rascality. That's a joke, boys.

Seriously now, the Three Rs were on television with Beltran recently, facing a formidable phalanx of Catholic priest scholars headed by Monsignor Ted Bacani. I hate to say this, but Ronald Remy and Roger Arienda were more than a match for Bishop Bacani and his *summa cum laude* theologians.

Remy was knowledgeable, charming, earnest, expansive, with a smile he must have filched from his beautiful daughter Jackie Kookooritchkin, "How can I be mistaken about the Roman Church when I was educated by Jesuits in Ateneo for 12 years?"

Poor Bacani, he can only murmur, "The Jesuits taught you the wrong things."

Roger Arienda showed flashes of his old self as the irrepressible, irreverent and blasphemous Bomba, with his thunderous "If you are not born again, you cannot be saved!" and "I am glad this is the 20th century because if we were in the Middle Ages, we would be burned at the stake by Bishop Bacani!" *Touche*!

Indeed, compared to Ronnie and Roger who were enthusiastic and sincere advocates of born-again fundamentalism, Bishop Bacani sounded like Rizal's pendantic Dominican, Padre Sibyla, making distinctions, defining terms, and making ex-cathedra statements till you expect him to announce how many angels can sit on the head of a pin.

If our Catholic Church depends for its credibility on Ted Bacani, we are headed for another Protestant Reformation. Why can't our church authorities send instead Father Sonny Ramirez, or Father Ben Villote, or anyone of the young Jesuits (not Father Kinik Bernas)?

But Bacani -- he is the ConCom member who voted to retain the US bases and consign the Filipino people to nuclear cremation, to an agricultural colonial economy, and to a male chauvinist piggery ("The trouble with you, Bishop, is that you have never been raped!" cried a nun).

The man is basically pro-American and anti-Filipino. How can he defend our beloved Catholic Church in its new role as the protector of the poor and the hungry among us, the friendless, the cheated and the beaten??

Why doesn't our Church send Bernie Villegas, Archibald Alexander Gilles and Vaughn Monroe Montes of Opus Dei CRC to debate with Ronnie and Roger? Instead of bullying the Jesuits and our other priests, why doesn't the Opus Dei apply its vaunted skills to obliterate the enemies of our Church?

April 1, 1989

Part 48. Anding Roces for Secretary of Tourism

Anding Roces may not be able to sell brassieres or swimming suits, nor is he the type like Edward VIII later Duke of Windsor who could not discharge his duties without the support of the woman he loves, but he has been the best Education

Secretary we ever had, and will make a very good Secretary of Tourism to replace Speedy Gonzalez who resigned to pursue his Malou apostolate.

His political credentials are perfect. He was a colleague of Ninoy Aquino since the 1960s when we both served in the Macapagal Cabinet. He and Ninoy were candidates of LABAN in the 1978 campaign along with Soc Rodrigo and Charito Planas, running against the Marcos candidates, Imelda and Carlos Romulo. And he is the only one in history to be arrested for not voting in the 1980 elections.

His credentials as a thinker and doer, with initiative, imagination and talent for organization, is no less perfect. He is a art enthusiast and historian, writer and author, loquacious and eloquent, with a sense of humor and the ability to project the best in the Filipino, his culture and society, his history and vision of the future.

As UNESCO chairman here, he traveled extensively and has contacts all over the world among the intelligentsia and the elite, with close friendships among the greats and near-greats.

He is a delightful wit who could say with words pregnant with meaning, "Let me go to Bali and die," and have it quoted by the world's press -- an ability to command the attention of world media that will help him project an exciting image of the Philippines among tourists.

As Secretary of Education, he helped the Filipino find his soul, writing a series of books on the Fiesta, as he recently did in an article for Time magazine. He masterminded the June 12 extravaganzas that attract two million people in Rizal Park, never before and never again surpassed within memory.

He recovered the stolen manuscripts of Rizal's Ultimo Adios when everyone despaired of ever getting them back.

Ask him, President Cory. He may not accept, but try anyway. He may be flattered to know that you have not forgotten the heroes of EDSA. And the nation will rejoice at your choice.

Holy Carabao, President Cory, whoever talks you into appointing into your cabinet vacuum-weights with no track records, unknown quantities whose only qualifications are that they are recommended by the Council of Trent?

Are you really thinking of replacing Winnie Monsod as NEDA chief with a non-entity? She was the only one who gave you an alternative opinion on the IMF Letter of Intent, and you need dissenters in your cabinet to test the validity of the majority opinion.

If everybody agrees, if there is no exploration of alternatives or give-and-take pro-and-con discussions, what kind of government will we have -- a moronic monolith?

I have disagreed with Winnie many times, Mrs. President, and I am not particularly fond of her and her husband, but for what it is worth, I heartfully recommend that you keep her as NEDA chief, because she is the only with balls (courage) and marbles (brains) in that sorry lot in charge of our economy.

Hang in there, Winnie old girl, my favorite screaming banshee, you wicked Witch of the West, you are a better and gutsier economist than those Three Stooges of the IMF -- Jobo, Ting and Ernest Leung. Hang in there, Winnie.

Dear President Cory, here is an unsolicited advice you may want to throw into the wastebasket: Never depend on a second string player to win the game for you.

Remember how Sir Anthony Eden stood on the sidelines waiting for Prime Minister Winston Churchill to step aside? For a long time, with a handsome face and a top hat, he stood in the shadow of the great bull of a man, and everyone was in a hurry to move out Churchill to make room for him.

Finally, after almost 20 years Churchill retired, and Anthony Eden became Prime Minister. The whole of England watched with bated breath for the wonders that this handsome protégé will perform.

Six months later. they were still waiting. And all throughout Eden's incumbency, nothing happened. *Dribble ng dribble, pero hindi nag sho-shoot!* Like Ting Jayme, like Philip Juico, like what's his name, like the faceless wonders whose mugs blend with the wall-paper -- the vacuum weights who took the place of your super Cabinet of 1986.

Later Winston Churchill was seen jogging along Hyde Park, and was asked what he was doing. At 79 years of age, he answered, "I am getting back in shape. Anthony Eden is getting old enough to retire!"

I suggest Mrs. President, that you ask ex Education Secretary, ex UNESCO chairman, Bulletin president Alejandro Roces to don his jogging outfit and start running.

May 10,1989

Part 49. *Linoloko nanaman tayo ng mga traidor!*

Tang Ina, these idiots in Congress, not content with demanding *buko* quotas, going on expensive junkets abroad at our expense, betting our precious dollars at the gambling tables of Las Vegas, smuggling guns to secure their protection rackets and murder their political opponents, protecting crooks and murderers, paying themselves a million pesos a year, and inflicting their ignorance and stupidity on the Filipino people -- now are committing treason!

Consultation, my aching ass! What do Congressmen care about the opinion of the people?? Did they schedule a referendum about the Agrarian Reform Code that they and Hortense Starke mangled it in the interest of landlords?

Did they schedule a referendum on IMF conditionalities that keep us in perpetual poverty and controlled by American imperialists? Did they schedule a referendum on whether we should selectively repudiate immoral foreign debts that result in inflation and devaluation?

The trouble with these fossil brains in Congress is that they are selectively in favor of Americans against Filipinos. As long as a referendum favors Americans, they will insist on it.

Why don't they have a referendum on whether or not Jun de Guzman, Peping Cojuangco and Komong Sumulong should be expelled from the House?

Tang ina, but if a referendum might reject IMF conditionalities, or the possibility of nuclear destruction or the spread of AIDS virus through imperial assholes in the bases, or military fascism, or exploitive landlordism -- then no, Congress will not submit any of those questions to a referendum.

They will only submit those by which Americans take advantage of our colonial mentality, to which we seem incurably addicted.

Tang ina, colonial mentality is like an addictive drug, pushed by the pushy Americans, and we are the poor addicts. Our stupid leaders in Congress, rather than prescribing a cure for this fatal and malevolent obsession, instead propose to ask the drug addicts if they want to continue taking drugs from the drug pushers. That's real dung.

What they are doing is to give the neanderthal Americans the opportunity to divide and conquer us, to bypass our leaders and deal directly with our people, to bribe them, to corrupt them, to intimidate them, in the same way these no-good Congressmen win elections.

Tang ina, this happened once before during the 1946 elections and subsequent sellout on the bases. Nationalists like Recto, Laurel and Ninoy's father were jailed by Dugout Dog MacArthur, and others were harassed by Army men and war veterans, believing in their miasmic minds that to be against Americans is to be a communist.

Afterwards in an effort to get Congress to ratify the treaty, the traitorous lackeys of Americans even went to the extent of expelling three senators (among them the father of Pepe Diokno) and seven representatives from the House to comply with American demands.

In the senate, the treaty won approval by only ONE vote purchased with a massive bribe.

In the House, the expulsion of then Congressman Luis Taruc convinced him and the peasants that their only chance to redress their grievances is through revolution. Instead of pursuing their aims in peace, they plunged us into a civil war that is still going on today.

Tang ina, in 1946 we gave these neanderthals our Bases for 99 years when Japan lay in defeat and Russian was a US ally. We gave them Parity Rights to exploit our natural resources and operate public utilities -- without getting reciprocal rights in the USA where such rights are given only by individual states.

We extended the Free Trade with them till 1973, for almost 50 years, in exchange for a pathetic amount of Sugar Quotas that only perpetuated a landlord elite allied with colonial interests against our Industrialization and Land Reform.

What did we get in return? Asshole promises that never materialized -- war damage payments that covered only five percent of the actual damage done by American and Japanese forces -- war surplus junk already fully depreciated at war's end, and worth less than one percent of American valuation based on original cost – veteran's payments worth only one peso for every dollar given to Americans and volunteer Poles and Chinese, which today is worth one twentieth of ordinary GI benefits.

Tang ina, all those "benefits" like the PAP promises today, were given under excremental conditionalities similar to that of IMF-WB -- so that the Philippines was driven to bankruptcy in 1949, a mere three years after we received those handouts from Mother America.

Above all, it gave the CIA a chance to intervene in our domestic affairs to this very day, and bend us to their evil will.

Tang ina, won't we ever learn?

October 2 1989

Part 50. Posterity will stand in judgment of us

Lorna Verano-Yap, representative from Pasay City, born in 1952, stood up in the House and delivered one of her finest speeches against the proposed referendum on the Bases, proposed by Antonio Cuenco and Pablo Garcia of Cebu and Magdaleno Palacol of Laguna:

I stand before you as a representative of a new generation born after World War II, a generation born without an umbilical cord to the colonial past, a generation which has never known what it means to be under a foreign master, which never had to fight America's wars in Korea and Vietnam. We are the First Citizens of our free Republic.

We of this generation live under conditions not of our own making, born out of colonial mentality not our own. We live at a time when a foreign power and the IMF could with impunity call the shots in the formulation of our economic policies and keep us mired in subsistence agriculture while neighboring nations progress to the status of being new industrial countries (NICs). We live at a time when our own Army pursuing the LIC bloodbath policy of a foreign power has become the avenging angels of Imperialism, plunging us deeper and deeper into a never-ending civil war.

Old and mentally decrepit men of a previous generation made the bed on which we lie. They are responsible for the darkness of our nights, these Gunga Dins and modern Humabons from Cebu who say, "We owe our democracy to the United States." These colonial cretins give lie to the truth that the generation of Rizal, Bonifacio and Aguinaldo set up the first democracy in Asia without the United States which made war on us and destroyed it.

Those of you in the previous generation who vote for a referendum on the bases even before the ratification of the Senate -- who persist in this betrayal of our nation in behalf of a foreign power -- are recreating colonial conditions which you will never live to see. We of the new generation strongly protest that we shall be heirs to this abomination and ignominy. And we and future generations will stand forever in judgment of you.

It is the characteristic of a spoilsport, even in the days of our childhood playing *patintero* or basketball, to say that it is a great game when they are winning, but always when they lose to say, "*Ayaw ko na, mandaraya kayo. Ulitin natin ang laro at palitan natin ang patakaran!*"

It is characteristic of a colonial spoilsport who seeing the end of America's colonial adventure in our poor suffering country, now say, "Let's start all over again, and change the rules specifically promulgated in our Constitution for the resolution of American military bases."

The Constitution is the ultimate will of the people, ratified by 85 percent of the electorate, and specifying the procedure with which the American bases may be extended beyond 1992. For the benefit of old and decrepit cretins who do not know how to read, Section 25 of the Transitory provisions, say: "After the expiration in 1991 of the Agreement between the Republic of the Philippines and the United States of America concerning military bases, troops, or facilities, shall not be allowed in the Philippines except under a treaty duly concurred in by the Senate and when Congress so requires, ratified by a majority vote cast by the people in a referendum..."

The law is clear. The general tenor is not to allow foreign bases after 1991, except under a new treaty concurred in by the Senate. Senate concurrence is mandatory. Ratification by referendum is only permissive, but if permitted, ultimately final.

Colonials among us would make use of the general provisions of Article XIII Section 16, providing for the right of the people and their organizations to effective and reasonable participation at all levels of decision-making, to demand a referendum on the bases before the Senate is able to act on it.

That is being a spoilsport, that is changing the rules of the game. We all know that a specific provision always prevails over a general provision of law. What these colonials are actually proposing is government by referendum, decision-making by public opinion poll, the rule of the mob.

But we know it is selective, only in cases where the interest of the United States may be advanced. Otherwise, why don't they propose as well a referendum on IMF conditionalities, on repudiation of foreign debt, on Salary Standardization and Minimum Wage, on the fitness of Jun de Guzman, Antonio Cuenco, Pablo Garcia and Magdaleno Palacol to sit in this august chamber??

This is a question of leadership, and its responsibility to render a sober, mature and wise judgment without inflaming the passions and prejudices of the mob.

In Matthew, Luke, John and in Mark (Chapter 15, verses 6 to 15), it is written that Jesus Christ was also subjected to a referendum:

At every Passover Festival, Pilate was in the habit of setting free any one prisoner the people asked for. At the time a man named Barabbas was in prison with the rebels who had committed murder in the riot.

When the crowd gathered, he asked "Do you want me to set free for you the king of Jews?" He knew very well that the chief priests had handed Jesus over to him because they were jealous.

But the chief priests stirred up the crowd to ask instead that Pilate set Barabbas free for them. Pilate again spoke, "What then do you want me to do with the one you call the king of the Jews?"

They shouted, "Crucify him!"

"But what crime has he committed?" Pilate asked. They shouted all the louder, "Crucify him!"

Pilate wanted to please the crowd, so he set Barabbas free for them. Then he had Jesus whipped and handed him over to be crucified.

Who is here among you who will crucify your own country on behalf of a foreign power? Who are the Chief Priests of Pharisee Shammai, the leaders of Lapiang Demokratang Pilipino, who would inflame the colonial mentality of the people against their own national interest?

Who is the Pontius Pilate in the palace of power who would wash his hands of this monstrous crime and submit to the rule of the mob?

Who are the Roman soldiers, the Council of Trent and the military, who would strip and mock their country, put on its head a crown of imperialist thorns, nail its hands and feet to the imperialist cross, and roll the dice for the only property it has on this earth, the meager resources of a colonial plantation economy?

What you are trying to do with this monstrous act are these:

First, you are trying dangerously to impinge upon the prerogatives of a co-equal branch of Congress, the Senate which is loathe to abdicate its constitutional mandate to pass judgment on the military bases agreement, and whose concurrence is needed for the referendum. The Senate will never agree to this, unless bribed or threatened by the CIA.

Second, you are blackening the image of Congress at the time its credibility and moral leadership are at a perigee, its lowest point -- by representing the Senate as insensitive to public opinion, and worse and more believable still, that the Lower House, which smuggles guns and demands *buko* quotas, has stooped so low as to be bribed into treason, treason, treason.

Third, you are putting yourself in the danger of being condemned by historians like the Congress of 1946 which first gave the Americans military bases and extraterritorial rights for a mess of potage. The Congress of 1946, unlike you in this chamber, did not have the lessons of History to guide them. If they are misguided, you suffer from stupidity and self-delusion, even more to be condemned by future historians.

Fourth, you are destroying the bargaining power of the Executive Department, whose posture is enhanced by an apparently intractable Senate. Faced with this, the Americans will have to make an offer that the Senate cannot refuse -- like a $3 billion a year grant without conditions. With a referendum that is likely to coerce the Senate to approve any treaty, the Americans can easily get away with offering a measly miserly $500 million a year for the bases.

We cannot change the minds of congenital colonials who crawl on their bellies every time they meet Americans. But we hope to change the minds of those intelligent and patriotic ladies and gentlemen who merely look on this as an exercise in party politics, a chance to embarrass the Senate and cater to the colonial appetites of the unruly mob.

We demand and expect a Conscience Vote, conscious of the judgment of history and of posterity.

May it not be said that Rizal, Recto and our heroes lived for a lost cause, that they are the last of the True Filipinos.

May it not be said that Ninoy Aquino who submitted to US Congressman Solarz two months before he died, a Declaration of the United Opposition opposing the continued presence of military bases in our country -- and those including Cory Aquino, Mitra and Salonga, who signed the Convenor's Pledge to do away with the Bases --

May it not be said that they spent themselves in a meaningless battle, to save a nation that refused to repent and be saved, and clung to its fleshpots and brazen idols, afraid to cross the burning desert into the Promised Land, a nation that no longer believed itself to be a nation.

If the cause of Filipino nationalism should die with us in this chamber, then it will deserve to die.

October 16-18, 1989

Part 51. Eldon's boss PNB President? Ridiculous!

Ramon del Rosario Jr., affectionately known as "Boy Blue," a blue-blooded member of the Council of Trent and boss of Eldon Cruz, will be accorded his due this month:

1. His teeny-weeny Asian Savings Bank has just been given a license to operate as a commercial bank, a privilege no longer extended by the Central Bank to others. Even existing banks find it extremely difficult, to get CB nod to open up branches.

2. He is due to be appointed as President of the Philippine National Bank (PNB) in place of Ed Espiritu who resigned after Trentists undercut his bid to be CB governor.

Boy Blue is the boss of Eldon Cruz, presidential son-in-law. Eldon is Boy Blue's ace, his ticket to see President Cory any old time he wants, even after Cory reprimanded him for giving her false information about the Neptunia investment in San Miguel.

Yeah, Boy Blue and I were on the same side in the PCGG-Soriano controversy over San Miguel. He was the one who was always going to Malacañang, so *kampateng kampante*, as if he actually lived there. His father Monching through PHINMA was able to acquire the Island Cement cheap through the APT and Debt-Equity swap, for a price equal to one year's profits.

Boy Blue, one recalls, was one of the original members of the Council of Trent, who spent the EDSA Revolution safe in the upper floors of the Cojuangco Building in Makati. He was one of Cory's Seven Dwarfs, with Father Kinik Bernas as Doc, Jimmy Ongpin as Grouchy, Noel Soriano as Sleepy and Boy Blue as Dopey.

Boy Blue was so called because he was born a premature blue baby. His father Monching is already short, about 5'3", but Boy Blue grew up even shorter.

In time Boy Blue developed a Napoleonic Complex. In La Salle where he studied, his classmates called him Boy Blue reportedly because he was always blowing his own horn, as the ditty goes: "Little Boy Blue, come blow your horn,/ The calf's in the meadow, the cow's in the corn..." What is this Asian Savings Bank? It is a teeny weeny bank, which if it were a part of the PNB, would be classified as a Class C branch.

It has total assets of P1.2 billion and total deposits of P989 million at the end of 1989 -- compared to the Buendia Branch of PNB, which a total assets of P7.4 billion and total deposits of P5.7 billion in the same year's end.

Boy Blue's Asian Bank is one sixth of the PNB's Buendia Branch which is managed by one of 37 PNB vice presidents. PNB has in addition 10 Senior Presidents and two Executive Vice Presidents.

Asian Bank can be literally be placed in the pocket in PNB's Buendia branch, and if Boy Blue were to join the PNB, his corresponding rank will not be even be that of an Assistant Vice President because Class C branches are not even entitled to Vice Presidents.

And Boy Blue aspires to be PNB President? It is ridiculous!

Despite the ridiculously Lilliputian size of Boy Blue's Asian Bank, CB Gov. Jobo Fernandez gave it a license to operate as a commercial bank, provided it raises its capital to P500 million -- that is a stupid hypocritical condition because anyone given such a license can easily raise a billion. Such a privilege was given to a favored person, boss of the presidential son-in-law, a certified Malacañang crony and member of the Council of Trent.

There is this famous painting of The Boy in Blue by Thomas Gainsborough and a famous poem entitled Little Boy Blue by Eugene Field.

Field's poem spoke of the Little Boy Blue who kissed and took care of his toy friends, and concluded, "Oh the years are many, the years are long,/ But the little toy friends are true."

We imagine Eldon Cruz is one of those true blue "toy friends" of Boy Blue.

There is joke going around that Boy Blue comes early to work and stands by the main door as his employees walk in. Knowing Boy Blue's antipathy towards those taller than he is, most employees reportedly crouch, heads between their legs, and/or walk on their knees as they filed in.

The joke is that Eldon Cruz is the only one who walks by with head high, because even on his high heeled shoes, he is shorter than Boy Blue.

And that is why Boy Blue chose him as his assistant, side-kick, and Malacañang Connection, and allows him to come to office any time he wants, according another employee, and waste time reading newspapers and doing nothing.

And that is why Boy Blue gets an undeserved commercial license for his minuscule bank, and will get an undeserved appointment as the president of the Philippine National Bank.

No wonder the military keeps plotting coups "as protectors of the people." This government really belongs to presidential relatives and the Council of Trent.

And no wonder even the Americans are worried.
February 16, 1990

Part 52. Propagandists are inspired idiots

The practice of Public Relations may be an honorable profession, if one considers that one of its earliest practitioners is James Boswell (1740-1795), author of Life of Samuel Johnson, probably the greatest biography in literature.

A journalist skilled in biographical research, Boswell displayed a genius for dramatic narrative, and for all his hero-worship, his book is not only an intimate portrait of the Great Lexicographer, but also an encyclopedia of 18th century social life.

But Macaulay, the most powerful influence on Victorian literary taste, has his own judgment on Boswell the Biographer: "Eclipse was first and the rest nowhere." What of Boswell the Man? "Servile and impertinent, shallow and pedantic, a bigot and a sot."

But how could such a man have written the greatest biography in literature? Macaulay is ready with his famous *lucus a non lucendo*: "If he had not been a great fool, he would never have been a great writer." This is known as the "inspired idiot" theory.

Surely there are many respected practitioners of public relations, "inspired idiots" who are primarily involved in public information rather than outright propaganda. The former is the dissemination of truth, the latter often is the spreading of rumors and lies, and the manipulation of the people and the media.

One gets into propaganda if he has a pleasant smile, good connections, no talent for mathematics, a poor scholastic record, and nothing else worthwhile to do. There is something disreputable about being a propagandist. It is as if one sells his mind, voice and pen to the highest bidder, so that what comes out of him is not his own opinion, but that of his master.

He comes in many forms: embassy apologists for imperialist policies; propagandists for Cesar Buenaventura, Reinerio Reyes and the Council of Trent, trying to defend the indefensible; PROs of officials, like Charlie Fiel of Mayor Binay; Buddy Gomez who is a far cry from Teddyman Benigno; and those who infest coffee shops, spread malicious rumors and cadge drinks from everyone.

Take Charlie Fiel. He reads a joke I write about Jojo and he flies off the handle because that is what he is paid to do. He is after all the hired hack and paid piper of Mayor Jojo Binay, even if he is the father of Corito Fiel, a fine writer and my friend.

What Charlie does not know is that I like Jojo, and that I make fun of him for a very good reason: to deflate his ego as mayor of the richest town of the nation, and bring him back to the days when he was a humble likeable squirt of a hick.

I knew Jojo from the days of the Snap Election, when he and Anding Roces took charge of Makati's participation. Frankly I thought Jojo was Anding's driver, but Anding explained that he and Jojo were aspiring to run for mayor and vice-mayor respectively. Anding of Dasmariñas Village said that he chose Jojo as his running mate because he represented the poor side of Makati where most of the votes are.

When Cory became president, Joker Arroyo got Jojo Binay appointed the OIC Mayor, and Anding found himself shunted aside.

Jojo whom we used to ask to get us a jeepney when we were tired of walking during the campaign, suddenly became Mayor of Makati, a courageous partisan of Cory, and clearly the best mayor of Makati, considering the only other one was Mayor Yabut.

Mayor Binay has his faults. At one time he was pushing his weight around with a horde of goons, but that time is past. He has been accused of graft, of putting up a "private foundation" to fund his political patronage. But no one has able to present proofs to our satisfaction.

We like, respect and admire him, and cannot bring ourselves to repeat charges hurled at him by Councilor Brilliantes.

But we enjoy making fun of him, calling him a tadpole at birth, held by tweezers while being baptized with a grain of salt and a drop of water from an eye dropper, fertilized with manure to make him grow, and often mistaken for a watch-your-car-boy, a flower vendor, and a juvenile delinquent.

Jojo never takes offense at my jokes, even when radio commentators repeat the jokes in Filipino with derisive laughter, because he knows in an election I am his best booster.

Since I do not walk with downcast eyes, I rarely see Jojo who moves close to the ground. I caught him once hiding behind a post in a hotel lobby. "Hey, Jojo!" I yelled, "Whom are you hiding from?"

He answered, "I was hoping you wouldn't notice me, Larry, because every time you do, you write another of your corny jokes about me."

"Don't give it another thought,'" I said, "I usually cannot see you without a microscope."

Unless that jackass Charlie calls attention to you.

February 21, 1990

Part 53. Ramsey Clark on the Bases Treaty

Ramsey Clark, world citizen and human rights advocate, former Assistant Attorney General of President John F. Kennedy and Attorney General (the equivalent of our Secretary of Justice) of President Lyndon B. Johnson, came for a two day visit to the Philippines recently, and granted an interview exclusive to the Inquirer, on his current mission, and on the present controversy of the Bases Treaty being considered for ratification in the Senate.

Question: You have been a frequent visitor to our shores in the past, to what purpose, Mr. Clark?

Answer: I first came to the Philippines as a 17-year-old with the Marine Corps just after the war, and have come back many times. In the mid 1970s I came to petition for the release of Ninoy Aquino, and later I came back to again petition for his release so he can have heart surgery performed in Houston, Texas. Again I came to protest an international convention of lawyers in Manila, ``World Law through Peace," to point out the irony of a military dictatorship hosting an international meet of lawyers committed to peace and the rule of law. I came back many times to document abuse of human rights and summary executions by the military and armed vigilante groups. I came back to witness some of your elections, the democratic processes being one of my primary interests. I was here when Filipinos rose as one to topple Marcos in one of the greatest demonstrations of people power the world has ever seen. I came to break bread with dear friends, like Senator Jose Diokno, the Tañadas, and many of those who were exiled to the United States during the Marcos period.

Question: You have come to the Philippines presently in a most crucial time of our history, when the Bases Treaty between the Philippines and your country is being debated upon and considered for ratification. What can you say about the Treaty?

Answer: Ordinarily I would leave the question to Filipinos themselves. It is their own internal affair. But I must speak as an

American. I am opposed to the Bases Treaty. The presence of a foreign military bases on the soil of any nation is a hallmark of Colonialism, one aspect of which I had an occasion to protest in support of Senator Jose Diokno sometime ago. This was the case of some 2,000 Filipino families privileged to be given allotments for the right to scavenge for garbage in the Clark Air Base and the Subic Naval Base. Outrageous! That is no way for any people to live. Where is your dignity as human beings? your sense of self-worth as a people? Where is your sovereignty, your right to self-determination? As an American I do not want a American base in the Philippines, because I love its people and I hate militarism. This base should have been closed down long long ago. The arms race of which the USA is a major contributor, is the greatest crime against humanity and against history. From the viewpoint of the Filipino people, you must get on with your lives without interference, take off the yoke that has been on your back since the Philippine American War when Americans slaughtered hundreds of thousands of your people. Your spirit will not be free, your economy will not improve till you get these Americans off your necks and out of your system.

Question: One of the issues being raised is the policy of the United States never to affirm or deny the presence of nuclear weapons in the Bases. What do you say about that?

Answer: Confirm or deny, the nuclear weapons are there. That is what Bases are for, as a forward storage space for the speedy delivery of lethal weapons to the combat area. Everybody knows that, these ships and planes do not throw their weapons in the air when they come to port, juggle them in the air, and catch them again after refueling. Of course there are nuclear weapons on your soil, as there are in Japan, New Zealand, Australia, Fiji, Spain and other American bases. Sadly every one of those governments ignore the presence of the nukes, pretend they do not know, or claim that the USA would never do such a thing. But there is a difference between the other bases and the Philippines. In Spain and elsewhere, the bases are remote from populated areas and the people hardly know they exist. Here in the Philippines the American base is the largest outside the United States, and the American presence is massive and intrusive, bringing in its wake, political corruption, moral decay, AIDS and venereal diseases, and a master-servant relationship that is fatal to the Filipino soul.

Question: Do you think the United States will get its way?

Answer: Let me warn you that the USA plays for keeps in matters like these. The examples are too numerous to mention, but let me cite just one. There was a time when a naval base on the island of Fiji was being considered as an alternative to Subic Bay. At the time, a great leader rose in the person of Timoteo Bavandra, who achieved a coalition of native Fijians and Indian immigrants, and was elected President. I spent much time with President Bavandra who made it clear after his election that he was going to make Fiji a nuclear-free zone. Former US Ambassador to the United Nations Vernon Walters, up to his usual tricks, paid a visit, and threatened Bavandra, ``You don't really want to do that, would you?'' A month later the newly elected president was ousted from office in a coup supported by two aircraft full of US Military Police. One plane came from Hickham Air Base in Hawaii, the other came from Clark Air Base. Bavandra was never restored to power, and the US military had their way.

Question: Is there really a need for a US naval base in the Philippines?

Answer: If there ever was such a need, it disappeared with the collapse of the ``Evil Empire'' of the Soviet Union, its economy, its unity as a nation, and its military capability. Yet the USA goes on seeking military and naval bases, because it has an ulterior purpose which is to establish a new world order based on the dominance of the US military force and the threat of economic coercion. That is the reason we destroyed Iraq, an overkill that established our dominance and control over oil fields on which Europe and Japan depend. We will have a permanent military base in the Persian Gulf and in West Africa (in Liberia and its neighbors). And we will maintain a base in Subic or somewhere nearby to control the sea lanes between Japan on one hand, and Indonesia and Brunei on the other, to dominate the passage to the Indian Ocean and to the Persian Gulf, to control Southeast Asia and the Pacific Rim, to maintain the Pacific as an American lake.

Question: If the USA needs the bases so much, why are they offering so little, practically nothing for it?

Answer: You have never heard of the Yankee trader? The Americans want the naval base alright, and if they offer a cheap price for it, it is because they really believe the Filipino people will buckle down under pressure and give it for nothing, and your own highest officials assure them that it will be so. Just think of the many billions of dollars that it would take the Americans to set up another base like Subic, and the many billions they actually spend to pay for landing rights in other nations, yet they refuse to pay even a little for the privilege of staying here among people who have been their staunchest allies in a dark period of their history. I believe that no price is high enough for you to accept the master-servant relationship that the Americans want to extend to the next century. I believe that the United States owes the Philippine much more, in reparations for the damage it has inflicted during the Philippine American War, payment in gratitude for Filipino loyalty during all the wars the Americans were involved in, and compensation for its exploitation during the entire period of American influence, including the imposition of the dictator Marcos on the Filipino people.

Question: Exploitation?

Answer: How can it be that this loyal courageous people which in the 40s, 50s and 60s, had the most dynamic economy in the region, now is the most impoverished, with one fourth of the per capita income of Malaysia, and one tenth of that of Taiwan. How come your beautiful and talented nurses which take care of Americans with such tender loving care, cannot even provide the least care for their own countrymen? How come your beautiful island of Negros which has the resources to feed the entire archipelago of 60 million people, cannot even feed itself and is mired in poverty and malnutrition, so that the Philippines has become the third most malnourished country in the world? How did it all happen? It happens because of Colonialism, because servile governments dedicate their energies and resources to the interest of the USA, instead of to the interest of their own people.

Question: As a former US Attorney General, and as an international lawyer, what is your opinion of the difference between a US treaty ratified by the US Senate, and an Executive Agreement unratified by the Senate?

Answer: The US Constitution make international treaties part of the supreme law of the land, but it requires that the treaties be ratified by the US Senate. It does not always happen. The US Senate refused to ratify the Treaty that created the League of Nations after World War I. Many people feel that the failure of a great power like the United States to join the League of Nations was a contributing factor to World War II. When the time came that the US signed a agreement hosting the United Nations headquarters in New York, the US President did not even bother to submit the agreement to the Senate for ratification. This critically important agreement among all the countries of the world, on which the independence and integrity of the United Nations depend, is not even a treaty. The President admitted that he did not want to risk a Senate debate that may promote polarization and adverse world opinion. So what was to be a treaty became instead an executive agreement. This may not be a tight commitment of the American people because it lacks political support from all sectors of the country represented by the senators. In legal or political terms, this may not have as much force as a treaty, but morally it certainly has. But, as a lawyer I cannot reconcile it with the intent of the US Constitution. From a historical viewpoint, the US executive department has found a way to usurp the powers of the legislature over war, peace and many other things. A treaty cannot be abrogated without debate and consent of the Senate, but an agreement by be abrogated by the executive alone, paying of course the stipulated penalties in the escape clauses.

Question: Unfortunately there is not even an escape clause in the Bases Treaty. As a matter of fact in the Treaty, while the Philippines is fully committed, with the ratification of the senate, to ten years occupation of the base lands, the US without the concurrence of its Senate, promises only to pay compensation on the basis of ``best efforts'' on the part of the US executive. Was it a fair agreement?

Answer: ``Best efforts'' in the agreement is a sure sign that the contract is not between equals. If I say I'm tired, I got a splitting headache, I am doing the best I can, but I cannot help you, there is no real commitment or consideration, no real enforceable contract. You are left in the tender mercies and goodwill of the other contracting party. Would you enter into an agreement selling your house on the basis that the buyer will take possession of it and say that he will exert his best efforts to pay you? You are a fool if you do.

Question: How about the ``side letter'' of President Bush to President Cory Aquino, does it have any binding effect?

Answer: Such letter has no binding effect, legally speaking, specially when it is nothing more than just a declaration of intentions with qualifications and conditions. But it does suggest strongly that President Bush really intends to get that treaty at whatever cost; he has in effect tipped his hand. He wouldn't bother to write such a letter otherwise. It also shows that Bush is not forthright about his real intentions about getting the treaty. He does not feel he has to be, because he assumes he is dealing with a weaker party.

Question: You have come a long way since your stint in the Attorney General's office in the Kennedy and Johnson administrations, what is your mission in life?

Answer: All my life I was involved in the US civil rights movement against racism and the exploitation of Afro-Americans. As the Assistant Attorney General of John F. Kennedy and as Attorney General of Lyndon B. Johnson, Civil Rights were our special concern and the noblest quest of the American people. It was a moment of high idealism when we tried to establish racial equality at the polls and in public facilities, eliminate poverty, control violence and gun proliferation, extirpate sexism and prejudice against women, also injustice against minority groups. For ten years there were no judicial executions, no death penalty in our prisons. We wanted to end poverty and war, and moved the nation closer to the end of the Vietnam war. After my stint, I moved into the field of international human rights, which is merely an extension of the civil rights movement.

Question: Go on, what kind of activities did you have in the field of international human rights?

Answer: I found myself in the boards of international organization involved in human rights. My training in international law and criminal law came in handy in addressing the human rights problem all over the world. Our credibility depended so much on the consistency and commitment we showed in civil rights and human rights. We were in Leningrad to defend the skyjackers, in Chile to monitor abuses by the Pinochet military, in South Africa protesting apartheid and murder of blacks. In Great Britain, we supported Bobby Sands in his self-imposed hunger strike for recognition of his dignity as a human being in the face of the cruel indifference of Prime Minister Margaret Thatcher, till he died of voluntary starvation, dignified to the end. In the so much on the consistency and commitment we showed in civil rights and human rights. We were in Leningrad to defend the skyjackers, in Chile to monitor abuses by the Pinochet military, in South Africa protesting apartheid and murder of blacks. In Great Britain, we supported Bobby Sands in his self-imposed hunger strike for recognition of his dignity as a human being in the face of the cruel indifference of Prime Minister Margaret Thatcher, till he died of voluntary starvation, dignified to the end. In the so much on the consistency and commitment we showed in civil rights and human rights. We were in Leningrad to defend the skyjackers, in Chile to monitor abuses by the Pinochet military, in South Africa protesting apartheid and murder of blacks. In Great Britain, we supported Bobby Sands in his self-imposed hunger strike for recognition of his dignity as a human being in the face of the cruel indifference of Prime Minister Margaret Thatcher, till he died of voluntary starvation, dignified to the end. In the so much on the consistency and commitment we showed in civil rights and human rights. We were in Leningrad to defend the skyjackers, in Chile to monitor abuses by the Pinochet military, in South Africa protesting apartheid and murder of blacks. In Great Britain, we supported Bobby Sands in his self-imposed hunger strike for recognition of his dignity as a human being in the face of the cruel indifference of Prime Minister Margaret Thatcher, till he died of voluntary starvation, dignified to the end. In the nto actions to justify war and US domination of the Gulf; that from August 2, 1990, Bush planned to destroy Iraq economically and militarily; that he ordered the destruction of facilities essential to life and livelihood, and of non-military targets like hospitals, mosques, residences; bombed indiscriminately throughout Iraq, used excessive force, killed soldiers seeking to surrender; used prohibited weapons capable of mass destruction and unnecessary suffering; ordered the invasion of Panama; obstructed justice in the UN; usurped the power of Congress to commit crimes against peace; encourage Shiite Muslims and

Kurds to futile revolt against Iraq; deprived the Iraqi people of essential medicines, water and food; violated and condoned violations of human rights in Kuwait and Saudi Arabia; demanded reparations that will impoverish Iraq and spread famine and epidemic; manipulated the press to achieve propaganda support for his goals; secured permanent military presence, control of oil resources and geopolitical domination of the Middle East.

Question: Who are making these charges and before whom?

Answer: A Commission of Inquiry into US War Crimes was formed, and it will assemble evidence for a forthcoming International War Crimes Tribunal which will render judgment in February 1992. The Commission has brought formal charges against George Bush, Dan Quayle, James Baker, William Webster, Colin Powell and Norman Schwarzkopf for war crimes against peace, humanity, the Charter of the United Nations, International Law and the US Constitution.

Question: Who initiated this, and how did it come about?

Answer: I initiated it. The Commission will coordinate evidentiary hearings throughout the world, including Jordan, Iraq, Malaysia, Philippines, Japan and Australia. On March 21, 1991, the UN reported that the situation in Iraq was near apocalyptic. I traveled 2,000 miles there in February during the massive use of 88,000 tons of explosives and can attest to the systematic destruction of human life. No running water or telephone exchanges. No food production, storage and distribution centers. All essential civilian services were destroyed. International law forbids attacking civilians; US bombing killed at least 25,000 civilians indiscriminately. Up to 300,000 persons were killed in Iraq, with US casualties only 350 -- a horrifying ratio to all who revere human life. Further deaths are expected from famine, epidemic and violence unleashed by US assault. We must never rest till we know what the US government did.

September 1991

Part 54. Dynamic Dodo Lina; CIA election meddling

We hope that with the new compromise formula for a three year withdrawal period, the divisive debate on the Bases

Treaty and Dynamic Dodo Joey Lina's referendum proposal will die a natural death.

But unless the contemplated executive agreement emphasizes a total and irreversible withdrawal of the Americans by 1994, along with the complete turnover of dry dock facilities as the British did in Singapore in the 1960s, we risk a turbulent election manipulated by the CIA and local traitors, and the kind of rampant, malicious and cruel vandalism that the Americans perpetrated on Sangley and Camp John Hay.

Already obscene leaflets depicting the anti-base senators as the Dirty Dozen and Twelve Apostles of Satan are being mailed and faxed, the only logical source of which are the control freaks of the CIA ensconced in the Magsaysay Building on Roxas Boulevard.

Despite President Cory's statement that she will no longer seek a referendum due to the Senate consensus on the withdrawal period, somebody ought to petition for declaratory relief from the Supreme Court on these four basically constitutional issues:

o Will a referendum be able to negate the Senate non-concurrence resolution?

o If so, can it in effect ratify the rejected treaty?

o Will a new senate next year be able to reconsider the rejected treaty and ratify it?

o Can a new administration renegotiate a new treaty allowing the American bases to stay, considering that foreign bases are in the Transitory Provisions meant to self-destruct after 1991?

If the answers are No, No, No, No -- then we will be able to dispense with all the debate, and go on with the tasks of reconciliation and nation-building. But if there is one single Yes among the answers, then the Bases Question will be a major issue in the next elections, and we may be in for a turbulent CIA-manipulated period of our history.

Mayor Dick Gordon in a Rotary Forum with Joey Lina, Johnny Enrile, Joe Concepcion, Tony Abaya and myself, proposed a referendum that will allow the people to select between the Constitutions of 1935, of 1973 (without the Marcos amendments) and of 1987. That is a possible repudiation of the Cory Constitution.

The Dynamic Dodo Senator Joey Lina is latching on to the Bases issue because he cannot get headlines or win an election without it. Anding Roces (who at last resigned from the Bulletin) says he first saw Joey swatting flies and pushing papers in the office of Peping Cojuangco. Then he saw him during the snap elections, as a cheer leader mouthing nothing more intelligent than "Cory, Cory, Cory!" Previously he ran for city councilor and lost miserably.

Joey is no leader. Of Cory's Eleven Dwarfs, he is known as Dopey, with little support from his betters, Shahani, Gonzales, Romulo, and totally abandoned by Makati Business Club, Council of Trent, PCCI and even Donald Dee Duck.

The Americans said once that the bases talks have nothing to do with US aid and trade, and that's a lie. Also that they will pull out immediately after the bases treaty is rejected, that's a lie too. They now say they will support Cory's proposal for a three year withdrawal, that is also lie because the CIA is already moving to influence the elections.

Unless the Supreme Court acts, we will see major political re-alignments. Issues will dominate the election -- on foreign bases, IMF conditionalities, foreign debt, import liberalization, and Cory's performance as President.

In this Cory will be the greatest loser. Despite threats to run again, she probably won't, and will stay on the sidelines as a non-candidate and a lameduck without the popular support she had at EDSA. Newsweek reported that her "one-million people" Luneta Rally even with *hakot* and *bayad*, only brought out 50,000 people.

She will be attacked for the lousy treaty she negotiated, the ZERO condonation of our debts, the disastrous economic policies that make us the world's worst basket case, and her subservience to American interest. And LDP candidates will not waste time defending her.

The anti-base faction has superior brains on their side: Saguisag, Ponce Enrile, Guingona, Salonga. The pro-base faction will no longer have Stanley Schrager and Marjorie Niehaus to call the shots for them. These two and the rest of their team were recalled to Washington in disgrace (like Phil Kaplan of old who is still rotting in the State Department without any new assignment) -- for assuring their bosses that only four senators will vote against the Treaty, and for despising Filipino leaders as whores for sale.

The CIA boys will prove unsuccessful too. Unlike in the 1950's, most Americans with brains stay in the USA making a good living in high-paying jobs. Those in the CIA nowadays are stupid red-necks, white trash jerks and low class losers, thank the Lord.

October, 1991

ooooo

END OF BOOK